WE'RE COMING FOR YOU AND YOUR ROTTEN SYSTEM

Seattle, Washington was the first major city to mandate a $15 minimum wage; the first to implement a payroll tax on Amazon to build affordable housing; the first to secure a bevy of renters' rights laws, making good on the slogan, "Housing is a human right."

Behind these remarkable breakthroughs in the 2010s stood a small but feisty Marxist movement, Socialist Alternative, and the City Council member they helped to elect, Kshama Sawant. In a municipal government dominated by pro-business Democrats, Sawant and the popular street movements she led against major corporations headquartered in the region—including Amazon, Boeing, Microsoft, and Starbucks—won battles that would transform the city's trajectory for years to come.

We're Coming for You and Your Rotten System tells this extraordinary story from the inside. Author Jonathan Rosenblum, who worked in Sawant's office and alongside community activists throughout this dynamic decade, weaves together intimate story-telling and political analysis to show how and why the Marxist-led movement succeeded where other progressive outsiders—such as Bernie Sanders and Alexandria Ocasio-Cortez—have failed. Waging major legislative battles and winning four consecutive elections, Sawant brought the movement with her into City Hall, demonstrating a distinctive theory of political power. This theory, shaped by 175 years of experience, is not new to socialist discourse, but its application is new to the US political landscape. The Seattle socialist experience represents a sharp counterpoint to the dead-end inside-the-party strategies favored by The Squad and other progressive activists.

For political activists searching desperately to make sense of the world after the reelection of Donald Trump, the Seattle experience offers a vital framework for fighting our way out of the despairing miasma of 21st-century capitalism.

WE'RE COMING FOR YOU AND YOUR ROTTEN SYSTEM

How Socialists Beat Amazon and Upended Big-City Politics

BY JONATHAN ROSENBLUM

O/R

OR Books

New York • London

Published by OR Books, New York and London

Visit our website at www.orbooks.com

All rights information: rights@orbooks.com

First printing 2025

The manufacturer's authorised representative in the EU for product safety is Authorised Rep Compliance Ltd, 71 Lower Baggot Street, Dublin D02 P593 Ireland (www.arccompliance.com)

Typeset by Lapiz Digital. Printed by BookMobile, USA, and CPI, UK.

paperback ISBN 978-1-68219-636-6 ebook ISBN 978-1-68219-637-3

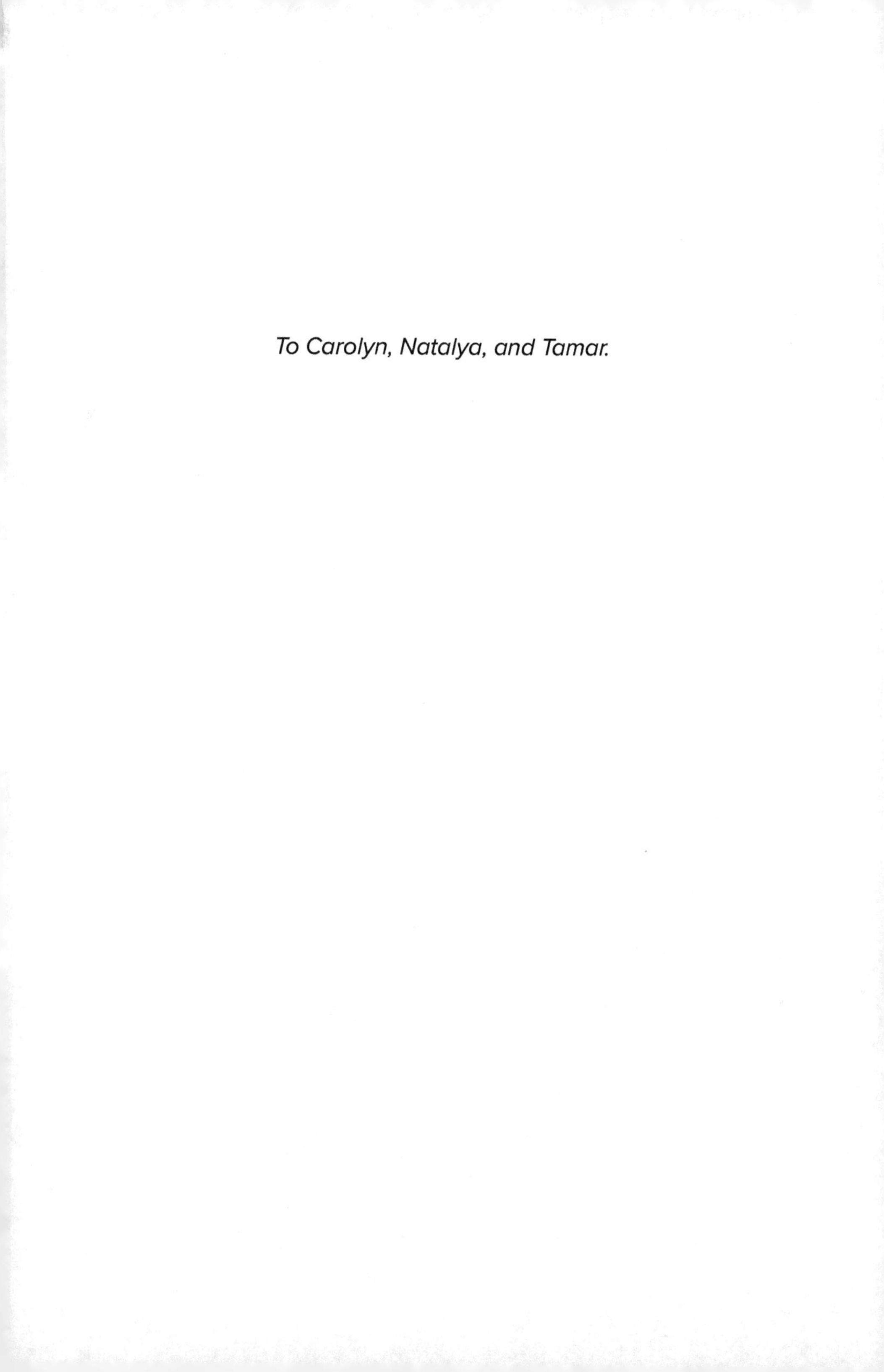

To Carolyn, Natalya, and Tamar.

Table of Contents

Foreword

"The best defense is a good offense."
Kshama Sawant[1]

What liberal pundits are calling a "crisis of democracy" is really just the escalation of class war. Most of the policies and executive orders issued by the Trump administration and informed by the Heritage Foundation's notorious Project 2025 are aimed at working people. A cabal of unelected billionaires are actively obliterating what's left of the social safety net, workers' bargaining rights, occupational safety, Medicaid, public health safeguards, regulations on pollution and fossil fuel extraction, investments in renewable energy, housing assistance to low-income renters, and enforcement of civil and disability rights. We've witnessed the

1 Kshama Sawant, "Amazon vs. the Socialists in Seattle," *Counterpunch* (September 23, 2019), https://www.counterpunch.org/2019/09/23/amazon-vs-the-socialists-in-seattle/

elimination of some 12 percent of the federal workforce through firings, layoffs, and buyouts during the administration's first three months. They are working overtime to gut the Labor Department and dismantle the National Labor Relations Board. And as the administration defunds essential social services, it has dramatically increased the budget for the Department of Homeland Security in order to accelerate its mass deportation plan—a direct assault on the working class.

Liberals who attribute the state's seemingly sudden fascist turn to a crisis of democracy propose returning to the status quo, a Democratic Party whose neoliberal policies have strengthened corporate power at the expense of working people. We know this is a failed strategy. If we are to defeat fascism *and* neoliberalism and save the planet, we need to build worker power and a strong, multiracial Left. Capitalism is not working for us, and merely reforming an exploitative system that produces poverty, immense income inequality, and ecological devastation is unsustainable. The question, of course, is how? The answer—at least in principle—can be found in the pages that follow.

Jonathan Rosenblum's illuminating account of Kshama Sawant's decade as Seattle's first and only socialist city councilmember and the dynamic movement she led is a model for how to build working-class power through class struggle. Rosenblum knows what he's talking about. He not only worked closely with Sawant but has been a labor and community organizer for four decades, building trade unions, securing affordable healthcare, resisting the onslaught of neoliberalism in the historic 1999 Battle in Seattle, and organizing a successful campaign for a $15 minimum wage. His book *Beyond $15: Immigrant Workers, Faith Leaders,* *and the Revival of the Labor Movement*, is a beautiful example of what it means to build a broad-based, worker-led, multiracial, nonviolent social movement.

We're Coming for You and Your Rotten System is not a biography or a hagiography lionizing Kshama Sawant. Although her unique and singular role in Left politics is undeniable, this is a movement history. Without Socialist Alternative (SA) or organizers such as Jesse Inman, Logan Swan, Rihanna Martinson, Alycia Roberts, Rev. Robert Jeffrey, Sr., Rev. Angela Ying, Eva Metz, Matt Smith, Kailyn Nicholson, Natalie Bailey, and many others (including Rosenblum), there would be no movement, no victory over Amazon and its political backers, no corporate tax to fund affordable housing, no Kshama Sawant, and no book. It is a testament to the organized power of the working-class when armed with a sophisticated analysis of the balance of forces, the possibilities and limits of strategic alliances, a clear-eyed assessment of the political terrain, and above all, what Rosenblum calls a Marxist theory of insurgent politics. The key elements of the new insurgent politics are a "class struggle approach, bold movement-building demands, and movement democracy," broadly speaking. Democracy is not just elections but assemblies, community forums, direct participation, and the democratizing of social movements themselves. Horizontalism and collective decision-making replace top-down, charismatic leadership.

Rosenblum recounts in breathtaking detail the movement's deployment of creative maneuvers and tactics to defeat Amazon, corporate-funded Democrats, and their well-connected allies at the helm of organized labor. But don't be fooled. The secret to Sawant's victories is not a series of clever ploys but worker mobilization pushing bold transitional and transformational demands. The point is not to outsmart the ruling class; it is to outorganize them.

Municipal government was never considered the ends for achieving power or "representation" on behalf of working-class voters, but rather an instrument through which the mass of working people could exercise their collective power. It was precisely the mobilization of class power outside the halls of government, not shaky coalitions or milquetoast compromises, that enabled Sawant to make things happen. Whereas the heads of organized labor were quick to make deals with establishment leaders at the expense of their own rank-and-file, Sawant and Socialist Alternative trusted the rank-and-file and their collective capacity to stand up to the public-private partnership we know as the neoliberal order. She trusted the people and earned their trust by recasting her role as "the shop steward of Seattle's working class." Where and when she entered, the people followed. They took over city hall, flooded meetings, held rallies, and challenged the status quo in the open, not behind closed doors. Their ability to practice a politics based on principle rather than riding the coattails of Democrats is a critical lesson we all need to learn, especially now. Socialist Alternative won not in spite of their name but *because* it overtly embraced a militant socialist agenda.

Kshama Sawant's and SA's ability to prevail as Amazon, the Democratic Party, the mayor, the courts, the police, and certain labor leaders waged war on them can be read as a classic David and Goliath story. But in this saga, there is no single hero armed with a slingshot and a smooth stone, but instead a phalanx of Davids, as well as Dianas, Dakotas, Delias, Diegos, Deeqas,

Daouds, Dinhs, Diwas, and so forth, who collectively and boldly demonstrate the power of an organized working class. Perhaps a more apt analogy might be drawn from the Greek myth of Hercules battling the Hydra, the many-headed serpentine monster who lived in the Lake of Lerna. Every time Hercules cut off one head, two would grow back. With the advent of capitalism, Hercules had come to represent capital, and the Hydra an insurgent working class. The lesson here is that organized workers threaten ruling-class power; united, they are the real giant capable of crushing Goliath or the sword-wielding Hercules.

And for Seattle's insurgent socialists, "workers" meant all workers. They understood how the Right and its corporate allies won over a segment of the working class by appealing to race, nationalism, citizenship, masculinity, and homophobia. Besides weakening potential solidarities, these kinds of appeals work on white men whose anger with the system is mobilized by politicians, right-wing forces, and the media against immigrants, women, Black, Asian, Indigenous, queer and trans people—essentially, any social group subject to displaced social anxieties. Sawant and her Marxist insurgent movement did not ignore these social anxieties or the various ways the working-class is differentiated by race, gender, sexuality, nationality, and citizenship status. They did not direct constituents to leave their other struggles or identities at the door when joining the class struggle, or issue empty assurances that racist policing, mass deportations, and the epidemic of anti-trans violence will disappear after the revolution. Instead, they joined with Black Lives Matter (BLM), protested police violence, fought for reproductive justice, and defended LGBTQIA rights. They understood that class struggle means fighting for the entire class.

Sawant also understood that class struggle and movement democracy entailed more than confronting power. They had to address divisions within their movements and coalitions. When BLM leaders accused the Tax Amazon campaign of co-opting their message during the George Floyd protests, Sawant publicly discussed the issue with a large group of Black organizers. Rather than dismiss those who wanted to separate the demand to defund the police from the other class demands as narrow identity politics, she instead listened, debated, and taught—laying out the connections between an inflated police budget, tax-exempt corporate profits, and the lack of affordable housing and living wage jobs. She pledged her solidarity even when they disagreed. As a result, they built a stronger movement. Similarly, when rank-and-file members of the Carpenters union split with their leadership, Sawant, Logan Swan, and other SA members supported the rank-and-file's fight for better wages and conditions, winning over workers who had been hardcore Trump supporters.

If we learn anything from this book, it is that we cannot retreat. We cannot be afraid of rejecting reformism, refusing politics-as-usual, or embracing socialism. The great radical intellectual W.E.B. Du Bois warned in 1956 that the ruling class would label any reform designed to give workers power over capital a communist plot. The ruling class is not entirely wrong. He writes:

> government ownership of the means of production; government in business; the limitation of private profit; social medicine, government housing and federal aid to education; the total abolition of race bias; and the welfare state. These things are on every Communist program; these things are the aim of socialism. Any

> American who advocates them today, no matter how sincerely, stands in danger of losing his job, surrendering his social status and perhaps landing in jail.[2]

As I write these very words, billionaires and their fascist agents are coming for our movements. They don't need to win in the electoral arena if they can lock us up by invoking emergency measures, dismantling democracy, and declaring us a national security threat by calling us Marxists, communists, and radical socialists. Rather than shrink from these labels, we should embrace them. The yet unfinished story of Kshama Sawant and Seattle's insurgent politics proves that socialists not only fight for the working class—they also win.

Robin D. G. Kelley
Los Angeles
May 21, 2025

---

2 W.E.B. Dubois, "Why I Won't Vote," *The Nation* (October 20, 1956), http://www.hartford-hwp.com/archives/45a/298.html

1

A Political Earthquake Strikes Seattle

Like many others, I failed to recognize the first tremors of the socialist political earthquake that struck Seattle in 2013.

It was July, in SeaTac City Hall, 15 miles south of Seattle. I was director of the SeaTac Airport workers Fight for $15 campaign, and workers had gathered to navigate a hostile City Council hearing to get our $15 minimum wage measure on the November ballot.

The SeaTac workers knew that to win the historic initiative they'd have to persuade a conservative electorate of 11,000 mostly white voters to enact a 63 percent pay hike for an overwhelmingly immigrant airport workforce. Drawn by the novelty of the bold demand, regional and national media were swarming into SeaTac. Accordingly, we instructed our hearing speakers to refrain from harsh rhetoric and instead focus on their personal economic struggles and how a raise for the lowest wage workers was good policy for the community and for local businesses.

I was surprised to see Kshama Sawant, a Seattle City Council candidate, and her coterie of red-shirted campaigners at the SeaTac hearing. Ballots had just gone out to voters in Seattle's summer primary election, where Sawant, a member of Socialist Alternative (SA), was an extreme long-shot challenger to City Council President Richard Conlin, a Democratic fixture and four-term City Hall incumbent. What was Sawant even *doing* here? Shouldn't she be door-knocking voters back in Seattle?

When Sawant's turn to speak came, she held nothing back. "The rich are getting richer, and they are the ones who are getting the free lunch!" she declared. "The SeaTac workers have shown that we as working people need to fight for our own interests. We cannot rely on corporate politicians. We need to . . . come together independent of the two big business parties to fight for our own interests!"[3]

This was about a million miles off the campaign's disciplined messaging. I was in the back of the hearing room, gritting my teeth and dreading how our corporate-funded opposition would demonize us by replaying Sawant's blistering, polarizing rhetoric to SeaTac's conservative electorate.

That evening, after the hearing, I debriefed with a group of workers and union staff. What was the highlight of the event? I asked them. The clergy who spoke movingly about justice? The community

---

3 [YouTube.com]. (2013, July 23). SeaTac City Council Meeting on $15/hr Min Wage [Video]. YouTube.com. https://www.youtube.com/watch?v=u59p7jnZIHk

members who extolled the local economic benefits? The workers' answers came quickly: None of the above. "We liked that Indian lady from Seattle!" a worker exclaimed. "Yes—she was the best," said another. Heads nodded in agreement: Sawant's lashing assault on corporate greed had stirred their passions and provided a level of moral clarity that had been absent from our polished talking points.

I was far from the only activist jarred by Sawant's sharp rhetoric. But as I drove home that night, I thought the airport workers might be onto something that the rest of us had missed: Here was a person whose words distinctively captured their anger, tapping the frustrations of the millions of low-wage workers who had suffered through the Great Recession while billionaires got richer; who had been promised better times under Obama only to fall victim to bankruptcies, evictions, foreclosures, and pink slips, while Wall Street got bailed out; who had been told to support Democrats because Democrats supported workers only to get stiffed, time and time again.

The airport workers sensed that Sawant was an unusual political ally, and they were elated. Her words brought them dignity. For the rest of us, it would take a few more shockwaves before fully understanding that Sawant was a different kind of radical—and that a scrappy band of socialists who had never won elected office were about to spark a revolution that would transform the region's political landscape.

This book tells the story of that revolution. It is not just the story of policy battles and Sawant's four consecutive electoral victories, but of how a distinctive theory of political power was put into practice. Sawant was not simply more radical than other US elected officials who, over the years, have claimed the left side of the political spectrum. She and Socialist Alternative exercised political power differently. Their insurgent politics combined bold demands, a class struggle approach, and hard-hitting tactics with grassroots organizing and participatory democracy, raising the socialist banner to achieve breakthrough gains for working people.

Under Sawant's leadership—through three hotly contested re-election campaigns, against the combined forces of big business and the Democratic Party establishment—grassroots movements won a $15 minimum wage, bans on evictions, limits on rent increases, and breakthrough renters' rights protections. They saved low-income public housing for thousands of residents and rescued the Central Area Senior Center and the neighborhood post office from the steamroller of gentrification. They replaced Columbus Day in Seattle with the annual Indigenous Peoples Day holiday. They secured funding for LGBTQ community services, millions of city dollars for youth mental health services, and millions more for sheltered housing. And they won a historic tax on Amazon to fund affordable housing and Green New Deal projects.

Sawant's Marxist orientation to political struggle is not new to worldwide socialist discourse, but its application is new to the US political landscape. The Seattle experience during Sawant's political tenure offers vital and unique lessons for people everywhere who are struggling to tackle the political, economic, and social crises of our times. Seattle's $15 minimum wage battle was the first demonstration of this new theory of disruptive political power.

This is a story I will tell from the inside. For the decade beginning with our first awkward encounter in SeaTac, I worked closely with Sawant—initially as a union activist, curious but a bit skeptical about this novel political development. But I overcame my doubts as I saw the movement's resounding results. I went on to work with her and Socialist Alternative members on three re-election campaigns and served for several years on Sawant's organizing staff in the City Council office. My work in the office and on campaigns put me at the center of the legislative fights, the electoral battles, and countless strategic discussions. I worked intimately not just with Sawant and Socialist Alternative members, but also with community activists who formed the core of the extraordinary grassroots coalition that disrupted the political system and produced historic wins.

Two weeks after the SeaTac hearing, Sawant scored 35 percent in a three-way race, well behind Conlin but enough to put her on the November runoff ballot. Sawant and Socialist Alternative ran on a demand to raise Seattle's minimum wage from just over $9 an hour to $15 an hour. SA members and supporters—many recruited out of the 2011 Occupy movement—staged rallies for a $15 minimum wage, door-knocked aggressively, and were a constant presence at union and community social justice actions. Conventional electoral wisdom says that to win a general election, a left-wing candidate must pivot rightward to draw moderate voters into her coalition, but Sawant's literature and stump speeches contained no such restraint. Sawant issued unabashed calls for worker justice, rent control, and a tax on millionaires. She pledged that, if elected, she would take home only $40,000 of a city councilmember's $117,000 salary, donating the rest to worker and social justice causes. Sawant's bright red "$15 Now!" yard signs sported the image of a shouting worker with a raised fist—hardly the stuff of moderation.

Fortuitously for Sawant, a synergy developed between her campaign and SeaTac's. The prolific coverage of the SeaTac $15 initiative by Seattle's TV and radio stations, newspapers, and blogs raised the visibility of Sawant's own signature issue. In her speeches she frequently hailed the airport workers and their initiative.

Many progressive activists in unions were glad to see Sawant's candidacy but dismissed any idea that she could prevail. Over the years Seattle has seen its share of radical candidates who occasionally rattled the political establishment but ultimately fell well short of winning office.

In this case, Richard Conlin seemed virtually bullet-proof, the political insider's insider. Elected four times as a prototypical Seattle liberal, he advocated strongly for good-government environmental policies while forging close ties with business CEOs and union leaders alike. Twice he had been elected by his City Council colleagues to serve as council president. His most obvious political misstep had been to oppose a popular paid sick leave ordinance in 2011, a point Sawant raised at every opportunity. But by 2013, most union leaders had forgiven Conlin, handing him their endorsements and checks, not wanting to cross the candidate they assumed would easily return to office.

But in the weeks leading up to November's election, I would drive along the residential streets in my working class neighborhood in south Seattle and see Sawant's "$15 Now!" signs newly planted in front yards or taped to apartment building windows. It seemed that this year, with the synergy between the SeaTac initiative and the Seattle race, a socialist actually might win.

Conlin campaign staff likely reached the same conclusion at around the same time. In late October, Conlin reached out to union leaders with urgent, personal requests for door knockers. But he was too late: the union leaders who endorsed him wouldn't turn out for his last-minute get-out-the-vote push, not because they didn't want to, but because anyone with a union card and an interest in electoral work was committed to knock on doors in SeaTac.

Come Election Day, Conlin held a narrow margin over his challenger, but as late votes were tallied in succeeding days, Sawant surged ahead. She won by 3,000 votes out of more than 180,000 cast. Under the banner of a $15 minimum wage, Seattle had elected its first socialist in a century, breaking the monopoly power that the Democratic Party held on Seattle City Hall and setting off a local and national media frenzy to try to understand who Kshama Sawant and her Socialist Alternative organization were.

Born in 1973 and raised and educated in Mumbai, India, Sawant moved to the US for work as a software engineer. "Coming from India, what was striking is that you expect that in the wealthiest country in the history of humanity, there shouldn't be any poverty; there shouldn't be any homelessness," Sawant told a reporter years later. "But when I came here, I found it was exactly the opposite."[4] She returned to school to get a PhD in economics from North Carolina State University in 2003, and three years later moved to Seattle, where she was hired as a part-time economics instructor at Seattle Central Community College.

---

4 Kamb, L. (2013, August 11). Growing wealth gap spurs on socialist in Seattle council race. The Seattle Times. Retrieved March 20, 2023, from https://web.archive.org/web/20190227182356/https://www.seattletimes.com/seattle-news/growing-wealth-gap-spurs-on-socialist-in-seattle-council-race/

In Seattle, Sawant joined Socialist Alternative, the US branch of International Socialist Alternative (ISA), a socialist organization with chapters in 30 countries. ISA calls for a complete rejection of capitalism and for working-class struggle to build socialist democracies worldwide.[5]

The Seattle branch of SA was small but feisty. Members had mobilized for the historic 1999 protests against the World Trade Organization, marched in protest as the US ramped up its wars in Iraq and Afghanistan, and organized students against military recruiters. Sawant and others in SA were enthusiastic participants in Seattle's 2011 Occupy movement. When the mayor ordered the Occupy encampment in downtown Seattle to disperse, Sawant and other members of her college educators union, the American Federation of Teachers Local 1789, offered to bring the encampment to campus over the objections of college administrators. For several weeks, Occupy tents were pitched outside the main campus building at Seattle Central. Sawant and her union colleagues helped organize support for the occupation and led an all-night teach-in on political activism.

SA had never run a candidate for political office in Seattle, but in 2012 the chapter voted to put Sawant forward against State Representative Frank Chopp. It was a Sisyphean task: Chopp was the long-time speaker of the State House and the Democratic Party's regional power broker. Sawant had been a reluctant candidate, but as a stirring, disciplined orator who connected easily with workers and students, she helped put SA on the political

---

5 Madsen, B. (2012, January 24). Answering Common Questions – Socialism FAQs. Socialist Alternative. Retrieved March 20, 2023, from https://www.socialistalternative.org/2012/01/24/answering-common-questions-socialism-faqs/

map. She called for a $15 minimum wage, got arrested with other activists trying to block an eviction, and emerged on election night with 29 percent of the vote. Given the imbalanced matchup, that was a respectable result, and it whet the appetites of SA members to try again the following year against the second biggest local Democratic politician, Richard Conlin.

After Sawant's 2013 electoral victory, political insiders predicted she would have to tone down her rhetoric in City Hall or face quick political irrelevance. The first weeks of 2014 proved them dead wrong on both counts. That January, nearly one thousand people crowded into City Hall for the inauguration of newly elected city leaders, including Ed Murray, a Chopp protégé making history as the city's first gay mayor. But most people were there for Sawant.

"Shamefully, in this, the richest country in human history, 50 million of our people—one in six—live in poverty," Sawant declared to the crowd after taking her oath of office. "Around the world, billions do not have access to clean water and basic sanitation, and children die every day from malnutrition. This is the reality of international capitalism. This is the product of the gigantic casino of speculation created by the highway robbers on Wall Street. In this system, the market is God, and everything is sacrificed on the altar of profit. Capitalism has failed the 99 percent."

Directly addressing the questions swirling around in the media, she continued, "Here in Seattle, political pundits are asking about me: Will she compromise? Can she work with others? Of course, I will meet and discuss with representatives of the establishment. But when I do, I will bring the needs and aspirations of working-class people to every table I sit at, no matter who is seated across from me. And let me make one thing absolutely clear: There will be no backroom deals with corporations or their political servants. There will be no rotten sell-out of the people I represent."

"To all those prepared to resist the agenda of big business—in Seattle and nationwide—I appeal to you: Get organized! Join with us in building a mass movement for economic and social justice, for democratic socialist change," Sawant declared, "whereby the resources of society can be harnessed, not for the greed of a small minority, but for the benefit of all people."[6]

The crowd went wild with applause. Well, most of the crowd. Scattered through the assembly I could see small clusters of establishment politicos—elected officials, City Hall staff—wearing expressionless faces as the activists around them waved their arms and chanted wildly. Perhaps they were coming to terms with what the SeaTac Airport workers had recognized months earlier, that Sawant's rise was a harbinger of a dramatically shifting political terrain. As one of nine city councilmembers, she was outnumbered. But then there were the hundreds of boisterous Sawant supporters who had used their power to take out Seattle's most powerful city councilmember.

The looming problem for the political establishment wasn't one socialist councilmember. It was the growing movement of workers and students who, having sent their demand for change reverberating through City Hall, weren't about to stop.

6 Council Connection, "Councilmember Sawant City Council Inauguration Speech," January 6, 2014, http://council.seattle.gov/2014/01/06/council member-sawant-city-council-inauguration-speech

Logan Swan was one of hundreds of young workers who got swept up in the excitement of Sawant's campaign. A few years earlier, he and his brother had migrated from the Bay Area to Seattle, where they cycled through the low-wage job circuit: lumber mill, food processing plant, restaurants. In 2013 Swan was operating a 20-ton crane at a non-union steelyard, making poverty wages for exceedingly dangerous work and living in low-income housing.

Swan read political books—his father had earlier given him Howard Zinn's *A People's History of the United States*, which helped persuade him not to join the military—but he was not politically active. "I knew that unions were good, that I supported workers getting organized," Swan recalled to me a few years ago. But Swan stayed on the sidelines until after Sawant made it through the 2013 primary. "My partner at the time was like, 'There's all that shit that you and your brother sit on the back porch and smoke too many cigarettes and bitch about. There, it's happening. Don't talk about it, be about it.' Which she probably later regretted because, yeah, we both went out to volunteer for the campaign, and I stuck with it."

"I wasn't a socialist at the time," Swan said. "It was more like I just looked around, and didn't see any organization fighting for workers, being a weapon in the hands of working people." While politicians betrayed Boeing workers and teachers, and union leaders equivocated, "the only voice on the side of the rank and file was Kshama Sawant." So he thought: "Okay, I'll join the crazy socialists."

After the November election, Swan and Socialist Alternative continued door-knocking and tabling, not for a candidate but for a $15 minimum wage in Seattle. The SeaTac Airport workers south of Seattle had narrowly prevailed in their $15 initiative, and while their victory was held up in court by an alliance of Alaska Airlines, the Chamber of Commerce, and the Democrat-led Port of Seattle commission, their historic ballot box win gave momentum to the Seattle drive.

Six days after Sawant's inauguration, the new 15Now coalition kicked off its Seattle campaign with a boisterous rally of 400 people in Seattle's Labor Temple. Led by Socialist Alternative, the 15Now coalition included several groups that had not supported Sawant's electoral drive but joined up as they saw the growing momentum. This included the Martin Luther King County Labor Council; Working Washington, the umbrella group formed by the Service Employees International Union (SEIU) for the SeaTac campaign; and SEIU 775, the politically powerful homecare union led by David Rolf.

At the 15Now kickoff rally, everyone in the hall nominally was united. But over the coming weeks, the fractures between Sawant and union leaders would break into the open, foreshadowing a decade of struggle between the rabble-rousing socialists and many leaders in the progressive movement. The conflict was not just about strategy or tactics; it was over the socialists' insistence that class struggle replace the polite lobbying and backroom negotiations that unions and political officials were used to.

Most of the union leaders were operating with their well-worn political playbook: Give rousing speeches in public, stage rallies, then get down to deal-making with the political establishment in private. The socialists weren't about to let them do that without a fight.

SA leaders made two significant announcements at the rally: First, they were forming neighborhood and campus action groups throughout the city and inviting anyone to join; and second, they were preparing to launch a citizen's initiative drive if the City Council and mayor failed to act. Both signaled a commitment to continue building a politically independent movement from the streets.

Sawant and the socialists knew that while Democrats on the City Council were at least rhetorically warming to the idea of a $15 minimum wage, they would nonetheless cave to business interests when push came to shove. "It was clear to us that we could not be complacent," Sawant later recalled. "Yes, we won the historic election victory, yes, we had captured the imagination of Seattle's working people, and there was every chance of winning $15 an hour. But we also saw that this was going to be a huge shift, having a 65 percent or so wage increase. We were very clear this is going to invite the ire of big business like nothing that Seattle has seen in decades."

What would be decisive, the socialists understood, was relentless grassroots pressure, not business-as-usual politicking. Just as workers exercise power by going on strike, "we recognized we had to have a credible threat, and that's how the ballot initiative came about," Sawant said. "That has to be an essential component. It was not a side issue."

But that clash between the socialists and union officials would come later. In the Labor Temple that January afternoon, speaker after speaker, including the head of the local labor council, railed against greedy corporations and vowed to bring SeaTac's victory to Seattle. Inside the room, the movement felt unstoppable. A January 2014 union-funded poll showed an undeniable mandate: Some 68 percent of Seattle voters supported an immediate minimum wage increase to $15, without exemptions or phase-ins.

David Goldstein went home and dashed off his political column for *The Stranger*, a popular local alternative newspaper. "Seattle's business establishment would be stupid to think that they are facing just a bunch of idealistic lefties or a disorganized group of occupiers," he wrote. "There was something special going on at the Labor Temple today. Something exciting. Something smart. Something potentially much bigger than all the individual parts. So if I were Seattle's business establishment I'd negotiate the best deal that I can at Mayor Murray's table rather than risk the will of newly radicalized Seattle voters at the polls."[7]

Indeed, Ed Murray, a career politician, was already working that strategy aggressively. As a mayoral candidate he had announced his support for a $15 minimum wage, but said he would do it by bringing labor and management together "to adopt a $15 wage standard. . . in a way that does not hurt small businesses" by phasing in pay raises and exempting some companies.[8] He secured the endorsement of the local Chamber of Commerce and the restaurant association – two employer groups who invested heavily against SeaTac's $15 initiative. The two big SEIU local unions, including Rolf 's SEIU 775, also endorsed Murray, not because his position on $15 was stronger than his opponent, but because

---

7 Goldstein, D. (2014, January 12). Supporters Pack Labor Temple at 15Now.Org Rally as Minimum Wage Momentum Builds. The Stranger. Retrieved March 22, 2023, from https://www.thestranger.com/blogs/2014/01/12/18665570/supporters-pack-labor-temple-at-15noworg-rally-as-minimum-wage-momentum-builds

8 Connelly, J. (2013, October 3). Ed Murray's Vision: Meat and potatoes, no greens. Seattle P-I. Retrieved March 24, 2023, from https://web.archive.org/web/20131004010346/http://blog.seattlepi.com/seattlepolitics/2013/10/03/ed-murrays-vision-meat-potatoes-no-greens/

union leaders believed there was a better chance that Murray could negotiate a wage agreement with big business.

This classic liberal coalition of big unions and big business swept Murray into office in the same race that saw Sawant elected. Three years later Murray's career would come to a calamitous and sudden end amid numerous allegations of child abuse and rape (which he denied).[9] But in 2013 he was riding high as the political establishment's best hope to avert class warfare over a $15 minimum wage.

Three weeks before his installation as mayor, Murray unveiled his blue-ribbon commission to develop a minimum wage increase proposal, with a charge to finish the work within four months. Murray's inelegantly named "Income Inequality Advisory Committee" (IIAC) was composed of twenty-four handpicked business, political, community, and labor leaders. It was a classic Seattle "stakeholder" group: The Chamber of Commerce and large and small business executives, Democratic City Council members, philanthropic and non-profit organizational leaders, and union leaders from the center-left side of the political spectrum. There was not a single minimum-wage worker on the panel.

Not everyone on the IIAC was equally sanguine about their charge. Community and labor leaders were pleased to be negotiating higher wages, but to some of the business representatives the IIAC was necessary root canal surgery to prevent a bigger abscess. "It was too big of an issue to be the first issue the mayor

---

9 Grinberg, E. (2017, September 12). Seattle Mayor Ed Murray resigns after latest child sex-abuse allegation. CNN. Retrieved March 28, 2023, from https://www.cnn.com/2017/09/12/us/seattle-mayor-ed-murray-resigns/

had to deal with," recalled Bob Donegan, CEO of the Ivar's restaurant chain. "But I understand why he had to do it. Kshama put him in that position."[10]

Murray also asked Sawant to join the IIAC, presenting the socialist with her first tactical quandary as a councilmember. "I was just nerve-wracked," Sawant later recalled. Joining the mayor's commission would open her to charges that she was allowing herself to be co-opted by the mayor and undermining the street movement; refusing to join would allow Murray and others to plow ahead and claim she had abdicated leadership on the issue. SA members discussed the matter internally, and, Sawant recalled, "we all agreed that it would be a bad mistake if we did not agree to be on it. But we also figured out a strategy of what we were going to do being on it."

Sawant informed the mayor that she would join the IIAC, but on her terms. While IIAC panel members took turns extolling the mayor's leadership at the press conference announcing the committee, Sawant declared she would sit on the committee as the shop steward of Seattle's working class. "I'm not there to serve the committee. I'm there to serve working people," she said. "To the extent that you genuinely are going to push for this, I want that, and I appreciate you taking a position. But to the extent that I feel that anything that happens on the committee is undermining working people, I'm going to speak up publicly about it.'"

---

10 Feit, J. (2014, July 30). *What Do We Want? $15! When Do We Want It? In a Little While! The secret history of Seattle's minimum wage law.* Seattle Met. Retrieved January 24, 2023, from https://www.seattlemet.com/news-and-city-life/2014/07/history-of-seattles-minimum-wage-law-august-2014

Mayor Murray and his IIAC co-chairs recognized that if they didn't steer the minimum wage negotiations from City Hall, Sawant's movement would lead it from the streets. Murray would have to manage his business and labor constituencies closely to make sure things didn't blow up. The payoff for a successful deal would be his coronation as a "big tent" mayor. He tapped SEIU's Rolf and Howard S. Wright, scion of one of Seattle's richest families and part owner of Seattle's iconic Space Needle, to co-chair the panel, which set to work in early 2014 with public forums and a slew of media appearances, including a weekday symposium with national speakers. The media marveled at how the mayor's co-chairs were "men on opposite sides of the debate,"[11] but that description overlooked the more salient truth that the two co-chairs, along with the mayor, shared a common goal.

Wright, a practical businessman, understood that if $15 wages were coming to Seattle, it was his responsibility to deliver an agreement that mitigated damage to business, phasing in the mandate over as long a period of time as possible. The negotiations also provided businesses an opportunity to win something they had not been able to achieve yet in the state of Washington: the ability to count tips and benefits toward employees' overall wages. Wright's goal would effectively create a subminimum wage for thousands of workers in restaurants and cafes, hotels, hair salons and barber shops, and other places where workers depended on gratuities.

---

11 Weise, K. (2015, May 8). How Seattle Agreed to a $15 Minimum Wage Without a Fight. Bloomberg.com. Retrieved April 2, 2023, from https://www.bloomberg.com/news/articles/2014-05-08/how-seattle-agreed-to-a-15-minimum-wage-without-a-fight

Meanwhile, Rolf wanted to harvest the local movement's momentum and claim the mantle as SEIU's national go-to leader as the fight for $15 ramped up in cities around the country. Having pushed Murray to embrace a $15 minimum wage, Rolf was now obliged to demonstrate that he could make the unions deal peacefully with business.

Though nominally in support of Sawant's 15Now movement, union leaders took steps to create daylight between themselves and the socialist. They set up a rival coalition, "15 for Seattle," and under that banner mobilized fast-food and other low-income workers to rally and turn out for the IIAC forums. Unlike the 15Now meetings, which were open to everyone, 15 for Seattle meetings were invitation-only sessions of organizational leaders and their deputies.

In February, 15Now neighborhood action groups held meetings throughout the city, planning a week of action in March and a huge rally on May 1, the day after the mayor's deadline for the IIAC to finish its work. They also began to lay the groundwork for a spring signature drive for a ballot initiative. Rank-and-file union members participated heavily in these neighborhood meetings. Even though their union leaders were opposed to the ballot strategy, rank-and-file union members recognized that to win, power had to be flexed outside City Hall.

Politicians on the other side of the fight also conceded the power of the initiative threat. "I hate the idea that we're sort of pressured to make a decision by this ballot threat," groused Democratic Councilmember Sally Clark, the chair of the City Council's special minimum wage committee. "I'm going to try to stay focused as much as possible on what's the best package, what's the right way to do this."[12] She was supported by the SEIU's Rolf, who told a reporter in a not-so-veiled warning to 15Now, "It would be unwise for any group to assume future significant SEIU financial support for an initiative as long as there's a viable path to achieving a new minimum wage policy through the council."[13] Rolf's rebuke was disturbing. The union leader was using his position to discourage workers from using their most powerful tool.

The leaders of the labor council, SEIU, and the United Food and Commercial Workers union were intent on working with, not against, the political establishment. Street marches and mobilizing workers for IIAC events was one thing, but when Sawant and other SA representatives continued to insist on the ballot initiative strategy, the union leaders were "very hostile," Sawant recalled. "They kept telling us, 'Look, we're not going to do it. You need to drop it. If you want to be part of 15 for Seattle, you need to drop this.'" Eventually, the shaky alliance between SA and labor leaders reached a breaking point. "We refused to drop the initiative, and so after a few meetings of that kind, they said, 'Well, we're not going to stand for it. You need to leave.'"

Outwardly, Sawant and the 15Now activists maintained a cordial détente with the 15 for Seattle union leaders, marching at rallies together and putting on a united front before the media. Some 15

---

12 [Seattle Channel]. (2014, March 28). *City Inside/Out: Minimum Wage Hike?* [Video]. Seattle Channel. https://www.seattlechannel.org/CityInsideOut/episodes?videoid=x20864

13 Feit, J. (2014, March 12). Minimum Wage Task Force Co-Chair Says Discussions are "On Track". *Seattle Met.* https://www.seattlemet.com/news-and-city-life/2014/03/minimum-wage-task-force-co-chair-says-discussions-are-on-track-march-2014

for Seattle leaders, including those from the hospitality workers union UNITE HERE and from the Washington Federation of State Employees, warmed to the ballot initiative strategy and continued to play central roles in 15Now. But the overall schism persisted through the end of the $15 minimum wage fight and would crop up repeatedly in other fights in the following years.

In late March, Sawant and 15Now announced they would begin drafting several potential ballot initiatives in time to begin collecting signatures in May. They announced a 15Now conference for April 26, where workers would democratically decide which ballot language to take to voters. The proposals all would include a $15 minimum wage to be implemented January 1, 2015 in all big businesses and a three-year phase in for businesses with fewer than 250 workers. The small business phase-in conceded that opponents were making headway on that issue in the media and in the IIAC. By agreeing to this concession, 15Now activists believed they would tamp down some of the opposition coming from small businesses.

Business leaders on the IIAC pushed for other concessions. Recognizing that the union leaders were loath to join Sawant's class war, they pressed for myriad loopholes: They demanded a first-ever tip penalty, in which tips would count against a worker's minimum wage, and for health benefits to count against wages as well. They wanted the definition of "small business" to encompass practically all employers in the city, and for phase-in periods of up to 10 years. Behind the genteel veneer of the IIAC's "big tent" was hard-knuckle bargaining by the corporate representatives.

At one point, union representatives nearly buckled in the face of corporate pressure. During a labor caucus, Sawant recalled, union leaders began talking about climbing down from $15. The

CEOs "want to meet us halfway," but as for $15, "they just can't get there," one of the union leaders told the labor caucus, according to Sawant. "At first there was a whole series of outraged reactions," Sawant recalled of the labor leaders, "Like, 'No, this can't be happening. Come on. No.' But then within minutes, practically all of them were ready to fold and basically say, 'Yeah, what can we do?'"

Sawant exploded. "I don't believe that you're saying this, at a time when the support for 15 is the strongest," she told them. "It's shameful that you're doing this," she said, and vowed to call a press conference to denounce their capitulation. Her sharp words brought the meeting back in line: The union leaders knew her threats weren't idle.

As the end of April deadline approached, negotiations in the IIAC tapered from all 24 members to a subcommittee of six, excluding Sawant. Meeting in private, the group came up with a late-night deal on April 23, a complex phasing-in of the $15 wage with varied wage schedules depending on the size of business and whether they offered benefits. Mayor Murray announced a press conference for noon the following day, expecting to celebrate the achievement. Newswires lit up in anticipation of the historic news. But noon came and went and the door to the mayor's office stayed closed. The secret deal had unraveled due to objections from the Chamber of Commerce and other business leaders. That afternoon, a dour mayor exited his office to inform the media: "Regrettably, and I know many of you have been here since this morning, waiting, but we don't have an agreement yet."[14] With

14 [Seattle Channel]. (2014, April 24). *Mayor's Press Conference: Minimum Wage Proposal* [Video]. Seattle Channel. https://www.seattlechannel.

co-chairs Rolf and Wright flanking him, he blamed the delay on all parties' hopes to avoid a "mini version of class warfare."

That evening, Sawant held her own press conference. "The committee has failed. And it is not a surprise," she said. "The committee had people with completely divergent goals. The goal of business is to keep wages as low as possible, continue to have their workers living in poverty, and they are only accountable to their private profits. Our goal is to make sure that poverty is ended among Seattle's workers." She called on all working people to join the 15Now conference, which was scheduled for just two days later: "Hold the City Council's feet to the fire so that we make sure that 2014 sees a strong $15 measure in the city of Seattle."

A reporter asked her, "The mayor said that if we go to a ballot battle in the fall, particularly a multi-initiative ballot, then that poses the danger of class warfare. What say you to that prospect?"

"We live in a capitalist system," Sawant rejoined. "If you look at the overwhelming race to the bottom for the 99 percent, it has been aerial bombardment from the 1 percent to the rest of us. So, like it or not, this is class warfare. What is different about Seattle this year is that workers are finally starting to speak out with one voice."[15]

Two days after the IIAC talks collapsed, more than 500 community members gathered for the first 15Now national conference

org/mayor-and-council/mayor/mayor-murray-(2014-2017)-archive-videos?videoid=x20749

15 [Seattle Channel]. (2014, April 24). *Councilmember Sawant Responds to Mayor`s Minimum Wage Proposal* [Video]. Seattle Channel. https://www.seattlechannel.org/mayor-and-council/city-council/city-council-all-videos-index?videoid=x20750

at a Seattle high school gymnasium. This was a giant, diverse gathering: healthcare workers, bus drivers, teachers, machinists, teamsters, hotel workers, homecare aides, students, construction workers, unemployed workers, and unhoused people, all coming together to debate and decide the movement's next step. While drawing workers from cities across the country, many of whom were starting their own 15Now chapters, the all-day conference focused on the immediate Seattle battleground. "The most dangerous thing we could do is be passive at this crucial moment or rely solely on negotiations with big business leaders in the [IIAC]," read the draft conference resolution. "We came this far because of grassroots power and pressure from below. The key to winning is taking our movement to the next level."

Sawant recalled sitting by herself during the lunch break, gathering her thoughts. "It was one of the most incredible feelings. What was happening there was a taste of what could be possible with worker-led organizations, where we're not just talking on the side, but genuinely discussing actionable things, something that actually could change material circumstances, where we could change the balance of power."

That afternoon, the conference attendees took up the main resolution, titled, "Onto the ballot and into the streets," which called for volunteers to collect the 50,000 voter signatures needed to put the $15 measure on the Seattle ballot. UNITE HERE members proposed an amendment to exempt hotel employers who negotiate full family health coverage with their union members. Some attendees were opposed to the exemption, calling it a handout to one sector of business. They were worried that it could be a slippery slope to more concessions. Sawant and SA members supported the amendment—it went against their ideological instincts, but they understood the practical importance of building the coalition by embracing the union members' demand. After hearing from pro and con speakers, the attendees passed the amendment handily. Then the conference took up the main resolution and boisterously adopted it. The debate and vote represented a vivid illustration of the "coalition from below" that the 15Now organizers were intent on building, a stark contrast to the top-down alliance of union officials and business leaders in the IIAC. Once lawyers completed drafting the conference-approved ballot—a two-week process—initiative petitions would be on the streets.

Following the 15Now conference, Mayor Murray promptly called the IIAC members back for urgent talks. "No matter what happens in the $15 wage debate, Seattle City Councilmember Kshama Sawant has already won," opined *Seattle Times* editorial writer Jonathan Martin three days after the 15Now conference decision. "In process-loving Seattle, the minimum wage is happening as quickly as a lightning strike." And if the City Council failed to act on $15, Martin noted, "Sawant and $15 Now will get a prime-time political brawl with the National Restaurant Association and other opponents. . . . and that offers $15 Now a chance to harness pure grassroots electricity."[16]

On the morning of May 1—five days after the 15Now conference, while thousands of Seattleites gathered for a huge May

16 Martin, J. (2014, April 29). Kshama Sawant has already won the Seattle $15 wage debate. *Seattle Times*. https://www.seattletimes.com/opinion/kshama-sawant-has-already-won-the-seattle-15-wage-debate/

Day march—Murray announced the IIAC union and business negotiators had reached a deal. "This is a historic moment for the city of Seattle," the mayor said. "We are going to decrease the poverty rate in this city by raising the minimum wage. We are going to improve the lives of workers who can barely afford to live in this city. At the same time, I think we do it in a way that doesn't harm those folks who are the great job creators of this city—the entrepreneurs, the homegrown businesses."[17] It was indeed a historic victory in the fight for $15, but the deal that Murray's IIAC crafted contained numerous concessions demanded by big business. The policy included an extended phase-in period: three years for businesses with more than 500 workers nationally, and seven years for other businesses. The proposal also included a tip and health benefit penalty for workers: For a period of up to 10 years, depending on the size of the business, employers could count tips and the cost of health benefits against the new wage rates.

With the proposal moving to City Council, 15Now adopted a two-track approach: Fight for the best legislation possible but keep the initiative path open. On May 15, as fast food workers in 150 US cities and in 30 countries worldwide were walking off the job over pay, Seattle union and community members joined Sawant to launch initiative signature-gathering. "I stand in solidarity with the fast food and low-wage workers around the world who are taking action for $15 an hour and the right to organize

---

17 [Seattle Channel]. (2014, May 1). *Mayor's Media Availability: Minimum Wage Proposal* [Video]. Seattle Channel. https://www.seattlechannel.org/mayor-and-council/mayor/mayor-murray-(2014-2017)-archive-videos?videoid=x20726

without retaliation," Sawant said. "These workers can't wait till 2025. The mayor's proposal is a step forward, but it falls short of what workers need by adding unnecessary delays of three, five, or even 10 years before getting up to an inflation-adjusted $15." She vowed to put forward amendments in City Council to close the corporate loopholes, retaining "the back-up option of letting the voters decide in November." Sawant noted that a new poll showed support for the $15 minimum wage in Seattle had increased from January's 68 percent approval level to 74 percent, and that many voters disapproved of the tip penalty and the other corporate loopholes.[18]

Before voting on the bill, City Council scheduled a series of hearings nominally intended to gather public input, but which also served the purpose of diverting street energy away from the ballot initiative. Small business owners, often fronting for the Chamber or major corporations, showed up to denounce the wage package. The union leader-controlled 15 for Seattle mobilized workers to testify in support of the IIAC proposal and called on the council to "adopt the mayor's proposal," refusing to point out the flaws. Only 15Now turned out workers to denounce the corporate loopholes and demand that the council strengthen the final bill.

This debate format allowed Democrats to embrace the IIAC proposal as a "sensible compromise," but that didn't mean they were done adding further concessions to the bill. Before forwarding

---

18 Minard, A. (2014, May 14). New Poll on the $15 Minimum Wage Shows Support in Seattle is Higher Than Ever: 74 Percent. *The Stranger*. https://www.thestranger.com/blogs/2014/05/14/19538144/new-poll-on-the-15-minimum-wage-shows-support-in-seattle-is-higher-than-ever-74-percent

it to City Council, the mayor tacked on a subminimum training wage that would harm mostly teenagers and immigrant workers.[19] And at the final committee meeting before the full council vote, Councilmember Clark surprised the crowd with an amendment to delay implementation of the minimum wage by three months, to April 1, 2015. Ironically, she claimed that because the new law was so complex—at the CEOs' insistence during IIAC negotiations—employers would need more time to adjust their payroll systems. It felt like a spiteful slap at workers. The 15Now activists in the crowd disrupted the amendment votes with howls of protest but the Democrats approved these further concessions.

On June 2, the City Council met for a final vote on the measure, concessions included. More than 150 workers filled seats in City Council chambers and spilled out into the hallway, holding up signs. Sawant had prepared her own amendments to strip out the concessions that the Democrats had added. Beating back those changes would not be realistic. But by making this last-ditch effort, she and the 15Now movement could publicly expose the Democrats' capitulation to big business, even as the movement made history.

"When you consider tips, when you consider training wages, when you consider the start date of this, think of those who had so little and risked it all in order for us to be here at this moment," Jesse Inman, a mental health worker and member of SEIU 1199NW, told the council. "This movement did not come about because

---

19 Martin, J. (2014, May 15). Murray adds a 'training wage' to $15 minimum wage proposal. *The Seattle Times*. https://www.seattletimes.com/news/murray-adds-a-training-wage-to-15-minimum-wage-proposal/

of meetings that were held. This movement did not come about because of politicians. This movement came about because of people in the streets taking risks, walking off their jobs, and organizing their workplace."

Next came Rihanna Martinson. She drew a standing ovation when she announced that, on May 15, she had walked out with her Target co-workers. "I went on strike in order to demonstrate that we do have power, and for all of the other workers out there to realize that they also have power, because change doesn't happen unless you actually make it," she said. "I make about $9.61 an hour right now, and I work very, very hard for it. What $15 means is that workers like me are able to afford basic necessities. Rising housing costs are only part of the problem. Things like healthcare, things like being able to afford new shoes before our shoes fall apart, being able to go to the dentist if we get a cavity without worrying about it completely destroying our lives. I'm worried that my mother right now is getting old and she's going to work until the day she dies, and I want to be able to take care of her, and I don't want to work until I die either. I would really like to be able to save money for retirement or even for something, if something happens to me so that I don't end up on the street."

Following public comments, the council took up debate on the bill and Sawant's amendments, including her call to require big businesses to pay $15 upfront, without the three-year phase in.

"In all the hundreds if not thousands of people that I've spoken to, the vast majority of whom are not socialists, I have not met a single person who claimed that McDonald's, or Starbucks, or any other big business needs any kind of phase-in," Sawant began. "Everybody understands they make such enormous profits, in the billions of dollars, that they are able to end the poverty of their workers today, but they don't want to. They pay poverty wages because their business model depends on it."

She asked, "Who here thinks that Target should get another couple of years of phase-in before workers like Rihanna can get a decent wage and get rid of this terrible anxiety that plagues them about what is going to happen to them if there's one financial backslide in her life, she is going to become homeless? . . . Why is it that the council is not fighting for workers like Rihanna?"

The crowd erupted in applause. The Democrats rejected all four of Sawant's amendments before taking the bill to a final vote. All eight Democrats took turns with flowery speeches extolling the $15 wage and thanking workers. Yet none of their words could erase what they had displayed the previous hour: When push came to shove, they served the interests of Target and the rest of big business, not Martinson and other low-wage workers.

Before the final vote, when it was Sawant's turn to speak again, she echoed Inman's earlier remarks: "We did this. Workers did this. Today's first major victory for 15 will inspire people all over the nation. We need to recognize what happened here in Seattle that led us to this point. Fifteen was not won at the bargaining table as the so-called 'sensible compromise' between workers and business. It was not the result of the generosity of corporations or their Democratic Party representatives in government. What was voted on in the city council was a reflection of what workers won on the street over this last year. . . . Our victory is not complete, but we have fought until the last day, the last hour, against all the loopholes demanded by business."[20]

At the final vote, the crowd erupted. First, 15 for Seattle leaders started their anodyne chant, "Good work!" only to be overtaken by the 15Now crowd bellowing, "We are unstoppable, we made 15 possible!" The cacophony was a fitting public demonstration of the divergence between the two camps—the union leaders thanking the councilmembers, the 15Now activists claiming the working-class victory. For that weekend's victory celebration, 15Now activists printed up hundreds of new signs that flipped the letters to read, "15Won."

The first major US city to approve a $15/hour minimum wage would raise pay for 100,000 workers, transferring an estimated $3 billion in wealth from businesses to workers over a decade. And because of the strong cost of living adjustment provision in the law, Seattle's minimum wage for all workers hit $20.76 an hour in 2025, protecting low-wage workers against the ravages of inflation.

Following the win, the $15 fight mushroomed out from Seattle. In the two years that followed—and just three and a half years since New York fast-food workers first hoisted picket signs calling for $15/hour and union recognition—some 17 million US workers won pay raises through voter initiatives, legislative action, administrative rule making, or because individual companies, facing

---

20 [YouTube]. (2014, June 3). *Kshama Sawant's speech at $15 minimum wage vote* [Video]. YouTube. https://www.youtube.com/watch?v=02PU5KoNhyc&t=15s

growing public pressure, raised base wages.[21] That number grew to 26 million workers over the span of a decade.[22]

Activists elsewhere drew lessons from Seattle. In San Francisco, where the mayor created a "big tent" labor-management wage committee, seeking to replicate the Seattle process, union leaders there took a strategic cue from Sawant and prepared to run an initiative. The leverage got them a better deal than Seattle—a three-year phase-in for all businesses to $15, with none of the tip or healthcare penalties that the Seattle labor leaders had conceded. Around the country, 15Now activists played key roles in many of the wage battles; unions and community organizations also were essential in mobilizing for and funding campaigns. In many cities and states, the wage fight linked up to related struggles. The Black Lives Matter movement joined with Walmart workers and allies to combine the fights against police brutality and economic inequality. Reverend William J. Barber II, the North Carolina pastor and founder of the Moral Mondays movement, marched with McDonald's workers, headlined a fast-food workers' convention, and made the Fight for $15 a central part of the Poor People's Campaign.

---

21 National Employment Law Project (2016, April 1). *Fight for $15 Impact Report: Raises for 17 Million Workers, 10 Million Going to $15*. Retrieved January 25, 2023, from https://cdn.cocodoc.com/cocodoc-form-pdf/pdf/130057978-Fight-for-15-Impact-Report-National-Employment-Law-Project-nelp-.pdf

22 Lathrop, Y., Wilson, M. D., & Lester, T. W. (2022, November 29). *Ten-Year Legacy of the Fight for $15 and a Union Movement*. National Employment Law Project. Retrieved July 19, 2024, from https://www.nelp.org/insights-research/10-year-legacy-fight-for-15-union-movement/

None of the wage victories, of course, happened out of political benevolence or enlightened business attitudes. In the aftermath of the Seattle breakthrough, Sawant and Socialist Alternative members emphasized that the fight for $15 was a class struggle, not a policy debate. Everything workers won was because of their power, and every shortfall was a consequence of not having enough power. And yet it was vital, Sawant noted, to claim every hard-fought victory, even partial ones. "As a socialist, as a fighter for the interests of the working class, I will fight every inch of the way. We should be doing that, we should be fighting until the last hour," Sawant told listeners on *Democracy Now!* three days after the historic vote. "But every gain that we can get has to be wrested, wrenched from the hands of the ruling elite, from the corporate politicians and the businesses that they represent. And so even a small raise in standard of living is something worth fighting for," she said.

The lesson of the Seattle fight "shows that we need to build an even more powerful mass movement everywhere around the nation, so that we are strong enough to fight against corporate loopholes," she said. "The outcomes of social struggle are a function of the balance of power. So the moral of the story is not that, well, we can't win; the moral of the story is we won a huge victory for the working class, but if we want to fight against corporations, then the only way to do it is to build mass movements."[23]

That was a lesson burnished into the minds of a new rising army of activists. For Logan Swan, the low-wage job-hustler, and for many

---

23 [Democracy Now!]. (2014, June 5). *Seattle's Socialist City Council Member Kshama Sawant Hails Historic Vote for $15/Hour Minimum Wage* [Video]. Democracy Now! https://www.democracynow.org/2014/6/5/seattle_s_socialist_city_council_member

other newcomers to political struggle, the $15 battle in Seattle showed a different, exciting way forward. Years earlier, Swan had been eager to vote for Barack Obama, only to be disillusioned when the new president failed to deliver on raising the minimum wage, and sold out workers to Wall Street. He was pissed off when he saw Seattle councilmembers, during public comment from low-wage workers, appear to gloss over or not even pay attention to what the workers were saying. In the community, he was frustrated with some of the activists who declared in meetings that "it has to be 15 now, no concessions." The Sawant-led strategy was different, a fighting approach that neither tried to cajole the political establishment nor issued inflexible demands. The $15 fight "really did allow me to see in contrast the movement-building approach of our council office—not some kind of weird liberal moralism or a pragmatism, but having a principled approach that's based on where consciousness is at, where the balance of class forces is at," he said.

What Sawant and Socialist Alternative had accomplished in Seattle was a lot more than a wage hike. They had introduced a new theory of political insurgency, successfully breaking through the inertia and resistance of the political establishment. By bringing a combative method to political struggle, mobilizing community members to challenge the establishment at every turn, and demanding grassroots decision-making on the key question of running a ballot initiative, they had stunned opponents and achieved transformational change that rippled out nationally and beyond.

This was a new weapon in the hands of the working class, and the emboldened Seattle activists couldn't wait to deploy it in the next battle. If we could win $15 in such dramatic fashion, what else was possible?

2

The New Political Insurgency

The Sawant-led movement was a shock to the political establishment. *Seattle Times* editorial writer Jonathan Martin credited the socialist for "coming out of nowhere to commandeer the city's political agenda."

"Who had heard of her before last August?" he wrote as the minimum wage battle peaked. "For that matter, who (aside from Socialist Alternative newspaper subscribers) had a quick jump to a $15 wage on their radar a year ago?"[24]

It wasn't just the bold demands made by the invigorated working-class movement. It was the forcefulness of the tactics that set

---

24 Martin, J. (2014, April 29). Kshama Sawant has already won the Seattle $15 wage debate. *Seattle Times*. https://www.seattletimes.com/opinion/kshama-sawant-has-already-won-the-seattle-15-wage-debate/

the establishment on its heels. Pundits were jarred by the activists who had packed City Council chambers. These people didn't sit passively while councilmembers read their scripted remarks from the dais. They brought signs, chanted, cheered Sawant, and booed Democrats during public comment sessions, readily fulminating against the politicians in front of TV cameras. And just as important, they showed a willingness, even downright enthusiasm, for deploying disruptive tactics like the ballot initiative. Politicians who were used to the fine arts of public pleasantries, backroom negotiations, and kumbaya press conferences suddenly found themselves in the unfamiliar terrain of open political combat. It rankled them that the socialists refused to follow their established rules.

For years before 2014, Seattle's political establishment—essentially a Democratic Party monopoly—had glided along in a political stasis. They cultivated the appearance of social liberalism, embracing—at least in rhetoric—the values of inclusion and diversity. But since the area served as homebase to Boeing, Microsoft, Starbucks, Amazon, and T-Mobile, among others, they mostly catered to the low-tax, low-regulation needs of modern capital. Municipal policy debates were usually genteel affairs culminating in unanimous votes and public statements of mutual congratulation.

As the minimum wage fight demonstrated, Sawant shattered that model of political consensus. Whether at public demonstrations, in press conferences, and in City Council debates, she used her new platform to bridge the daily struggles of working people with her vision of a socialist society, excoriating Democrats especially for claiming to stand with working people but lobbying to undermine their demands behind closed doors.

This was a political insurgency, a different way of engaging in struggle in the US. If asked to identify a socialist in elected office, local politicos previously might have pointed to Bernie Sanders, the genial senator from Vermont who called himself an independent socialist but caucused with the Democrats. Or perhaps they'd cite the three reformist Milwaukee mayors who, in the early 20th century, under the banner of "sewer socialism," successfully cultivated a series of municipal public works projects. Less charitably, they might cite images of the dour, greying leaders of the late Soviet Union.

Sawant was none of those. Her political organization emerged from a strand of Marxist activism that emerged after World War II as a sharp rejoinder to both the reform-minded international socialist movement and the bureaucratized and disfigured experience in the Soviet Union and its client states. To fully appreciate the ideological foundation of the contemporary Seattle activists, understand how exceptional the Sawant movement experience has been in the American political experience, and draw lessons for future political action, one must examine 175 years of socialist thought and experience.

What follows is not an expansive recitation of socialist history, which spans the globe from advanced industrialized countries to anti-colonial liberation movements, and ranges from protest movements to electoral work to armed struggle. Rather, I have chosen to focus on those strands of socialist struggle that most informed the Seattle movement's intervention in the political arena. Sawant and SA closely studied political history, so to fully appreciate Seattle we, too, must look back to see what ideas informed this extraordinary movement.

Socialism as an aspiration gained currency during the political explosions that rocked Europe in 1848 and 1849, first in Paris, where mass street protests forced the abdication of King Louis Philippe, and then in nearly 50 other European cities. People's demands for parliamentary democracy and civil rights were brutally repressed by the military and police. But in their wake, monarchs and the other ruling elites felt compelled to institute reforms, including parliaments, an end to serfdom, and voting and constitutional rights. The reforms were quite truncated—legislatures had limited powers and were still subject to the control of unelected sovereigns; farmers went from outright servitude to sharecropping and crushing debt; suffrage was limited to white men, and often only property-holders; and rulers banned political parties that they felt posed a potential threat. Yet it was a seismic societal shift, coinciding with rapid urbanization, the emergence of large capitalist enterprises with huge new productive capacities, and the advent of breakthrough transportation technologies, most notably railroad and steamship lines.

Just before the political convulsions of 1848-49, Karl Marx and Frederick Engels had published the *Manifesto of the Communist Party*, which declared that under the rapidly developing capitalist economy, "Society as a whole is more and more splitting into two great hostile camps, into two great classes directly facing each other—bourgeoisie and proletariat."[25] Marx and Engels observed that the bourgeoisie, or ruling class—the factory owners, financiers, and big landlords—made profits only by exploiting the labor of the proletariat, the workers. To build a society free of

25 Karl, M., & Engels, F. *Manifesto of the Communist Party* (1948th ed., p. 9). International Publishers.

exploitation, workers would have to wrest control of the means of production from the bourgeoisie and operate them democratically for the benefit of all, not for private profit. And the bourgeoisie would not yield willingly. It would take a popular revolution—a communist revolution—to win a society in which production and wealth was held in common, “from each according to his ability, to each according to his needs,” as Marx later elaborated.

The advent of parliaments, even in limited form, forced early socialists to confront the question of whether and how to engage in these new political spaces. Prior to that, revolutionaries had mostly employed mass strikes, industrial sabotage, and direct armed rebellion as primary tactics. Elections and parliaments held the potential to raise the prominence of workers’ pressing demands and even win reforms; on the other hand, a parliamentary focus threatened to divert energy into the narrow strictures established by bourgeois governments, and away from the independent worker self-organization and action necessary for revolution.

The *Manifesto* recognized that liberal forms of government under capitalism were only façades of democracy, structures intended to uphold the capitalist order: “The executive of the modern state is but a committee for managing the common affairs of the whole bourgeoisie.” Marx and Engels believed that the working class could not gain its identity and program—develop its consciousness as a “class for itself”—in the electoral arena; that had to be established through struggles led by unions and socialist organizations. Nevertheless, in the aftermath of the 1848-49 political spring, Marx urged socialists to fight for political power through elections, not as a dominant strategy but as a tactical arena of struggle to support revolutionary organizing in factories and fields. "Even when there is no prospect whatever of their being elected," he told members of the new Communist League in 1850, "the workers must put up their own candidates in order to preserve their independence, to count their forces and to lay before the public their revolutionary attitude and party standpoint."

Another uprising in 1871 led to the creation—ever so briefly—of the worker-run Paris Commune. The revolutionary Parisian government abolished child labor, mandated separation of church and state, and permitted workers to take over factories that the bourgeoisie had abandoned. They barred perks for government workers and required that all public servants, including members of the Commune, be paid only average workers' wages. But the bourgeoisie were not vanquished. After two months of Commune power, the French army swept in and crushed the revolutionaries, killing up to 20,000 Communards and taking more than 43,000 prisoners. One lesson of the Paris Commune and its demise, Marx and Engels observed, was that to realize a true revolution, the entire governing structure—not just bourgeois parliaments, but also the army, as the enforcer of societal rule—had to be replaced with democratic forms of worker control. "The working class cannot simply lay hold of the ready-made state machinery, and wield it for its own purposes," they wrote.

The years after the Commune saw three tendencies develop in socialist practice. Syndicalists considered parliamentary politics to offer an illusory path to revolution, and they outright rejected engaging in bourgeois-designed elections. They urged "abstentionism" in elections and a complete focus on building the revolution at the point of production—in the factories and other major capitalist enterprises. Others, who called themselves revolutionary parliamentarians, hewed to Marx's original formulation of entering the political arena not with the hope of seizing power through that avenue but so that working class movements could "count their forces" and speak to a wider audience about the need for revolution. And the third tendency—which gained dominance over the other two—was reformism, also called "parliamentarism," the idea that winning political reforms under bourgeois systems could over time undermine capitalism and ultimately produce a socialist society.

Socialist reformists argued that movements should fight for "minimum demands"—higher wages, shorter work hours, voting rights—while articulating the "maximum demand" goal of a socialist society. They registered remarkable electoral victories in the decades following the Paris Commune. By the turn of the century, the Socialist Party of France had 3,800 representatives in municipal government, and the German Social Democratic Party (SPD) went from winning around 1.4 million votes—equating to 35 seats in the 397-seat Reichstag—in 1890 to 4.2 million votes—producing 110 seats, the most of any party—just two decades later. Socialists also held local and national offices in Austria, Belgium, Denmark, England, Norway, and Sweden.[26]

The success led reformists to believe that parliamentary activity would displace general strikes and mass uprisings as the pathway to socialism. Austrian Social Democrat Karl Kautsky asserted that parliamentary activity "is the most powerful lever that can be utilized to raise the proletariat out of its economic, social, and

26 International Workers League (2018, October 30). *The role of socialists in electoral politics during the period of competitive capitalism.* Revolutionaries and Elections. Retrieved January 13, 2023, from https://litci.org/en/revolutionaries-and-elections/

moral degradation."[27] But the price for electoral success was the integrity of the socialist agenda. The SPD and other parties watered down their political demands in order to expand their voter base and avoid invoking the ire of ruling elites. Elected leaders became careerists detached from working people and their struggles. They focused solely on "minimum demands" and jettisoned the "maximum demand," talking about socialism as a lofty ideal to be achieved in some hazy future era. They lost confidence in workers and maintained that capitalism was displaying adaptability that was taming, not inflaming, conflict between the bourgeoisie and the proletariat. To many, this was socialism stripped of its Marxist foundation.

But in fact, just as socialist reformism was gaining ascendency in the late 1800s, the conflict between the bourgeoisie and the proletariat was scaling up globally. What business enterprises did to individual groups of workers—extract profits by paying them less than the value of their labor—entire nations, backed by armies and navies, did to peoples in distant lands through brutal conquest and subjugation, exploiting new markets in Africa, Asia, and the Americas. This was the rise of imperialism, the system of capitalist exploitation raised up from the factory floor to encompass the entire globe.

The bourgeoisie in Europe and the United States competed against one another for access to these new markets and valuable goods—rubber, coffee, ivory, cotton, oil. In the years before and after the turn of the 20th century, states maneuvered to dominate as many new lands as possible for the benefit of their

---

27 Kautsky, K. (1971). *The Class Struggle (Erfurt Program)* (p. 2). W.W. Norton.

own capitalist classes. France, Britain, Russia, Germany, Austria-Hungary, Italy, and the United States raced to build empires around the globe, investing heavily in new and bigger weapons to conquer nations and peoples. Not coincidentally, the same armaments also were deployed to fend off challenges from rival capitalist states. To the "victors" went the spoils: vast profits "sold for a song or simply taken by force,"[28] as Dutch astronomer and Marxist Anton Pannekoek explained at the time. "Again and again, conflicts broke out, first over China, then over Turkey or Persia, then over Morocco. Each time, they were successfully settled until finally, in 1914, when none of the parties wanted to retreat, the great, long-awaited and long-prepared war, the war over world power, erupted."[29]

It was the beginning of World War I, the deadliest conflict to date in world history. Some 22 million people were killed over the following four years of war. The *Communist Manifesto* had declared that the working class has nothing in common with the bourgeoisie. But as World War I approached, workers in Europe found that years of socialist reformism had compromised their parliamentary representatives. In 1912, socialists from throughout Europe had gathered for an international conference in Switzerland to protest "against war, and declared that they would do everything in their power to prevent it," Pannekoek wrote. "But, behind this declaration, there lay much more fear of war than firm determination to take up the fight against it." The conference failed to

28 Pannekoek, Anton, *The Prehistory of the World* War, in Day, R. B., & Gaido, D. (2012). *Discovering Imperialism: Social Democracy to World War I* (p. 886). Haymarket Books.

29 Ibid, P. 887.

develop a plan to mobilize workers to oppose the looming war, and accordingly, "When finally the governments really wanted war, there was neither the strength nor the courage to take up the fight," Pannekoek wrote. Instead, most socialist leaders in European parliaments succumbed to nationalist war fever and voted for war funding. Some even joined war cabinets set up by the ruling elites, choosing national flag over international class. As Pannekoek wrote, "Internationalism went up in smoke."

Contributing to the European socialists' collapse was their failure to effectively confront European racism, a key pillar of the imperialist project. Bourgeois powers whipped up nationalist fervor to advance their colonial designs, winning over significant sections of the working class. Outpourings of racist images and stories depicting primitive, backwards people in Africa and Asia, combined with the allure of more and better jobs for workers at home as a result of these new foreign markets, won over large portions of the European working class to the program of imperial conquest.

Socialist civil rights champion W.E.B. Du Bois noted the diabolical ingenuity of imperialists in diverting European workers' attention from hard economic times at home to the glories of empire and the adventure of conquering foreign lands. "It is no longer simply the merchant prince, or the aristocratic monopoly, or even the employing class, that is exploiting the world," he wrote in 1915 as war raged. "It is the nation, a new democratic nation composed of united capital and labor."[30]

30 *The African Roots of War,* W.E.B. Du Bois (1915), reprint from *Atlantic Monthly* accessed March 6, 2025 in http://www.webdubois.org/dbAfricanRWar.html .

Rosa Luxemburg, a Polish socialist organizer and one of the leading polemicists against the reformist tendency, singled out the German Social Democrats, the single largest socialist parliamentary bloc in Europe. "The great historical hour," she said, demanded that they organize against the war drive. "Instead, there followed on the part of the parliamentary representatives of the working class a miserable collapse." The German Social Democratic Party "has wiped itself out completely as a class party with a world conception of its own, has delivered the country, without a word of protest, to the fate of imperialist war without [and] to the dictatorship of the sword within," she wrote.[31]

Moreover, the war demonstrated who was really in control of state machinery: certainly not the people, and not even government ministers and elected parliamentarians, but rather the big bourgeoisie. American socialist journalist John Reed observed that the US entry into the war in 1917 "completed the abject surrender of the government to the great financiers." In November 1916, Woodrow Wilson won reelection as US president on the slogan "he kept us out of war," but five months later the US joined the conflagration. Reed noted: "It had been clearly proven for almost two years that the forces which were pushing the country toward war were the great munitions interests, the bankers who had floated Alliance's loans, and the imperialist corporations, anxious to get a share in the redistribution of foreign markets."[32]

---

31 Quoted in *The Junius Pamphlet: The Crisis in German Democracy,* in Hudis, P., & Anderson, K. B., editors (2004). *The Rosa Luxemburg Reader (p. 327).* Month Review Press.

32 Quoted in International Workers League (2018, October 30). *The role of socialists in electoral politics during the period of competitive capitalism.*

Not all socialists fell down the reformist rabbit hole. In the late 1800s, while reformist parliamentarians were giving up on class struggle, socialist revolutionaries throughout Europe were leading mass strikes with demands for pay raises, shorter workdays, and political freedom.

Sometimes a small spark set off a giant conflagration. Luxemburg, who organized extensively throughout Europe, traced the origins of the first Russian Revolution, in 1905, to a cascading series of mass strikes in dozens of cities throughout the vast Russian empire beginning in 1896. Sometimes, she noted, "the immediate cause was trivial." In 1905 in St. Petersburg, bosses at the Putilov metal works fired two workers for union membership. "This measure called forth a solidarity strike on January 16 of the whole of the 12,000 employees in this works," she noted. Russian socialists extended strike demands to call for the right to unionize, an eight-hour workday, and freedom of speech and of the press. Within a few days, 140,000 workers throughout the region were on strike.[33]

When the St. Petersburg strikers and supporters marched en masse on the Tsar's palace, the police massacred hundreds, inaugurating 10 months of strikes and rebellion throughout the country—what's known as the first Russian revolution. Factory workers in dozens of cities began organizing into democratically-elected bodies of workers—both men and women—established initially to coordinate strikes but which quickly adapted into local legislative

Revolutionaries and Elections. Retrieved January 13, 2023, from https://litci.org/en/revolutionaries-and-elections/

33 Quoted in *The Mass Strike, the Political Party, and the Trade Unions,* in Hudis, P., & Anderson, K. B., editors (2004). *The Rosa Luxemburg Reader (p. 179).* Month Review Press.

bodies for the working class, similar to the Paris Commune. These were called soviets—literally, "councils" in Russian—and they were the living manifestation of what the Russian socialists considered true democracy in action. They rejected the notion that democracy was limited to electoral voting rights. For them it also encompassed the demand for democratic decision-making in the economic arena, all the way down to the factory floor.

In a country with no history of democracy, the newly formed soviets were a remarkably bold and creative assertion of worker control. The Tsar also made sure that they were temporary. Following the lead of 19th century monarchs, the Tsar created a bourgeois parliamentary system known as the Duma, to siphon energy from revolutionaries, while directing his police to crush the soviets with brute force.

While limited in its powers and with elections skewed to ensure few workers would get into office, the Duma became a proving ground for revolutionary parliamentarians—the left wing of Russia's Social Democratic Party, known as the Bolsheviks. In 1912, four metal workers and two textile workers, all Bolsheviks, won seats in the Duma and proceeded to wage battle against the autocracy from within the Tsar's own legislature. Vastly outnumbered in the chamber, and shadowed by the Tsar's police, they agitated for universal suffrage and a democratic republic, a national eight-hour workday, and the confiscation of landlord estates; they led street demonstrations, published a nationally-distributed party paper, and coordinated strike support; they forced parliamentary debates on deadly factory explosions, demanding punishment for the owners. Through these fights, the Bolshevik deputies became masters at Marxist political insurgency.

In a remarkable book, *The Bolsheviks in the Tsarist Duma*, one of these deputies, metalworker Alexei Badayev, recalled his first speech in the hostile Duma: "When I mounted the rostrum I felt very keenly the responsibility which rested on a workers' representative. . . . Here we, the representatives of the workers, stood face to face with the enemy, the age-long oppressors of the working class. We had to express directly and openly, without subterfuges or parliamentary tricks, all that the masses were thinking, to proclaim their needs and to hurl their accusations at the representatives of the existing regime."[34]

Badayev and the other socialist deputies frequently snuck out of Russia to consult with Bolshevik leaders who had been exiled by the Tsar. Bolshevik expatriate leader Vladimir Lenin counseled the deputies to "use the Duma for agitation and to help develop the revolutionary movement by exposing both the Tsarist government and the hypocrisy of the so-called liberal parties. . . . No doubt it is possible to move amendments and even to introduce some bills, but this must only be done in order to expose more effectively the anti-working-class nature of the Tsarist regime and to reveal the absolute lack of rights of the exploited workers. This is really what the workers should hear from their deputies."[35]

In the summer of 1914, Badayev and the other Bolshevik deputies were preparing to introduce a National Equality Bill banning a raft of antisemitic laws when the Tsar declared war on Germany. The Duma brushed aside the equality bill and voted to fund the war. The Bolshevik deputies—unlike their socialist compatriots elsewhere—declared their steadfast opposition to war. They

---

34 Badayev, A. (2012). *The Bolsheviks in the Tsarist Duma* (pp. 55). Red Star Publishers.

35 Badayev, A. (2012). *The Bolsheviks in the Tsarist Duma* (pp. 67, 117-118). Red Star Publishers.

published anti-war pamphlets, organized factory strikes against the war, and joined workers in the streets confronting the police. For their efforts, they were arrested, expelled from the Duma, and deported to Siberia. The antiwar strikes were suppressed.

This brief experiment in revolutionary parliamentarism would have been an inconsequential historic footnote but for the second Russian revolution that erupted just two and a half years later. In January 1917, having steered the country into a ruinous war, Tsar Nicholas II abdicated power, ending the 300-year Romanov dynasty. The streets flooded with workers and soldiers demanding peace, land redistribution, jobs, and civil rights. With a bourgeois-dominated provisional government fighting to gain power, socialist forces drew upon the lessons of the Bolshevik experience in the Duma along with the early soviet experiences in the 1905 revolution to navigate the chaos of a new society struggling to be born.

In cities throughout Russia workers began to establish new soviets, challenging the authority of the provisional government and demanding that workers run the state. The Bolsheviks defended the soviets and rejected a return to Duma-like structures. “We need not only representation along democratic lines, but the building of the entire state administration from the bottom up by the masses themselves, their effective participation in all of life’s steps, their active role in the administration,” Lenin wrote in April 1917 shortly after returning from exile.[36]

36 Lenin, V. (1974). *Lenin: Collected Works, Volume 24* (2nd ed., p. 181). Progress Publishers. https://archive.org/details/LeninCW/Lenin%20CW-Vol.%2024/page/n185/mode/2up

Speaking a month later to a congress of peasants' deputies, he explained why the Bolsheviks rejected the reformist provisional government in favor of the soviets: "The capitalists want to preserve the bureaucracy, which stands above the people, to preserve the police and the standing army, which is separated from the people, and commanded by non-elective generals and other officers. And the generals and other officers, unless they are elected, will almost invariably be landowners and capitalists. That much we know from the experience of all the republics in the world."

The Bolshevik Party, Lenin explained, "is therefore working for a democratic republic of another kind. We want a republic where there is no police that browbeats the people; where all officials, from the bottom up, are elective and displaceable whenever the people demand it, and are paid salaries not higher than the wages of a competent worker. . . . We want a republic where all state power, from the bottom up, belongs wholly and exclusively to the Soviets of Workers', Soldiers', Peasants', and other Deputies. The workers and peasants are the majority of the population. The power must belong to them, not to the landowners or the capitalists. The workers and peasants are the majority of the population. The power and the functions of administration must belong to their Soviets, not to the bureaucracy."[37]

The Bolsheviks began 1917 as a minority movement, even among Russians who considered themselves socialists. But

---

37 Lenin, V. (1974). *Lenin: Collected Works, Volume 24* (2nd ed., pp. 373-374). Progress Publishers. https://archive.org/details/LeninCW/Lenin%20CW-Vol.%2024/page/n185/mode/2up

through months of strikes and soldier rebellions, as the soviets gained sway, the Bolsheviks achieved ascendancy. Under the banner of "Peace, Land, and Bread," they united the two core but disparate Russian working class constituencies, urban workers and rural peasants. In October, masses of workers, soldiers, and peasants took to the streets, overthrew the provisional government, and declared a socialist republic run by democratically elected soviets.

The unfortunate history that followed—the Russian civil war stoked by hostile imperial forces; the crushing of incipient socialist revolutions in Europe and elsewhere, laying the groundwork for the eventual rise of fascism; missteps by the new Soviet leaders, including their failure to scale up the original democratic soviet model; Lenin's incapacitation and early death; and the resurgence of the very bureaucracy that the revolutionaries feared so greatly—is far beyond the scope of this book. Those developments led directly into the rise of Stalin's brutal dictatorship that, beginning in the 1920s, turned the idea of Marxist socialism, including the democratic character of the workers' councils, on its head.

But the experiences of 1917 in Russia, and the events in the years leading up to the revolution, provided vital lessons that have animated political revolutionaries—including those in Seattle—for more than a century. If you could transport metalworker Alexei Badayev to the present, he would immediately recognize the political congruence between Kshama Sawant's attacks on the political establishment in the $15 minimum wage fight and his own speeches in the Duma a century earlier.

In 1920, Social Democratic parties worldwide gathered under the flag of the Communist International and drew up a balance sheet on the parliamentary experience. Reformism waged under bourgeois governments had been a dreadful and costly failure. Under capitalism, legislative bodies are not neutral grounds but rather are basic instruments of state power, they declared. It was, in essence, "a machine for oppression and subjugation in the hands of ruling capital," and as such, socialists needed to return to Marx's formulation whereby they would use the parliamentary struggle "to count their forces and to lay before the public their revolutionary attitude and party standpoint." They would engage not as reformers, but as revolutionaries who have been sent by their party "into the enemy camp." As political combatants they should proudly raise the socialist banner in office, use the parliamentary platform to organize and agitate workers about mass struggles happening in the street and the workplace, unmask politicians who insincerely claim to support workers, and ultimately "help the masses from inside parliament to break up the state machine."[38]

This did not mean, however, abandoning the fight for the immediate needs of the working class, from higher wages to voting rights—in fact, socialists needed to be on the front lines of these battles. When socialist reformists severed the link between their minimum and maximum demands, they'd misled people into thinking that winning material improvements under

38 Third (Communist) International, Second Congress (1920). Theses on the Communist Parties and Parliamentarism. Equals Publishing. https://equals-publishing.wordpress.com/wp-content/uploads/2021/04/reader-ep_comintern_1920_theses-parliament.pdf

capitalism was either a sufficient end goal, or that it would somehow magically lead, step by gradual step, to a socialist society. Revolutionary parliamentarians recognized that the legislature was an *arena of struggle* between the bourgeoisie and the proletariat's opposing interests, a place to advance bold demands, confront and expose adversaries, and build working class consciousness. Any gain inside that arena for workers would be strictly a function of the power of the movement outside. And without a sustained insurgent working-class movement, any legislative victory would be rolled back as soon as the bourgeoisie found an opening.

In 1938, Russian revolutionary Leon Trotsky refined this approach with a lengthy paper that became known as "The Transitional Program for Socialist Revolution." By then, the Soviet Union under Stalin had degenerated into an authoritarian state, modernizing rapidly but intolerant of dissident viewpoints. Socialists who backed the original democratic soviet model were pushed out, exiled, or executed. Outside the Soviet Union, socialists organized a movement to counter Stalin. Trotsky, a leader in the Russian revolution forced out of the Soviet Union in 1929, played a central role in the opposition and drafted the Transitional Program from exile in Mexico. Trotsky's draft document was debated by socialists in countries worldwide for six months before being ratified at an international conference in France in September 1938.

"It is necessary to help the masses in the process of the daily struggle to find the bridge between present demands and the socialist program of the revolution," the program read. "This bridge should include a system of transitional demands, stemming from today's conditions and from today's consciousness of wide layers of the working class and unalterably leading to one final conclusion: the conquest of power by the proletariat."[39]

By "transitional demands" Trotsky aimed to create a link between what earlier socialists had labeled "minimum demands" and the "maximum demand" for a socialist society. Minimum demands include both economic demands, like raising the standard of living, and political demands, like the right to organize unions and political democracy. Transitional demands are more ambitious, such as calling for democratic control of industry. They are specifically put forward to demonstrate the inability of capitalism to meet the basic needs of working people, and to underscore the need for a socialist society. "On the economic level, transitional demands point toward the planned economy of socialism. On the political level, they center on the need for the workers to establish their own government," observed US socialist leader Joseph Hansen.[40]

In the decades following World War II, this updated form of revolutionary parliamentarism competed against reformism in countries with parliamentary systems.[41] Though battered by the pre-World War I experience, reformist advocates in these countries regained their ascendancy in the latter half of the 20th century. They offered

39 Trotsky, L. (1977). *The Transitional Program for Socialist Revolution* (3rd ed., pp. 148-149). Pathfinder Press.

40 Quoted in Trotsky, L. (1977). *The Transitional Program for Socialist Revolution* (3rd ed., p. 34). Pathfinder Press.

41 In countries and regions without a history of bourgeois parliaments, like Cuba and China, socialist revolutions followed a more direct path to power – popular overthrows of repressive regimes. These histories, ranging from inspiring to cautionary, are a far-reaching subject beyond the scope of this book.

voters a less confrontational path than their revolutionary counterparts: Challenge inequality under capitalism, without challenging the system that produced the inequality. Reformist parties once again gained traction in several developed countries, winning office and establishing themselves on the political landscape. They pointed to the increasingly ossified Stalinist model of the Soviet Union and its eastern European client states as a warning against full-on revolution.

In the United States, capital's undisputed political center, McCarthyism wrecked socialist movements and destroyed unions in the post World War II period, while the Democratic and Republican parties consolidated their joint electoral monopoly. Socialist political action, whether reformist or revolutionary, was pushed beyond the margins until the political uprisings of the 1960s. It's only in the decades following the 1991 disintegration of the Soviet bloc that the idea of socialism in the U.S. electoral arena has emerged however tentatively from the shadows of repression. Bernie Sanders, first elected mayor of Burlington, Vermont as an independent socialist and later to the U.S. House and Senate, was a rare breakthrough. In his second run for president in 2020, he defined his version of socialism as completing the "unfinished business" of Roosevelt's 1930s New Deal,[42] positioning himself well inside the historic left wing of Democratic Party politics. As such, he falls squarely in the reformist camp—fighting for social

---

42 Krieg, G., & Nobles, R. (2019, June 12). *Bernie Sanders makes the case for democratic socialism as Trump attacks and moderate Democrats worry.* CNN. Retrieved January 19, 2023, from https://www.cnn.com/2019/06/12/politics/bernie-sanders-democratic-socialism-speech/index.html

reforms and railing against corporate greed but not advocating for overthrowing the capitalist system.

Socialist Alternative emerged during the post-McCarthy period as one of many tiny US socialist organizations that raised a revolutionary banner. SA members draw on the lessons of Marx, Engels, Lenin, and Trotsky, among others, but are not doctrinaire about socialist forerunners, recognizing that past leaders can be wrong, and that history unfolds in ways that call for new approaches. Over the years, SA members have organized strikes, campus protests, and anti-war demonstrations. The group has its roots in the US branch of the Committee for a Workers International (CWI), formed in the 1970s by socialists from a dozen countries, which built relationships with revolutionary socialist movements in developing countries in Asia and Africa, and today—after rebranding as International Socialist Alternative (ISA)—encompasses groups in 31 countries. To the original CWI members, as with ISA, the new reformists were merely copying the mistakes of the pre-World War I social democrats.[43]

Until Sawant's 10-year tenure in Seattle City Hall, the group's most noteworthy foray into electoral politics was in 1980s England. The CWI-affiliate Militant maintained a strong organizing base in Liverpool, a port city of half a million people with a deep history of union power and strikes. In 1983, Militant members, running as Labour Party candidates, won majority power on City Council and led a campaign against the right-wing Prime Minister Margaret

43 *A Socialist World Is Possible*. Socialist Alternative. Retrieved February 27, 2023, from https://www.socialistalternative.org/history-committee-workers-international/

Thatcher, mobilizing workers throughout the city to fight for increased social housing and public jobs. Ultimately their program put the socialists on a collision course not just with the Thatcher government but also the national Labour Party, which expelled them and crushed the movement in 1987.[44]

In the first years of the 21st century, Socialist Alternative built chapters in two dozen US cities. Its members, mostly students and young workers, are well-studied in the theory and history of Marxism and are rigorous in their organizing. They have no pretensions of being a mass political party. Before Kshama Sawant, Socialist Alternative had never come close to winning a U.S. political office. Emerging from the 2011 Occupy movements, which energized a new generation of activists, SA members judged that the moment seemed favorable for the organization to, in Marx's term, "count their forces" in the political arena.

Sawant's upset 2013 victory heralded not just tremendous momentum for the fight for a national $15 minimum wage; it also set the stage for an extraordinary U.S. political experiment, unmatched in recent history: What happens when an avowed Marxist gets a foothold inside the halls of American political power? Over the course of the following decade, Seattle became a laboratory for the application of 175 years of Marxist theorizing and political practice. Certainly the level of revolutionary ferment in Seattle and the U.S. in the 2010s was nowhere close to the scale of social rebellion in 20th century Russia and other European countries. The overall balance of forces today tilts much more heavily in favor

44 Taafe, P., & Mulhearn, T. (1988). *Liverpool: A City That Dared to Fight* (1st ed.). Fortress Books.

of the bourgeoisie and against the proletariat. That plain reality makes the Seattle experience even more illuminating.

The victories, challenges, and defeats for workers that followed from the Seattle movement offer hopeful examples of what is possible with a Marxist approach to political struggle today. They also offer sobering reminders of the obstacles that such a movement faces. The 10-year Seattle experience sharply refutes the ideology and methods embraced by contemporary reform-minded socialists, including the dominant tendencies within the Democratic Socialists of America and European social democrats.

One hundred years ago, the 1920 Communist International Conference labeled their strategy "revolutionary parliamentarism." I am updating the term for this theory of power, calling it "Marxist insurgent politics," to incorporate new ideas based on the Seattle experience, and to reflect its applicability at all levels of political office.

I've distilled the three key pillars of Marxist insurgent politics that distinguish Sawant's movement from other contemporary socialist and progressive political movements: a class struggle approach, bold movement-building demands, and movement democracy.

The first pillar, a class struggle approach, is borne out of an understanding that *the state is a hostile force that must be confronted by organized working-class power.* By "state" I mean the full range of institutions that establish, maintain, and enforce the rules governing civil society—the executive and legislative branches of governments, the bureaucracy, court system, and the police, along with adjacent institutions including the two main US political parties and the media. Surveying bourgeois parliaments in his day, Lenin observed that "the state is an organ of class domination, an organ of oppression of one class by another; its aim is the creation of 'order' which legalises and perpetuates this oppression by moderating the collisions between the classes."[45] Sawant's movement has been guided by this foundational recognition that the political arena in capitalist society is not an open ground for the contest of ideas. Rather, the political arena and other elements of capitalist civil society are specifically designed and structured to uphold and reinforce the capitalist status quo.

This basic power analysis has eluded most progressive movements in the US. Often they have foundered on the mistaken assumption that state power, whether a mayor or a governor, a legislative body or a court, stands apart from the conflict at issue, and to succeed the movement must simply persuade the state to take the movement's side against its opponents. At other times, progressive movements have recognized the need for struggle and conflict, but lacking a clear analysis of competing class interests, they have underestimated the forces needed to win. In contrast, Sawant's movement recognizes that state institutions are not neutral mediators; they are the political instruments through which economic powers maintain and reinforce their domination and control. In taking on the state, workers challenge ruling class power.

The tension in Seattle between the 15 for Seattle coalition, led by union officials, and the 15Now movement, led by SA, offers a vivid example of the political friction between progressive and Marxist forces. The union leaders believed that persuasion—sometimes

45 Lenin, V. (1917). *State and Revolution* (1983 ed., p. 9). International Publishers.

through public demonstrations, often through backroom dealing—was the pathway to win $15. They saw the Democrats as politicians who might need some bolstering from time to time, but who fundamentally were allies to workers. This misguided approach is not a new phenomenon. Reformists as far back as the 19th century up through today have mistaken tactical concessions by state power as proof that establishment politicians were allies to workers. Sawant and the 15Now movement, in contrast, recognized that the Democrats were obstacles, regardless of their sympathetic rhetoric. Democrats' late amendments watering down the wage legislation underscored whose side they were on in this class struggle. To win, activists would have to force the political establishment to concede through confrontation and the threat of a ballot initiative.

On a larger scale, we can see how in recent decades capitalist states have conceded to reforms that relieve social pressure but retain bourgeois control over government and the economy. This "moderating the collisions between the classes" is intended to forestall deeper unrest. Obamacare is one such example: Faced with growing pressure to make healthcare universally available, the government agreed to expand coverage and benefits while protecting the private profit-making structure responsible for the healthcare crisis in the first place.

As social pressure subsides, we see that capitalist states waste no time in clawing back popular gains from earlier times: attacks on voting rights, the explosion of anti-union open-shop and anti-strike laws, the evisceration of programs and laws meant to counter systemic racism, and the obliteration of national abortion rights are but four recent examples of reversals when the balance of power shifts.

The Seattle experience offers a very different way to approach these and other major struggles, whether locally or nationally.

When Sawant was first elected, mainstream political pundits—and a fair number of progressive activists—took offense at the new movement's tactics. Why were they flooding into City Council meetings, openly challenging liberal councilmembers as corporate sell-outs? Why was Sawant publicly calling out other elected officials and community leaders who sided with the establishment, instead of working collegially with them to craft legislation? Why did the movement brush aside the normal decorum in favor of in-your-face demands for immediate change?

Time and again, when I was working as a community organizer in Sawant's council office, I'd field calls from union officers or staff pleading – sometimes demanding – that the socialist councilmember and her acolytes play nice with the Democrats. Their protests betrayed a lack of understanding of the fundamental struggle.

To overcome state resistance would take a fighting movement willing to challenge the politicians head on, not more PowerPoint reports, blue-ribbon commissions, and earnest persuasion. Notwithstanding their socialist beachhead in City Hall, Socialist Alternative members understood that bourgeois state power was still firmly in control. Their strategy, including the ballot initiative plan, recognized the adversarial nature of the struggle. The eight other councilmembers flanking Sawant were the epitome of what Marx and Engels called "a committee for managing the common affairs of the whole bourgeoisie."

The second pillar of Marxist insurgent politics, a movement-building approach, is *taking the struggle around bold material demands outside the halls of power*, explicitly connecting them to the call for broader societal change. In the $15 minimum wage battle, Sawant used her new public platform to speak out about the inherent injustices of the capitalist system and the need for fundamental change. Following Trotsky's 1938 Transitional Program, which recognized movement-building as a decisive factor in winning reforms, she approached legislative battles—such as expanding tenant and workplace rights, taxing big business, and funding services such as social housing—with the announced goal of building an independent, worker-led force that could, over time, grow to challenge state and economic power.

In the $15 wage battle, Sawant used her new public platform, whether at demonstrations, in press conferences, and in City Council debates, to speak out about the inherent injustices of the capitalist system and the need for fundamental change. Sawant also distinguished herself from other politicians by rejecting the financial sinecures of elected office. When she first entered City Council in 2014, Seattle councilmembers were paid $117,000 a year, the second highest city council salary in the country. Taking a cue from socialists as far back as the Paris Commune, Sawant announced she would take home only $40,000, the salary of an average Seattle worker, and put the remainder of her salary into a social justice fund. Over her 10 years in office, Sawant donated hundreds of thousands of dollars from the fund into movement-building, giving money directly to support worker organizing and strikes, climate justice campaigns, and fights against racism.

This stands in sharp contrast to other self-described socialists who have been elected to Congress and state legislatures in recent years and toned down their ideological rhetoric once in office.

Sawant's target audience in her speeches was not the media, City Council peers, or policy experts. Rather, she spoke expressly to working class community members, organizing them into action around immediate demands while also making an overarching critique of the capitalist system and calling for a socialist end-goal. Her use of the council seat to educate and mobilize workers into action corresponds closely to how Alexei Badayev and his Bolshevik comrades employed the Duma more than a century ago.

The third pillar is *popular movement democracy*, the ongoing engagement of community members in setting demands and in deciding strategies for how to wage the struggle. Popular movement democracy as practiced by Sawant and Seattle movement activists, with a particular focus on involving people from marginalized communities, is much broader than the customary definition of "democracy" in bourgeois society. In the United States in particular, people are taught to think of democracy in extremely limited terms—mostly by voting a couple of times a year. Yet in the United States and other industrialized capitalist countries, elections typically offer an extremely limited range of choices. That's by design—bourgeois elections are structured forms of state power intended purposely to restrict debate and reinforce the status quo.

"One of the most important aspects of power," political theorist Michael Parenti observed more than half a century ago, is "not to prevail in a struggle but to pre-determine the agenda of struggle—to determine whether certain questions ever reach the competition stage."[46] In the US, the state limits electoral choices

46 Parenti, M. (1970). Power and Pluralism: A View from the Bottom. *Journal of Politics*, *32*(3), 501-530. https://doi.org/10.2307/2128829

through a combination of levers—rules regarding ballot eligibility that reinforce today's two-party duopoly, laws restricting what issues may get on the ballot, and most significantly, the vast sums of corporate cash that in the modern era are routinely deployed to purchase a desired election result.

Today's corporate-controlled media—technically independent from state power but functionally its pedagogical arm—assiduously steers political discourse into a very narrow spectrum of debate, breathlessly reporting on clashes between Democrats and Republicans while outright ignoring policy ideas that fall outside of those offered by the two parties. Linguist and social critic Noam Chomsky described it this way: "The smart way to keep people passive and obedient is to strictly limit the spectrum of acceptable opinion, but allow very lively debate within that spectrum—even encourage the more critical and dissident views. That gives people the sense that there's free thinking going on, while all the time the presuppositions of the system are being reinforced by the limits put on the range of the debate."[47]

It takes extraordinary disruption by grassroots movements to break out of those confines and force questions surrounding the minimum wage, let alone the benefits of socialism versus capitalism, into Parenti's "competition stage." That's not because dramatically higher pay, rent control, universal access to healthcare, or public control of industries are inherently unpopular concepts; it's because the political system—how it's structured, funded, and controlled—is designed intentionally to block these and other radical ideas from even entering public discourse.

---

47 Chomsky, N. (1998). *The Common Good* (p. 43). Odonian Press.

Furthermore, in modern bourgeois society the concept of democracy doesn't even apply to where people spend most of their waking hours: work. Every day, tens of millions of workers head to their jobs, many listening to or reading media reports that excitedly recount the latest jousting between Democrats and Republicans. Then they punch a time clock and instantly surrender their free speech and democratic rights in order to labor under autocratic rule. They are told what to do, when, and how to do it. They are increasingly tracked, surveilled, and monitored by managers. If they are among the 90 percent of American workers who lack union protections, they do not have free speech rights or due process rights if the boss wants to discipline or fire them.

The revolutionary socialists of the 19th and early 20th centuries conceived of democracy as extending far beyond public elections and into work and other aspects of daily life. While far from perfect models, the 1871 Paris Commune and the 1905 St. Petersburg soviets were examples of workers striving to create new forms of democracy in its fullest meaning. In demanding workplace democracy—such as the right to take over and operate factories under democratic rules—the early socialists were exposing and challenging the profoundly undemocratic nature of work under capitalism.

Sawant's popular movement democracy drew inspiration from this history, inviting community members into forums where they would discuss and decide what demands to place before City Council and how to wage the fights for those demands. The $15 minimum wage strategy was developed through neighborhood and citywide meetings, circumventing the established institutional structures. The decision to push for a ballot initiative as a backstop to the legislative fight was debated and approved at a mass meeting of hundreds of workers. This form of participatory democracy became a feature of Sawant's approach to movement work in the subsequent battles for tenants' rights, the tax on Amazon to build social housing, and in the annual city budget fights. Time and again during Sawant's tenure I would hear community members marvel about how wonderful it felt to be able to express their views in a meeting and be heard; how their ideas became incorporated into legislation that Sawant's office put forward. For the first time, many felt like active participants in the political arena, rather than just subjects.

Sawant and Socialist Alternative recognized the potentially decisive role that existing working class organizations play in creating and advancing popular demands. Herself a rank-and-file union member, Sawant regularly supported workers organizing unions and striking for good contracts. She walked picket lines, brought resolutions to City Council in support of worker organizing drives, spoke out publicly against union-busting businesses, and was arrested alongside workers in contract struggles. Sawant was doing more than solidarity work; she was underscoring the central role that unions must play in challenging the antidemocratic nature of work in our society.

Often in lifting up the voices of rank-and-file workers in these struggles, Sawant came into conflict with officers in progressive community organizations and unions. These officials were more accustomed to managing conflict than stoking it. Before the rise of Sawant, most Seattle progressive organizations and liberal elected officials enjoyed a stable, symbiotic relationship in municipal and state government. Union leaders could usually be counted on to tamp down the more militant urges of their members. In union strikes and organizing drives, Sawant sought out rank-and-file workers for their perspectives, frequently butting heads with more cautious union leaders intent on preserving their gatekeeping roles. Community leaders, purporting to speak for their constituencies, made demands on elected officials through the "Seattle process" of extended hearings, "all-stakeholder" task forces, and "listening sessions," culminating in backroom compromises and other "consensus" policies that fell well short of what working people demanded. Political gatekeeping throttled grassroots democracy, meeting the interests of both the political establishment and community leaders in reinforcing status quo relations.

The challenge that Sawant faced repeatedly in City Hall was not unlike what the Bolsheviks had to confront in 1917: Established legislative structures were effectively controlled by the bourgeoisie and their accomplices in the community. The soviets, then, countered the provisional government and gave workers an independent power base. While SA's popular assemblies may not have held the same lofty ambition of displacing state power, they still circumvented gatekeeping and discredited bourgeois institutions while building voice and power for workers. To the chagrin of establishment politicians and many leaders of unions and other non-profit groups, they disrupted relations throughout the city, and in doing so, they modeled a deeper conception of democracy.

These three pillars—class-struggle, movement building around bold demands, and popular movement democracy—successfully guided Sawant's decade-long movement in Seattle, a city home to many of the leading corporations of modern-day capitalism. It's understandable that political establishment figures would at first fail to recognize the seismic shift underway when Sawant first took office. Accustomed to tempering their own voluble campaign-trail promises once in office, they wrongly assumed—and perhaps earnestly hoped—that Sawant would do the same. Maybe they thought that Sawant would be another Bernie Sanders—rhetorically passionate and acerbic, but still willing to work within the political system. They were shocked when they saw an elected official operate her office as a base of revolutionary political activity. They shouldn't have been. They were part of a novel US experiment in the collision between Marxist insurgent politics, informed by 175 years of history, and modern capitalist state power.

3

The Disrupters

There was no respite for Sawant after the $15 minimum wage fight. Working with Indigenous community activists, she successfully pushed through legislation to replace Columbus Day with Indigenous Peoples Day. Sawant and community members organized a public forum to shed light on an uptick in anti-LGBTQ hate crimes, and she championed the demand to fund an LGBTQ youth shelter. She held evening public forums on rent control at City Hall, prompting a Democratic councilmember to grouse that Sawant had organized a "political rally designed to inflame emotions."[48] She rallied community members at the

48 Beekman, D. (2015, April 27). Complaints liken Sawant event on cost of housing to 'political rally'. *The Seattle Times*. https://www.seattletimes.com/seattle-news/politics/complaints-say-sawants-housing-meeting-was-actually-political-rally/

Council's annual city budget debate, successfully demanding that the Council hold evening budget discussions so that more members of the public could attend. At these evening forums, Sawant mobilized hundreds of community members to demand—and win—more funding for youth apprenticeships in the construction industry, a year-round YWCA shelter, and tenant education and organizing.

Sawant joined protesters in the streets after Ferguson, Missouri, police killed Michael Brown. When Seattle protesters interrupted a City Council meeting, chanting "Hands Up! Don't Shoot" and raising their arms, Sawant stood up, raised her arms in solidarity, and called on the Council to set aside regular business and get Seattle's police chief to address concerns about police violence. Sawant also rallied with Black Lives Matter activists against county plans for a new youth jail, and she was the sole vote against the jail when it came before the City Council. Along with SeaTac airport workers and a church minister, she was arrested at the corporate headquarters of Alaska Airlines, protesting the company's court challenge of the voter-approved $15 minimum wage initiative (The following year the company relented after losing its case before the state Supreme Court.).

In street protests and in the audiences at City Council meetings, Sawant's signature red placards became a regular feature—hundreds of cardstock picket signs with Sawant's Council office logo and movement slogans like "Tax the Rich," "Black Lives Matter," and "Support LGBTQ Rights." Community members would take the signs home from City Hall and from rallies, and the placards began to reappear in apartment windows, in coffee shops, and on telephone poles in working-class neighborhoods.

All this was a product of the spirited organizing work centered in Sawant's office on the City Hall's second floor. Until Sawant's arrival, the second floor City Council office suite was a business-like municipal legislative center. Lobbyists were quietly ushered into private conference-room meetings. Neatly dressed bureaucrats walked the hallways from one meeting to the next or plugged away at their high-tech workstations in orderly cubicles. Weekly City Council meetings and daily committee briefings, held in modern, airy chambers, were lightly attended most of the time.

The advent of Sawant disrupted that culture. As an elected councilmember, Sawant was entitled to one of the nine council offices on the second floor and her own budget, including funding for five staff. Sawant hired staff who used the office as a base to organize activist meetings, print leaflets and posters, run phone banks, operate social media, and mobilize people to public rallies and to City Council meetings.

Long-time Democratic Councilmember Jean Godden was appalled when Sawant set up shop. "As soon as she moved into the former Conlin office on the Second Floor, her office quickly was turned into a party headquarters," Godden recalled with horror. "There were red and white posters, some likely produced on city copying machines, stacked on desk tops. At the council's Monday morning council briefings, Sawant treated colleagues to rapid-fire anti-establishment rhetoric, backing rent control, millionaire taxes, and state takeover of Boeing, Microsoft, and Amazon."[49]

---

49 Connelly, J. (2021, November 28). Recall Sawant? Ex-Colleagues and Close Observers Weigh In. Post Alley. Retrieved April 16, 2023, from https://www.postalley.org/2021/11/28/recall-sawant-recall-ex-colleagues-and-close-observers-weigh-in/

The movement activists who shuttled in and out of Sawant's office didn't look at all like the other people roaming City Hall. Instead of Seattle business casual attire, they wore t-shirts bearing political slogans or work uniforms if they had just punched out of day jobs. Instead of carrying dossiers and laptops they lugged around flyers, posters and megaphones. They came and went at all hours of the day and evening.

The other eight council offices were tidy suites, tastefully decorated with art and awards on the walls. The two-room office that Sawant's staff occupied was not so orderly. Desks were strewn with papers, pens, hammer tacks, markers, rolls of duct tape, phone bank scripts and lists, and multiple drafts of press releases and speeches. Posters plastered the walls, demanding rent control, LGBTQ rights, taxing Amazon, supporting union workers, immigrant communities, and small businesses. Bookshelves were stuffed with socialist literature, reams of extra picket signs, and stacks of the latest rally flyer, along with clipboards and battery-powered megaphones. A sink was frequently overloaded with sticky plates and half-empty coffee cups, the product of evening phone banks that stretched into late night strategy sessions. It was a bit chaotic, and any visiting organizer would happily recognize it as a campaign nerve center in the pitch of righteous battle.

And yes, Godden was correct that the signature red posters had been produced on city copy machines, an entirely legitimate purpose. The high-volume copy machines were shared by all nine council offices. On one visit, the private vendor hired to replenish supplies elicited chuckles from city staff when he expressed wonderment about why the copiers always seemed to be running low on red ink.

In addition to the organizing, Sawant's council staff worked the legislative levers—requesting reports and briefings from city departments, ordering analyses and legislative drafts from the council's non-partisan policy and legal staff, guiding communications staff to issue press releases and pitch stories to media, and developing the legislation to propel forward movement demands.

The socialist foothold was an unwelcome imposition on Godden and the rest of the political establishment. Involuntarily, they had been assigned front row seats to witness Marxist insurgent politics.

Low income workers were elated with the $15 minimum wage win, but the first of each month, the majority of their paychecks would continue to go to one place: their landlords' pockets. The fight for affordable housing in "booming" Seattle, where the cost of living was skyrocketing, soon took center stage. Sawant, who had already been involved in tenants' rights protests following Occupy, continued to work closely with housing activists once in office. Public housing tenants were among the first to reach out to the new councilmember. They were facing the threat of mass evictions, and wanted help.

The Seattle Housing Authority (SHA), public landlord for more than 8,000 apartments and administrator of the federally funded housing voucher program, had just unveiled a scheme to increase rents and limit the number of years tenants would qualify for subsidized housing. Because of woefully underbuilt public housing, waiting lists extended years to get into these affordable apartments—a crisis mirrored in cities across the U.S. The idea behind

SHA's program, known as "Stepping Forward," was to push tenants into the private housing market, thereby making room for others languishing on the waitlist. For some tenants, SHA's rent increases would amount to 400 percent; in an Orwellian twist, they were "stepping forward" into an economic abyss.

Stepping Forward was a typical neoliberal scheme, dressed up in progressive sloganeering and paternalistic rhetoric about helping tenants train for higher paying jobs so they could afford more expensive apartments. But it was intended ultimately to strip away the remaining shreds of the New Deal-era social safety net, replacing them with austerity, means-testing, drug-testing, and surveillance. It reinforced institutionalized racism by demonizing poor people, especially women and people of color, and shunted the government's responsibility to provide peoples' basic needs into a shadowy web of nonprofit partnerships.

The SHA proposal owed its inspiration to Democratic President Bill Clinton and his pledge to "end welfare as we know it." His 1996 legislation limited benefit eligibility, set time limits, and made people jump through administrative hoops to qualify for housing, food, and other basic survival aid. The legislation cemented the neoliberal consensus among leaders in the Democratic and Republican parties, and encouraged local housing authorities to push tenants out if they couldn't find work or prove they were training for new skills. Dozens of other authorities across the country had already embraced Clinton's austerity framework. Federal budget cuts whipped policy at the local level.

Rebecca Snow Landa had lived on the streets and struggled with her mental health until she lucked out and received a North Seattle SHA apartment. She went back to school, earned a college degree, and worked part-time as a health aide—while also working full-time as a single parent of two children. Then, in 2014, SHA sent her a notice that her rent would be going up every year for six years until it quintupled, regardless of her earnings. "When I got that letter from SHA I could barely get out of bed for about a week," she told a local radio reporter. "It felt—it almost felt like a death sentence in a way. It felt like we don't have a chance."[50]

Indeed, SHA officials presented Stepping Forward as inevitable. SHA planned a series of informational sessions for residents over the course of two weeks in early September, mostly to go through the motions of community outreach. The agency intended to roll out the program by year's end. Legally, the City of Seattle couldn't order SHA to halt Stepping Forward. While the mayor and Seattle City Council have the authority to choose SHA's Board of Directors, SHA operates independently of city government. But that fact was no barrier to Sawant and Socialist Alternative.

Sawant's Council office staff went door-to-door with public housing residents in SHA complexes on Seattle's First Hill and in West Seattle to talk with neighbors about the threat and to organize a response. Many of the SHA tenants were recent East African residents, including a number of people who either worked at SeaTac Airport or who had volunteered on the historic 2013 $15 ballot initiative there. From the SeaTac victory they had gone on to participate in the Seattle $15 win. Activists from the Tenants Union of Washington, a grassroots group of low-income renters, joined in.

---

50 McNichols, J. (2014, September 23). Single Mom On Housing Authority Plan: 'We Don't Have A Chance'. KUOW. Retrieved January 30, 2023, from https://kuow.org/stories/single-mom-housing-authority-plan-wedont-have-chance/

SHA's September hearings—one in each of the five major SHA housing communities—grew increasingly contentious. Residents and their allies challenged SHA Executive Director Andrew Lofton as he gamely tried to run through his PowerPoint slide deck before he opened the room for "questions"—really an opportunity for the public to tee off against the cruel program. Residents described being stuck in low wage jobs year after year, the lack of affordable housing in the private housing market, and the fear of being tossed out on the streets by SHA.

The final hearing at High Point Community in West Seattle, a center of the East African community, saw some 200 people—residents, Sawant, her Council office staff, union members, and members of Socialist Alternative—crowd into the High Point meeting hall. They held up signs and interrupted Lofton's presentation, chanting "Show me the jobs!" and "No rent hikes!"[51]

Having faced two weeks of growing vocal resistance, Lofton allowed that he was open to tweaking Stepping Forward, or at least relaxing some training and job search requirements. What were some appropriate "hardship policies?" he asked. "We're looking for information back from people so we can design a policy with the right criteria that addresses" things such as "unforeseen circumstances or emergencies."

"How about you scrap the whole thing?" a man in the audience retorted.

51 This and following dialogue from West Seattle Blog. (2014, September 29). *Seattle Housing Authority Meeting in High Point* [Video]. YouTube. https://www.youtube.com/watch?v=cuwJVzJnf30&t=2418s

"Scrap the plan!" another shouted, and soon the entire room was chanting. No one was interested in working with Lofton to craft "the right criteria" for "unforeseen circumstances or emergencies." Many of the people in the room had escaped war in their homelands. They had survived years in refugee camps and other temporary waystations. They had endured hunger, disease, and forced separation from loved ones. They had traveled thousands of miles from home, built new lives in foreign cultures, learned new languages, and slaved away at dirty jobs under hostile, racist supervisors. Their lives had been one continuous string of unforeseen circumstances and emergencies. The last thing they needed from the privileged SHA bureaucrats was a PowerPoint slide show or lecture explaining how to try harder.

"This is clearly a plan that shows low-income people how they're going to be accountable," a woman said. "Where is the plan that holds developers accountable for creating more low-income housing that people can truly afford?"

"Who is motivating employers to hire people?" another woman challenged him.

"Andrew, just put that plan back in your pocket and get out of here," a young man demanded.

Lofton's aide, trying to rescue her boss, interceded. "We're not responding tonight," she said. "We're going to record all of your answers and questions. Staff will be available afterwards."

"What's the point if you're not going to answer the question?" a man shot back.

Abdinasir Mohammed stood to speak. A Somali refugee, Mohammed had played a central organizing role in the SeaTac campaign, and he was among the many East African tenants who'd been organizing alongside Sawant to resist Stepping Forward. "We have been talking and talking and talking endlessly," Mohammed said. "They are not answering our questions, and nobody is listening to us, whatever we say. Whatever we say, it doesn't make any sense to them. So we will walk out from this building—let them meet. Let's go!"

And with that, most of the attendees, including Sawant and other Socialist Alternative members, stood and headed for the door, chanting, "No means no!"[52]

The crowd reconvened on a basketball court next door to plan next steps with Sawant. "It has become clear to us that SHA will not change their policy on Stepping Forward," Sawant told the tenants, pausing after each sentence to let a Somali translator repeat her words. "They will go ahead with it even though they know that all the tenants are opposed to it. So we have no choice but to build our own strength, to keep building this movement so that we can actually stop this from happening. We have to now take this battle to City Hall," Sawant declared, garnering a big round of applause. Before leaving that night, the group committed to mobilize for a rally at City Hall in October.[53]

Three weeks later, more than 100 SHA tenants gathered in City Hall to call on the other Councilmembers to sign on to a letter

---

52 West Seattle Blog. (2014, September 29). *Seattle Housing Authority Meeting in High Point* [Video]. YouTube. https://www.youtube.com/watch?v=cuwJVzJnf30&t=2418s

53 West Seattle Blog. (2014, September 29). *The Other Housing Meeting* [Video]. YouTube. https://www.youtube.com/watch?v=s4I97eyxIds&t=141s

Sawant had drafted, leveraging the only power City Council had over SHA. Sawant's Council staff had determined that five out of the seven SHA board positions were going to be open in the coming six months. The letter would put councilmembers on record pledging to refuse to appoint anyone to the SHA board if they supported Stepping Forward. Without new appointments, SHA could not operate. Until this point, most of the other council members had stayed silent or offered only tempered concern about Stepping Forward. Sawant's letter would force them to declare whose side they were on: SHA, or the tenants.

"We need our City Council members to support us. This is our city. You are our leaders," Ubah Warsame told the Council. "Andrew Lofton makes $216,000 a year while he is pushing homelessness on the most marginalized people. This is the hard reality of Stepping Forward."

Warsame noted that SHA officials, even after the raucous public hearings, were sticking with Stepping Forward. "We need you elected officials to take decisive action," she said.[54] All eight other councilmembers signed on to Sawant's letter. The crowd celebrated, then headed upstairs to Mayor Ed Murray's office to demand his public support as well.

A month later, more than 100 SHA tenants crowded into an SHA Board of Directors meeting to present a letter signed by 30 unions and community organizations. SHA officials declined to publicly comment, but the pressure was building. Lofton had spent a 40-year career working with some of the most powerful

---

54 [YouTube.com]. (2014, October 24). SHA tenants rise up at city hall [Video]. S. Kimmerle. https://www.youtube.com/watch?v=LvgSQA2PBVY

elected officials in the city and state, cultivating connections in all the right places. But his Stepping Forward program had become politically toxic.

Just before the Christmas holiday, Lofton wrote to City Council and the Mayor to announce that SHA would not implement Stepping Forward. Stepping Forward had been killed not by any legislative vote but by a relentless and creative street movement led by a socialist politician and feisty immigrant tenants, many of whom were newcomers to political struggle in the US.

"This is what happens when amazing people get together and fight back for their rights," exclaimed Nimco Abdirahman, a teenager whose family lived in SHA housing. "This victory is only the beginning of change."[55]

Just as with the fight for $15, the battle against Stepping Forward offered another display of Sawant's new Marxist insurgent politics. She urged activists to escalate their demands. "Use the momentum from this victory to build an even stronger affordable housing movement to win rent control and a massive expansion of quality publicly-owned affordable housing, in order to address some of the root causes of the affordable housing crisis in Seattle," she told them.[56] SHA had made for an obvious first target, but

55 Tenant Union of Washington (2014, December 22). *Major Victory: Tenant movement puts brakes on Seattle Housing Authority 'Stepping Forward' rent hike*. SHA Tenants Organizing Project. Retrieved January 30, 2023, from https://stopsha.wordpress.com/

56 (2014, December 19). *Congratulations to Tenants on Defeat of "Stepping Forward" Rent Hike Proposal*. Councilmember Kshama Sawant. Retrieved January 30, 2023, from https://sawant.seattle.gov/congratulations-to-tenants-on-defeat-of-stepping-forward-rent-hike-proposal/

in speeches and meetings, Sawant and Socialist Alternative reinforced the broader political context to mobilize community members: Stepping Forward was born out of a bipartisan neoliberal consensus, and the local political establishment would not willingly come to the aid of the tenants. The battle over Stepping Forward was a struggle between conflicting class interests.

Sawant had effectively used—to borrow her socialist forebears' term—the "parliamentary rostrum" to mobilize workers, unmask SHA's hypocrisy, and force the political establishment to choose a side. Sensing the growing community blowback as the September hearings unfolded, the mayor and some councilmembers had begun to waver. One councilmember had urged federal officials to look into SHA's plans. But no one in the political establishment offered full-throated support for tenants like Sawant had, nor did any of them replicate her on-the-ground organizing alongside the Tenants Union.

That organizing created democratic spaces for the SHA residents to discuss and formulate plans to fight back. All eight of Sawant's Council colleagues ultimately accepted the movement's demand to sign the October letter to SHA, but the unanimity belied the truth that they had only sided with tenants because of the sustained grassroots pressure campaign. Defeating Stepping Forward was a powerful demonstration of the 1920 Communist International Conference's admonition for elected socialists to "help the masses from inside parliament to break up the state machine."

In celebrating the victory, Sawant urged the tenants to join the bigger battles that would dominate the housing struggle in the coming years: rent control and taxing big business to fund a massive upsurge in public, affordable housing construction.

But to have a shot at those bigger battles, the movement first would have to preserve the socialist beachhead in City Hall. In the same 2013 election that ushered Sawant into office, Seattle voters had approved a new City Council district plan. Beginning in 2015, instead of all nine councilmembers running at-large, seven would be elected to four-year positions by district, encompassing about 70,000 registered voters each, and two would be elected citywide.

Sawant lived right in the heart of the new District 3, which encompassed neighborhoods of apartments catering to young renters, college students, and LGBTQ community members; the historic Central District Black community; and other working-class homeowners. The district had a diverse working-class base but also was a prime target of gentrifying corporate developers, intent to convert single homes and older apartment buildings into multistory luxury condominiums and apartments. The new District 3 also included many elites of Seattle's ruling class, who lived in stately hilltop mansions and Seattle's "Gold Coast," which ran up the shore of Lake Washington and featured large estates with boat docks and stunning water-and-mountain views. Starbucks founder and CEO Howard Schultz and Alaska Airlines CEO Brad Tilden were among District 3's ultra-rich residents.

The political establishment was determined to shorten Sawant's City Hall tenure. They recruited Pamela Banks, a prominent member of the Black community, Central District resident, and leader of the city's Urban League chapter, to run. Managing her campaign was the mayor's chief political consultant; six of the eight Democrats on City Council endorsed Banks. Some 200 real estate developers and corporate executives donated the legal maximum of $700 to her campaign. Exactly as the establishment intended, support among the Black community was split, with older voters tending to support Banks, and younger voters backing the socialist.

"This is an extremely tough race for Banks," Democratic political consultant Ben Anderstone acknowledged in October. "It is going to require Banks peeling off votes that are leaning to Sawant. The negatives she's using that Sawant is ineffective and doesn't play well with others — well, she's going to have to be more specific, because a lot of people like the fact that she doesn't play well with others."[57]

Anderstone was correct to point out that Sawant had tapped into voter anger, but as with other establishment insiders, he missed the real point. Where pundits saw only frustrated voters, others saw a leader who inspired previously discouraged and disengaged people into action with an affirming message of hope through organizing. Sawant frequently punctuated her rally speeches with the call-and-response chant, "When we fight, we win!" There was no better living proof of that than people's experiences with 15Now and Stepping Forward.

Socialist Alternative ran an aggressive door-knocking campaign to reelect Sawant, touting her wins and making the case that a vote for her was a vote in support of rent control, affordable housing, and taxing big business. More than 600 tenants, rank-and-file

---

57 Rosenblum, J. (2016, January 13). *Socialism can win here, really: What Seattle means for the future of the American left.* Salon.com. Retrieved February 1, 2023, from https://www.salon.com/2016/01/13/socialism_can_win_here_really_what_seattle_means_for_the_future_of_the_american_left_partner/

union members, and other supporters knocked on 90,000 doors and made 170,000 phone calls.

In the end, the voters' verdict—56 to 44 percent for the Marxist over the Democrat—was as much a message about increasing confidence in collective struggle as it was a smackdown of the political insiders. Campaign volunteer Leticia Parks described it this way: "Every time there's a victory, I want to be a part of that."

Following her upset 2013 victory, the establishment hadn't taken her seriously, Sawant reminded a reporter on election night, as preliminary results showed her far outpacing Banks. "They said, 'What will a group of young radical socialists amount to? They won't get anything done.' We showed them the most transformative two years in Seattle politics."[58]

Even as Sawant was fending off the 2015 election challenge, the growing crisis for renters kept her Council office busy. One month before the November election, Sahro Farah reached out to Sawant's office. Farah, a home healthcare worker and single mother of five, lived in the dilapidated Charles Apartments in southeast Seattle. Cockroaches crawled in and out of the apartments through cracks in the walls. Three of Farah's four stove top heating elements were broken. Sparks occasionally shot out from wall outlets when she and neighbors plugged in cords. Water dripped from the ceilings, spreading mold in the apartments. And

58 Gupta, A. (2015, November 5). With Kshama Sawant Claiming Reelection Victory, Seattle Doubles Down on Socialism. *In These Times*. https://inthesetimes.com/article/seattle-kshama-sawant-reelection

now, Farah told Sawant, the new building owner, Carl Haglund, had just sent out notices he was more than doubling the rent and demanding that tenants pay up or leave by the end of the month.[59]

Haglund had a reputation among renters as a slumlord who did as little as possible to keep up his low-rent apartment buildings in Seattle's Rainier Valley, home to new immigrant communities from Asia and Africa. He also had a long-standing reputation as a bully, filing more than 200 legal actions against tenants during his 30 years of landlording.[60] While Seattle had a full set of tenant protection laws on the books, city housing officials were perennially understaffed and had a hard time keeping up with complaint investigations. Seattle landlords like Haglund, along with the corporate property management companies that were coming to dominate the multi-family housing market, knew full well that enforcement was lax, and they took full advantage of the situation.

Farah united with her neighbors. They began organizing with the Tenants Union to address the deplorable conditions and the rent hike when she called Sawant. The next day, Sawant came to visit the Charles Apartments. "My stove isn't working. My heat isn't working. My windows aren't working," Farah said after showing the councilmember her apartment. "But now we're going to be homeless."

---

59 [Firesteel]. (2016, June 20). *'I'll Never Give Up': Sahro Farah on Tenants' Rights* [Video]. Firesteel. http://firesteelwa.org/2016/06/ill-never-give-up-sahro-farah-on-tenants-rights/

60 Pulkkinen, L. (2015, October 9). Judge hammers 'Seattle Goliath of housing' who sued ex-tenant over Yelp review. *SeattlePI.com*. https://www.seattlepi.com/seattlenews/article/Judge-hammers-Seattle-Goliath-of-housing-6562124.php

Incensed by the "absolutely unacceptable" conditions, Sawant and the Tenants Union organized a rally outside of another Haglund-owned building the following week. "This is Seattle," Sawant said. "We have billionaires coming out of our ears in this city, yet we have people living in such terrible conditions."[61] More than 100 people gathered in the chilly morning rain to learn that the night before, Haglund had agreed to refund a month's rent to all the Charles Apartments tenants, and also pledged to not raise the rent until the numerous building code violations were fixed. Emboldened, the tenants and Tenants Union organizers agreed to take the fight to City Hall.

Sawant and Nick Licata, another councilmember who had joined her in visiting the Charles Apartments, introduced legislation banning all landlords from raising rents if their apartments had outstanding building code violations. Sawant dubbed it the Carl Haglund Law. Farah found a better place to live in the neighborhood but kept organizing with her former neighbors. Tenants Union staff turned out crowds for City Council hearings on the bill. Haglund was peeved that his name was publicly associated with the legislation. His spokesperson Roger Valdez asserted that low-income tenants ought to foot the bill for landlords who bought dilapidated buildings.[62] But in June 2016, the City Council unanimously passed the Carl Haglund Law. After the vote, a beaming

---

61 Beekman, D. (2015, October 1). Tenants of run-down building: Owner said pay more or get out. The Seattle Times. https://www.seattletimes.com/business/real-estate/2-city-council-members-decry-soaring-rent-at-run-down-south-seattle-apartments/

62 Groover, H. (2016, June 8). Stopping Slumlord Rent Hikes. *The Stranger*. https://www.thestranger.com/news/2016/06/08/24178683/stopping-slumlord-rent-hikes

Farah addressed tenants inside City Hall. "I'll never give up," she declared. Urging others to stand up for their rights as well, she added, "If you want a fight like this one, I'm here."

Carl Haglund wasn't giving up either. True to form, he sued Sawant and the City for $25 million, claiming defamation. (The case was dismissed two years later.)

The fight over the Carl Haglund Law brought the battle lines in Seattle's housing conflict into sharper relief. It also emboldened renters. Sawant and community members mobilized and won legislation limiting move-in fees that landlords could charge. They also won a new law that undercut systemic race discrimination in the rental market, by requiring landlords to accept the first qualified rental applicant in line and by banning criminal background checks. Seattle's Fair Chance Housing Ordinance was "one of the most far-reaching fair housing laws in the country," NBC reported.[63] Landlords sued to block these new renter laws–and lost.

These reforms, of course, did not achieve socialist goals, like kicking out Haglund and other slumlords and putting housing under public control. But the legislative battles taught community members about the necessity of organizing and reinforced class struggle principles. These lessons would be important foundational experiences for the bigger battles that lay ahead.

As for the political establishment, they accepted the Carl Haglund law and the other measures because they were still reeling from

63 (2019, May 19). *Seattle's fair housing law is the most progressive in the country. But now, landlords are challenging it.* NBC News. Retrieved February 2, 2023, from https://www.nbcnews.com/news/nbcblk/seattle-s-fair-housing-law-most-progressive-country-now-landlords-n1004321

their failure to unseat Sawant. They had not yet developed a viable strategy to neutralize the socialist movement, and their legislative concessions reflected a recognition that in these fights, the balance of power still lay with Sawant's forces. The same year, Sawant and the movement also recorded their first victory in the fight for more city funding for housing. It was relatively modest, the product of a community-led fight that began first with a demand not around housing but against police militarization. It also provided an instructive lesson about how far the Democrats would go to deny Sawant and the movement a political victory.

In May 2016, while Sawant was pushing through the Carl Haglund law, community activists learned of the mayor's plan to build a new police precinct station in north Seattle. With a $160 million price tag, it would be the most expensive free-standing police precinct in the country, a state-of-the-art building designed to withstand earthquakes and bombs and equipped with a basement firing range. Police claimed they needed a new north precinct building because the existing one was rundown.

The Seattle Police Department had a long-standing reputation in working class neighborhoods for brutality and racism. In 2010, an officer had shot to death John T. Williams, a Native American woodcarver, as he crossed a busy city street; another brutalized a Latino man in custody and threatened to "beat the fucking Mexican piss" out of him; a third punched a Black teenager in the face.[64] In 2012, the US Justice Department had placed the Seattle

64 Black, T. (2020, June 4). *What the federal consent decree means for Seattle Police Department*. King 5 News. Retrieved February 6, 2023, from https://www.king5.com/article/news/what-the-federal-consent-decree-means-for-seattle-police-department/281-1c410cb9-206c-4ff3-b6b9-e085ffb88648

Police Department under federal supervision. They ordered anti-bias and de-escalation training and promised to scrutinize every aspect of department operations. The Democratic political establishment welcomed the reform program; it promised a shiny public relations veneer that would allow them to claim they were opposing racism while functionally allowing the department to continue its repressive work. But in the four years since the start of federal supervision, Seattle police were still frequently accused of racist abuse and had killed another 16 residents, mostly people of color or people living on the street. That didn't stop Mayor Murray and the Democrats from pushing the north Seattle precinct project. Indeed, Seattle officials claimed the new building would somehow help reduce police abuse and mistreatment.

Community members called a meeting at the local library branch to discuss how to stop the project. While the meeting was underway, 50 armed police officers surrounded the building. The police later claimed their mobilization was a simple misunderstanding, but the message to the community was clear: Don't mess with the north precinct plans.[65]

Roused by the outsized police response, community members launched a petition and mobilized 400 people to disrupt a City Council meeting, demanding the city "Block the Bunker" and invest in housing and services instead. In August, when Sawant was out of town, the Democrats passed a resolution, 7 to 1, in favor of the megaproject. But community pressure was growing.

65 Hellmann, M. (2017, March 9). *Defunding Police—How Antiracist Organizers Got Seattle to Listen*. Yes! Magazine. Retrieved February 6, 2023, from https://www.yesmagazine.org/social-justice/2017/03/09/defunding-police-how-antiracist-organizers-got-seattle-to-listen

Young activists dogged the mayor at public events, and the idea of a swanky new police building came under increasing scrutiny.

Sawant returned to town and demanded that the police show her the supposedly rundown building that needed replacement. She toured the existing north precinct facility and brought along community activists, including Abdi Mohamed from the Stepping Forward fight and members of the Block the Bunker movement. Sawant emerged from the tour to declare that not only was the existing building not in need of replacement, but that the tour had revealed what really needed to be replaced from the ground up: the sick culture within the Seattle police department. In the building's locker rooms, Sawant and other tour participants had seen stickers with cartoon characters peeing on Obama symbols and a homophobic slur against the President. Author and activist Ijeoma Oluo, who joined Sawant's tour, asked plainly, "How is a new building going to fix your culture when you haven't even addressed something as simple as these images in your locker room?"[66]

At first, the police department said the stickers were simply First Amendment expressions of the officers. Within hours, facing withering public criticism, city media relations staff said the officers had been told to take the stickers down. But the damage was done. Sawant's tour exposed more about the Seattle Police Department

66 Beekman, D. (2016, September 9). *Sawant tours police station, isn't sold on need for replacement*. King 5 News. Retrieved February 6, 2023, from https://www.seattletimes.com/seattle-news/politics/sawant-tours-police-station-isnt-sold-on-need-for-replacement/

than the police ever had intended. For the political establishment, it was an unmitigated public relations disaster.

A few days later, Block the Bunker leader Rashad Barber confronted the mayor at a community event in support of stopping the Dakota Access Pipeline. The environmental activists eagerly gave the mic to Barber, who challenged Murray about the racist history of Seattle policing, the extravagant north precinct budget, and the desperate community need for basic services. Instead of $160 million on a new police building, Barber asked, "What about housing? What about rent control?"

The next day, Murray announced the project was being put on long-term hold. Sawant and the activists celebrated. "The only reason that this new police precinct is not going to go ahead in this year's budget is because of the Block the Bunker movement and because ordinary people, young people, and activists came and shut the city all down," Sawant said.[67] And since the city had $160 million to spend on a new building, that money should be dedicated toward affordable housing. With that money, Sawant calculated, Seattle could build 1,000 new apartment homes. She put forward a budget amendment to do just that.

Murray capitulated to the Block the Bunker movement just as the Council's two-month budget season was getting underway. Sawant and her staff mobilized a coalition of 70 unions, faith organizations, and community groups to demand that the City

67 Hellmann, M. (2017, March 9). *Defunding Police—How Antiracist Organizers Got Seattle to Listen*. Yes! Magazine. Retrieved February 6, 2023, from https://www.yesmagazine.org/social-justice/2017/03/09/defunding-police-how-antiracist-organizers-got-seattle-to-listen

Council adopt her amendment: $160 million to build 1,000 affordable homes. Activists postered in neighborhoods, waved signs at street corners, organized press conferences, and got neighborhood Democratic political groups to endorse the Build 1,000 Homes budget demand.

City Hall Democrats were in a political pickle. They had long preached their commitment to build affordable housing, and now the Block the Bunker movement was pointing them to a pile of money that clearly had no dedicated purpose. The solution seemed obvious. Yet adopting Sawant's proposal would give her a huge political win, and it would mean stripping any funding for a future new police building. Democrats wanted to hold that money in reserve so they could bring back the police precinct project in the future. They developed a two-fold strategy.

First, they united to reject Sawant's proposal to Build 1,000 Homes with the $160 million in undedicated funds. The vote was 7 to 2, with only Sawant and one of the Democrats objecting. And then, Democratic Councilmember Lisa Herbold scrounged up a surprise source of assets: $29 million in bond money for new affordable housing. Previously, Democrats had declared that this bond source was not available for housing. But now, suddenly, it was. Their reversal deftly covered two political bases: To those on the left, they could claim they were increasing funding for affordable housing; and on the right, they could claim that they had protected police money for the future. Herbold's $29 million bond proposal prevailed, 7 to 2, with six of the Democrats plus Sawant voting yes.

Pundits recognized how the new housing funding had come to pass. "Without the pressure built by Sawant's 'Build 1,000 Homes' movement, it's unlikely Herbold's proposal would have been at the table at all," political reporter Heidi Groover observed.[68] Sawant spoke caustically about the Democrats' Machiavellian tactic. "The majority of councilmembers refused to use public funds for housing—the very same public dollars they were willing to spend for a new police bunker in the north precinct," she said. "It is unconscionable to continue to prioritize an unnecessary new police precinct over the urgent needs of communities, especially people of color." To challenge the Build 1,000 Homes coalition, she said, "Corporate Democrats built their own Coalition of 1,000 Excuses."

But Sawant also urged community members to claim the win. "Let's be clear: We won this because we built our coalition and a movement. We made it impossible for corporate Democratic politicians to ignore our proposal to Build 1,000 Homes," she said. "Because of your hard work, because we got organized and fought, City Councilmembers were forced to concede even though most of them were loath to do so."[69]

The same month the movement registered its $29 million housing victory, a much greater national development overwhelmed the political arena: the first election of Donald Trump. As in other cities, Seattle's Democratic political establishment railed against

68 Groover, H. (2016, November 23). *Lisa Herbold Wins the Budget Fight*. The Stranger. Retrieved February 6, 2023, from https://www.thestranger.com/news/2016/11/23/24704627/the-winner-in-this-years-budget-fight-lisa-herbold

69 Sawant, K. (2016, November 17). Build 1,000 Homes Coalition Wins $29 Million for Affordable Housing! Councilmember Kshama Sawant Blog. Retrieved February 6, 2023, from https://web.archive.org/web/20190307204436/https://sawant.seattle.gov/build-1000-homes-wins-29-million/

Trump's fake populism, issued press statements, rallied against his xenophobia, and loudly declared that Seattle would be a sanctuary city for immigrants. But with unabashed chutzpah, they also perpetuated and even doubled down on local policies that fit very comfortably within the new Trumpian political agenda.

The final two years of Mayor Murray's administration, and in 2017, following the election of Jenny Durkan as his successor, the city cracked down on people living on the streets even as the housing affordability crisis worsened. Two Democratic mayoral administrations increased "sweeps" of homeless encampments, in which city officials confiscated tents and belongings and forced people to move, even if they had nowhere else to go. Often, people relocated to a new encampment only to be swept again a few days later. In 2016, Seattle carried out 601 sweeps, an average of more than two every weekday.[70] In 2017, city officials admitted to spending more than $10 million on sweeps. Police enforced the relocation orders, callously discarding people's belongings—their clothing, food, medications, identification papers, mementos—and threatening them with arrest.[71] On top of having to struggle daily to meet their basic food, shelter, and hygiene needs, now homeless people had to stay one step ahead of the police and their sweeping brigades.

---

70 Sawant et al., K. (2017, October 30). *Ending Displacement Requires A Movement*. South Seattle Emerald. Retrieved February 7, 2023, from https://southseattleemerald.com/2017/10/30/ending-displacement-requires-a-movement/

71 Hawkins, Jr., D. S. K., & Oron, G. (2018, May 15). *Seattle Spent Over $10 million on Homeless Sweeps in 2017*. South Seattle Emerald. Retrieved February 7, 2023, from https://southseattleemerald.com/2018/05/15/seattle-spent-over-10-million-on-homeless-sweeps-in-2017/

To put a liberal veneer on things, the Democrats on City Council established new social worker "navigation teams" who were supposed to accompany the police and offer shelter accommodations to the people being swept. But a report found that these teams offered shelter space to a paltry 4 percent of the people being swept. Often, the city conducted sweeps without informing the social workers, and when they were informed, the outreach staff had very few shelter beds to offer. Most of the people declined the shelter anyway:[72] Shelters were crowded, noisy, often bedbug-ridden warehouses that forced residents to leave every morning. Most weren't set up for families and didn't allow pets. The streets were preferable, where at least there was community, however fragile.

The Seattle Democrats also missed no opportunity to denounce Trump's vow to build a wall at the Mexican border. In her first year in office, Mayor Durkan made a show of visiting the border and condemning the president's plan. But back at home, Democrats deployed their own walls to push out campers. The Murray and Durkan administrations, along with state officials, installed miles of chain-link fencing, some as high as 10 feet and topped with sharp spikes, as a menacing warning against Seattleites struggling to survive on the streets. The fencing enclosed green spaces along highways, under viaducts, and on otherwise-unused vacant land and parklets—places where a homeless person might pitch a tent at night. In my neighborhood, where a tiny sidewalk peninsula

72 Bowman, N. (2020, February 27). *Seattle council slams Navigation Team on homeless camp sweeps*. MyNorthwest.com. Retrieved February 7, 2023, from https://mynorthwest.com/1737931/seattle-council-navigation-team-homeless-sweeps/

at a busy intersection served as a home for an elderly, wheelchair-bound man, the city booted him and erected a tall, ugly fence. People living on the streets would compare the number of times they had been swept—6, 7, 8 times, or perhaps too many to count—the same way war veterans might compare their wounds.

Nationally, Trump's border wall ambitions were stalled by politics and the courts. But in Seattle, Democrats overran local objections and protests to build miles of walls. They had succeeded where Trump had failed. Local political satirist Brett Hamil coined this "the proximity law of Seattle politics," calling out the rank hypocrisy of Democrats for shamelessly pointing fingers at distant cruelty but perfecting cold-heartedness at home.[73]

The same political establishment that meted out cruel treatment also assiduously documented the damage they inflicted, gathering data that showed the racist and xenophobic harm—and then they stayed the course. County authorities conducted a broad survey and found that 29 percent of the homeless population identified as African American, more than four times the area's general African American population; 14 percent were Latino, compared to 9 percent of the general population; 6 percent were American Indian or Alaska Native, compared with 1 percent of the general population; 18 percent identified as LGBTQ, compared to 5 percent of the general population; a full 40 percent were survivors of domestic abuse; nearly one in five had spent time in foster care.[74]

---

73 [South Seattle Emerald]. (2017, November 25). *The Proximity Law of Seattle Politics* [Video]. Facebook. https://www.facebook.com/watch/?v=941551632665526

74 All Home (2017, June 2). Seattle/King County Point-in-Time Count of Persons Experiencing Homelessness 2017. Cloudinary.com. https://res.

A second city study found that more than 40 percent of people living on the streets were working part- or full-time jobs. Fully 11 percent of homeless people were immigrants or refugees, precisely the population that Democrats claimed to be protecting against Trump.[75] This study also measured what any sentient being would expect: Nearly every surveyed person on the street said they would happily move into safe and affordable housing if it was available.

In advance of the City Council's fall budget debate, Sawant annually convened a series of People's Budget forums in City Hall in the evening for community members to organize around key budget demands. Different groups and activists also brought forward their own issues, which got added to the list. In 2017, Sawant proposed to the Peoples Budget forum that the movement prioritize defunding sweeps and taxing big business to build affordable housing. The demand, for $150 million a year in big business taxes, would build on the previous year's success in winning the $29 million housing bond.

Sawant put forward a budget amendment to redirect sweeps money into more mental health services, shelters, garbage removal and cleanup services, portable toilets, and access to showers and laundries. Activists postered neighborhoods and tabled at key transit stops in support of the anti-sweep budget

cloudinary.com/sagacity/image/upload/v1496345607/2017-Count-Us-In-PIT-Comprehensive-Report_uxjkdq.pdf

75 Applied Survey Research (2017, March 3). 2016 Homeless Needs Assessment. Seattle.gov. Retrieved February 8, 2023, from https://www.seattle.gov/documents/Departments/HumanServices/CDBG/CityOfSeattle2016-HomelessNeedsAssessment.pdf

amendment. In addition to turning people out for budget hearings, they collected supplies for campers—blankets, tarps, propane heaters, sleeping bags, tents, batteries, and toiletries. People living in encampments distributed leaflets and organized neighbors to turn out for City Council budget hearings.

Sawant's housing amendment proposed to revive a defunct city Employee Head Tax on businesses. Her original proposal—to raise $150 million a year—received no traction among Democrats. Under Sawant's submitted proposal, revised downward to get Democratic support, larger businesses would pay a small tax—$125 per year for every employee—with the $25 million in proceeds dedicated toward new affordable housing construction. She would have preferred a straight-up tax on corporate profits or revenue, but the Washington state constitution forbade cities from imposing all but a few types of taxes.

Sawant and the anti-sweep activists mobilized more than 400 people for the City Council's November 1 budget hearing. The line to get into council chambers snaked out of the second floor meeting room, down a long stairway, and through a large atrium. To dramatize the housing crisis, they planned to stay in City Hall overnight once the meeting ended, for a night of teach-ins, music, and perhaps a few hours of rest. The following morning would mark the two-year anniversary of the city's emergency homelessness declaration, and Sawant and the community activists wanted to underscore the two years of inaction by the political establishment. The City Council meeting extended late into the evening to accommodate all the speakers. The next morning, activists staged a die-in inside City Hall, calling out the names of all the people—including one baby—who had died on Seattle streets in the previous 10 months.

Two weeks later, the Democrats rejected Sawant's stop the sweeps amendment. And by a narrow 4 to 5 vote they rejected her business tax. But sensing the growing pressure to show they were doing something to alleviate the housing crisis, Democrats created a Progressive Revenue Task Force, "charged with identifying investments to assist people who are homeless or at high risk of becoming homeless in obtaining and retaining stable housing." They were loath to give Sawant credit. By creating the task force, they aimed to take charge of the process of coming up with a compromise tax plan, one that would avoid alienating big business.

The Democrats hoped that the task force would steal momentum from the growing community demand. But instead, they set in motion a roller-coaster series of events that over the coming years would escalate the fight over housing and big business taxation and put Sawant, Socialist Alternative, and their community allies in direct political combat with the most powerful political force in Seattle—Amazon.

4

Big Business Power Play

Rubi moved to Seattle in 2017 after a three-day road journey from southern California. She immediately found a secure home that met all her needs. She had it easier than the other Seattle newcomers who were blown away by skyrocketing rents. She didn't have to worry about finding a safe place nightly, like the 8,500 people living on the streets, under bridges, in abandoned buildings, in run-down recreational vehicles, and in shelters. And she didn't share the anxiety of the 100,000 Seattle households whose crushing rents were forcing them to scrimp on basic necessities of life.

How did Rubi luck out?

Rubi was a tree, a 49-foot Ficus Rubiginosa to be more precise, brought to the city in 2017 by one of the richest men in the world, Amazon CEO Jeff Bezos. Amazon gave her a cute moniker and her own promotional video about her journey and provided a comfortable home inside the company's ostentatious new Spheres.[76]

As Amazon developed its sprawling $4 billion Seattle headquarters, executives dreamt up the eye-popping crystalline biosphere—three interlocking glass spheres up to 90 feet tall and occupying half a city block in the center of the part of downtown now dubbed "Amazonia." In addition to Rubi, the Spheres housed treehouse meeting rooms, waterfalls, a suspension bridge, and 40,000 trees and plants from more than 50 different countries.

The biospheres were a fitting totem to the new Gilded Age heralded by Amazon—stunning, elegant, temperature-controlled palaces for plants, while in the surrounding neighborhoods thousands of people struggled to pay rent or shivered under makeshift plastic and canvass tents.

I happened to be in Amazonia the day Rubi arrived. An enormous hydraulic crane hoisted Rubi—all 18 tons of her—more than 100 feet into the air before gingerly maneuvering the tree down through a small temporary opening in the largest of the glass globes. It was a breathtaking operation, carried out with expert precision by the crane operator and dozens of crew members. Rubi was the climax in Amazon's paean to its own extraordinary wealth and power. The company never revealed how much the 70,000 square foot conservatory cost, but the year Rubi was

---

76 (2018, January 16). *1,200 miles with Rubi.* Amazon. Retrieved February 8, 2023, from https://www.aboutamazon.com/news/sustainability/1-200-miles-with-rubi

brought home, Amazon tallied $5.6 billion in US profits and didn't pay a dime in federal taxes.[77]

The Spheres project was just the tip of the iceberg. In the 2010s, the skies above Seattle were cluttered with cranes as Amazon built out its 10 million square foot headquarters, which eventually occupied more than three dozen buildings, fully one-fourth of all downtown prime commercial space. Its Seattle-area employment soared from 5,000 in 2010 to over 75,000 a decade later.[78]

Tech companies boomed in Seattle alongside Amazon: Microsoft, Expedia, Google, Facebook, F5, and others expanded their footprints while midsized companies and a slew of startups jockeyed for office space and talent. In the mid-2010s, an average of 1,000 people were moving to Seattle every week. It was a gold mine for developers and big landlords, who set to work jacking up rents and gentrifying previously affordable neighborhoods. Seattle's Central District, in the heart of Sawant's District 3, was a thriving African American community in the 20th century, but

---

77 Gardner, M. (2018, February 13). *Amazon Inc. Paid Zero in Federal Taxes in 2017, Gets $789 Million Windfall from New Tax Law*. Just Taxes Blog. Retrieved February 8, 2023, from https://itep.org/amazon-inc-paid-zero-in-federal-taxes-in-2017-gets-789-million-windfall-from-new-tax-law/

78 Soper, T., & Nickelsburg, M. (2021, January 6). *Amazon tops 75,000 employees in Seattle area as company looks elsewhere in region for growth*. Geekwire. Retrieved February 8, 2023, from https://www.geekwire.com/2021/amazon-tops-75000-employees-seattle-area-company-looks-elsewhere-region-growth/ and Rosenberg, M., & Gonzalez, A. (2017, August 23). *Thanks to Amazon, Seattle is now America's biggest company town*. The Seattle Times. Retrieved February 8, 2023, from https://www.seattletimes.com/business/amazon/thanks-to-amazon-seattle-is-now-americas-biggest-company-town/

that was rapidly changing. Formerly 70 percent Black, by the 2010s the Black population in the Central District had plummeted to 15 percent as swanky triplex condominiums replaced modest single-family homes. Well-paid tech workers, savoring the short commute to Amazonia, replaced Black homeowners—established families who had participated in the Great Migration and the Civil Rights Movement and were just one or two generations removed from sharecropping. Now they were forced again to be on the move, this time to the suburbs or other cities in western Washington. Likewise, LGBTQ renters of all ages on Capitol Hill found themselves economically evicted to make way for luxury condominiums and apartments. Pushed out of the homes they grew up in, residents became severed from their churches, grocery stores, parks, schools, coffee shops, bars, and other local gathering spaces.

The social upheaval also marked an enormous transfer of wealth, from Seattle rent and mortgage payers to big developers and real estate companies. Local company Goodman Real Estate ballooned to $5.2 billion in assets. It gobbled up 45 apartment buildings in the Seattle area alone. Goodman Real Estate owners John Goodman and George Petrie, taking a page out of slumlord Carl Haglund's playbook, doubled the rent on residents of the Lockhaven Apartments in Seattle and then evicted them.[79] Microsoft co-founder Paul Allen, one of the richest men in the

79 Herz, A. (2014, April 2). *Battle Between Vulnerable Tenants and Goodman Real Estate Gets To the Heart of What Kind of City Seattle Wants To Be*. The Stranger. Retrieved February 3, 2023, from https://www.thestranger.com/blogs/2014/04/02/19186415/the-battle-between-vulnerable-tenants-and-goodman-real-estate-gets-to-the-heart-of-what-kind-of-city-seattle-wants-to-be

world, started Vulcan Real Estate and snapped up huge swaths of land in Seattle's Central District for his gentrification projects. Cadence Real Estate, with 15 properties a relative guppy to the Vulcan whale, also got in on the gentrification game. Cadence boasted of its "mission of generating above market returns for our investors" by buying and flipping buildings that "are dated in appearance and have several deferred maintenance items. This allows us to reposition and stabilize at market rates."[80]

Not content just to watch the local billionaires and multimillionaires enrich themselves in the gold rush, foreign investors and international speculators increasingly got into the Seattle gentrification game. It was simply too profitable to pass up. In 2016, Seattle was the fifth hottest real estate market in the US for super-rich investors from countries like China, Canada, South Korea, and Germany.[81] Five years later, Seattle had moved up to number one, topping even Manhattan.[82] Taiwan-based Da Li Development Company Ltd. bought up vacant lots in Seattle's Chinatown/International District (CID), home to many working-class elders in the Asian community. Da Li could have built affordable housing for CID residents but instead chose to construct condominiums

80 (2018, March 5). *About Us*. Cadence Real Estate. Retrieved February 3, 2023, from https://www.cadencere.com/

81 Rosenberg, M. (2016, November 12). *Foreign investors pouring billions into Seattle commercial real estate*. The Seattle Times. Retrieved February 3, 2023, from https://www.seattletimes.com/business/real-estate/foreign-investors-pouring-billions-into-seattle-commercial-real-estate/

82 Dean, G. (2021, May 21). *Foreign investors pouring billions into Seattle commercial real estate*. Business Insider. Retrieved February 3, 2023, from https://www.businessinsider.com/manhattan-new-york-seattle-washington-real-estate-investment-foreign-overseas-2021-5

priced up to $1.4 million. The luxury units offered access to an elegant rooftop garden and a Tesla carshare.[83] Want a parking space to go with your luxury pad? Da Li charged an additional $65,000 for parking spaces, more than twice the annual income of a typical CID neighbor.[84] Community members protested and picketed, to no avail. Da Li developers "have no relationship to the history, to the land . . . no appreciation or reverence for the people that built this neighborhood and the people who continue to make it a special place," said community activist Alison Cheung. "They just see an opportunity to make a massive profit and displace everything that makes this home."[85]

More than money was at stake. Thanks to the federal government's EB-5 Visa program, rich people could buy a pathway to US citizenship by investing in luxury housing and other projects. The visa program, little known to the public, was primed for scandal. In 2014, Seattle Mayor Ed Murray joined Path America CEO Lobsang Dargey in a ceremony breaking ground on the Seattle Potala Towers, a 41-story luxury hotel-and-apartment skyscraper. Media snapped pictures of the ornate lion dance that celebrated

---

83 Kronen, M. (2019, April 13). *Update on Koda Condominium Flats in the International District*. Seattle Condo Review. Retrieved February 4, 2023, from https://seattlecondoreview.com/update-on-koda-condominium-flats-in-the-international-district/

84 Nelson, G. (2019, November 21). *How Seattle can slow gentrification — And why it must*. Crosscut.com. Retrieved February 4, 2023, from https://crosscut.com/opinion/2019/11/how-seattle-can-slow-gentrification-and-why-it-must

85 Ho Chang, S. (2021, June 26). *Community Groups Protest Grand Opening of CID's First Luxury High-Rise*. South Seattle Emerald. Retrieved February 4, 2023, from https://southseattleemerald.com/2021/06/26/community-groups-protest-grand-opening-of-cids-first-luxury-high-rise/

the new project. Dargey financed the development in part with money from 250 foreign investors, whom he promised an EB-5 path to citizenship in exchange for their millions. Instead, he squandered their money on a mansion for himself and his out-of-control casino habit. He pled guilty to fraud and spent three years in prison.[86] The project was sold to two new investment groups—one from Las Vegas, the other from China—renamed Arrivé, and finally opened in 2019, with monthly rents listed at upwards of $12,000.

Billions of dollars, clean and dirty, poured into the Seattle real estate market. Everyone was a winner—developers, selling agents, financiers, marketers; only the residents of Seattle got trampled in this stampede for riches. One investment advisory firm, in pitiless corporate-speak, put it this way: "Although affordability continues to be an issue for local residents, it does have a positive aspect for Seattle real estate investors. Owning a rental property in Seattle does mean high demand which translates into good occupancy rates and cash flow."[87]

Instead of building the affordable housing that the city so badly needed, global development firms scooped up choice downtown properties and hired workers to construct soaring multi-million-dollar condominium towers whose individual units sold for upwards

---

86 Stiles, M. (2017, May 8). *Once waylaid Potala Tower high-rise project has a new name*. Business Insider. Retrieved February 3, 2023, from https://www.bizjournals.com/seattle/news/2017/05/08/once-waylaid-seattle-high-rise-project-has-arriv-d.html

87 Shalhout, S. (2020, October 9). *Seattle Housing Market Forecast for 2021*. Mashvisor. Retrieved February 2, 2023, from https://www.mashvisor.com/blog/seattle-housing-market-forecast-2021/

of $10 million. Construction workers drove up to two hours in the pre-dawn hours to bring the international elite's elaborate architectural renderings to life. Hundreds of feet up in the air, they welded steel structures, sheet rocked and painted the walls, set the glass, poured the concrete, installed the elevators, plumbed and electrified the buildings, and then proceeded to the finish work: glistening infinity pools, heated limestone shower floors, rooftop decks, high-rise doggie runs and pet spas, indoor waterfalls, dazzling artwork installations, indoor putting greens, and the finest in imported cabinetry, countertops, and appliances. At the end of the workday, the workers drove back to the homes they could afford in the far-off suburbs. Some of them forsook family life and slept in their cars overnight to avoid the long commute. They never imagined, of course, living in these spectacular homes.

Neither, apparently, did many of the condo owners, though for very different reasons. A study found extraordinarily high vacancy rates in these new luxury buildings. At one building only 39 percent of the people listed as condo owners were even registered to vote at that ownership address, a figure 40 percent below what one would expect based on state averages. At another tower, 99 Union, just up the street from Seattle's iconic Pike Place Market, nearly half of the condo homes were not even owned by human beings, but rather were held by trusts or limited liability corporations. At the 440-foot tall Fifteen Twenty-One Second Avenue, whose developers plumped it as "a microclimate for luxury in-city real estate," one out of every five condos was owned by a trust or corporation, many of them shell companies whose true ownership remained hidden. Former Microsoft executive Jyoti Paul owned three of the six penthouses at the top of the tony Escala high-rise but never lived in them. Starbucks founder Howard Schultz owned a $7.5 million condo at the Millenium Tower, a peculiar location for a second residence as it was less than four miles away from his main home on Lake Washington. Indeed, these were not places to live in; they were entertainment centers, lucrative investments, tax shelters—sparkly trophies for the uber-wealthy.[88]

Back in the neighborhoods where people actually lived, big landlords took full advantage of the overwhelming legal power they'd bought and paid for. In 1980, the Seattle tenants movement put local rent control on the ballot. The landlord lobby raised record funds to defeat the initiative at the ballot. But they didn't stop there. The following year, lobbyists went to the state Capitol and won a statewide ban on residential rent control. To anyone with a shred of moral fiber, slumlord Haglund doubling the rent on Sahro Farah and her children was unethical and outrageous. But it was perfectly legal, and precisely what the real estate lobby fought tenaciously for the right to do. They intended to suppress any future talk of rent control, and they were successful for decades—until Sawant's election.

Further benefiting big landlords was a dearth of affordable housing, which drove working class households to desperation any time they had to find a new place to live. Politicians issued glowing press releases and staged festive ribbon-cutting ceremonies any time a new affordable housing development opened. But no

---

88 (2019, October 1). *Who Is Buying Seattle?* Institute for Policy Studies. Retrieved February 3, 2023, from https://inequality.org/wp-content/uploads/2019/10/IPS-SEATTLE-REPORT-FINAL.pdf and (2013, January 11). *Fifteen Twenty-One Second Avenue Now 97% Sold; Just Four Homes Remain.* Realogics Sotheby's International Realty. Retrieved February 13, 2023, from http://1521second.com/pdf/1-11-13_1521.pdf

amount of mediagenic fanfare could refute the lived reality for working people or the hard data that a few hundred new affordable homes every year was a drop in the ocean. In unguarded moments of honesty, establishment representatives admitted that the profiteers were to blame for the housing crisis. A report by the McKinsey & Company consulting firm, commissioned by the local Chamber of Commerce, reported that during the 2010s the Seattle area lost 40 percent of its affordable housing stock—more than 112,000 residences—even as the population and housing needs grew. The study concluded by saying the quiet part out loud: "This has happened largely because rents on existing units rose faster than incomes, and lower-cost units were demolished to make way for more expensive ones."[89] In 2017, a local government study corroborated the McKinsey study and estimated that with the destruction of affordable housing combined with population influx, the Seattle area needed 156,000 new affordable homes immediately, and another 88,000 by 2040.[90]

If quashing affordable housing supply wasn't bad enough, big landlords and realtors also began price-fixing to boost rents as high as they possibly could. Technically, it would be illegal for landlords to share pricing information directly with one another. Instead, in

89 Maritz, B., & Wagle, D. (2020, January 22). *Why does prosperous King County have a homelessness crisis?* McKinsey & Company. Retrieved February 2, 2023, from https://www.mckinsey.com/industries/public-and-social-sector/our-insights/why-does-prosperous-king-county-have-a-homelessness-crisis

90 (2017, October 31). *King County Housing Affordability: Understanding the Need.* King County Housing Affordability Task Force. Retrieved February 4, 2023, from https://kingcounty.gov/~/media/initiatives/affordablehousing/documents/Meetings/CAI-RAH-Deck1031.ashx?la=en

the 2010s big data companies like RealPage began doing the job for landlords. They aggregated rental information from millions of apartment units and instructed their corporate clients exactly how much they could upcharge every apartment they controlled. RealPage billed handsomely for their services and boasted that its clients could "outperform the market 3 percent to 7 percent." RealPage's big data took negotiations and human contact out of the pricing process and helped landlords boost their profits. The problem with property managers talking with prospective renters, the RealPage program architect said, was that "there's way too much empathy going on here."

RealPage also drove housing inflation in cities like Seattle. By 2016, the company boasted that its participating landlords controlled 60 percent of the core Seattle apartment building market and 57 percent of the greater Seattle market—enough to constitute what multiple lawsuits labeled a cartel. In the Belltown neighborhood, just north of downtown Seattle, it was even higher. Some 70 percent of the major apartment buildings were controlled by corporate landlords that set rates using RealPage, according to a ProPublica investigation. Not surprisingly, rents skyrocketed in the neighborhood under the new algorithm.[91] RealPage, one class action lawsuit asserted, "developed and used proprietary artificial intelligence and algorithmic decision-making systems to help big housing landlords operate as a cartel to push up rents above

91 Vogell, H. (2022, October 15). *Rent Going Up? One Company's Algorithm Could Be Why*. ProPublica. Retrieved February 4, 2023, from https://www.propublica.org/article/yieldstar-rent-increase-realpage-rent

competitive levels, all to increase profits at the expense of thousands of unwitting tenants.[92]

Apologists for the housing market would maintain that since capitalists were putting their money on the table, they were entitled to the rewards. Roger Valdez, the Haglund ally and a frequent spokesperson for Seattle's landlord lobby, argued, "The essential idea of a 'free market' approach is for government to allow private investors to take the risk so it doesn't have to." But there's nothing "free" about landlords fixing prices and destroying affordable housing supply while the political establishment stands back and applauds at every new luxury development groundbreaking.

Between 2012 and 2016, Seattle area rents soared 29 percent, reaching a median of $2,031 in mid-2016. That earned Seattle the dubious title of having the highest rent increases in the country.[93] Median area single-family home prices that year topped $666,000,[94] on their way to a mind-boggling $781,000 by the end of the decade.[95] The staggering increases put Seattle home own-

---

92 (2022, November 10). *Matthew Alvarez and Scott Halliwell v. RealPage et al.* DocumentCloud.org. Retrieved July 13, 2023, from https://s3.documentcloud.org/documents/23309703/realpage-complaint-alvarez.pdf

93 Rosenberg, M. (2016, July 21). Seattle rents now growing faster than in any other U.S. City. *The Seattle Times*. https://www.seattletimes.com/business/real-estate/seattle-rents-now-growing-faster-than-in-any-other-us-city/

94 Rosenberg, M. (2016, July 6). Seattle's devilish new home price record: $666,000. *The Seattle Times*. https://www.seattletimes.com/business/seattles-devilish-new-home-price-record-666000/

95 (2021, February 22). *Mortgage Affordability Worsens in 51 of 100 Largest U.S. Cities in the Past Decade*. Point2. Retrieved February 13, 2023, from

ership out of reach for all but the lucky or rich. By the mid-2010s, more than 100,000 Seattle households—more than one-third of all homes—were by official standards cost-burdened, meaning that by federal standards they were forced to forgo at least some basic necessities of life.[96]

The skyrocketing housing costs translated into a profound human toll for people struggling at the bottom of the economic ladder. With great flourish, in 2015 Mayor Murray had proclaimed a state of civil emergency to address the homelessness crisis in Seattle, but that was just performative lip service. A year after the emergency declaration, as Sawant was agitating that the City Council repurpose the $160 million police precinct allocation for affordable housing, the number of people living on area streets or in shelters hit a new record—10,730—an increase of 21 percent in four years.[97] Some 7 percent of all Seattle public school students were homeless, on average more than one child in every classroom.[98] The number of people dying every year on Seattle-area

https://www.point2homes.com/news/us-real-estate-news/affordability-evolution-100-u-s-cities-decade.html

96 (2015). *2015 Washington State Housing Needs Assessment*. Washington State Department of Commerce. Retrieved February 4, 2023, from http://www.commerce.wa.gov/wp-content/uploads/2016/10/AHAB-needs-urban-Seattle.pdf

97 (2016, October 12). *HUD 2016 Continuum of Care Homeless Assistance Programs Homeless Populations and Subpopulations*. US Department of Housing and Urban Development. Retrieved February 2, 2023, from https://files.hudexchange.info/reports/published/CoC_PopSub_CoC_WA-500-2015_WA_2016.pdf

98 Dornfeld, A. (2017, October 18). *District didn't want us to visit this struggling Seattle school*. KUOW.org. Retrieved February 2, 2023, from https://kuow.org/stories/district-didnt-want-us-visit-struggling-seattle-school/

streets soared from 78 in 2012 to 169 in 2017—more than double in just five years.[99]

That was the scene as 2018 began. Accordingly, the timing seemed auspicious for winning a first-ever Seattle tax on big business to fund affordable housing. Even after Sawant's tax proposal the previous fall was narrowly defeated in City Council, opponents conceded that something needed to be done. The City Council Democrats had diverted Sawant's big business tax legislation into a broad-based study group, the Progressive Revenue Task Force. They appointed housing advocates, union staff, business owners, and non-profit housing developers and tasked it with drafting a proposal in two months. Pointedly, Sawant was not included, and only one of the 16 task force members had experience being homeless. The Democrats' redirection was quite purposeful: They sought to cobble together a tax plan that would relieve political pressure, a plan that would demonstrate their progressive bona fides while staying on the good side of business executives. Sawant had been increasingly ratcheting up the call for Amazon to pay for the housing. Mindful of how Sawant and the movement had driven the $15 minimum wage debate, the Democrats were determined to call the shots; they sidelined the socialist councilmember at every possible turn.

Two crucial events in late 2017 weighed heavily on the Democrats' minds: A gauntlet thrown down by Amazon, and the November municipal elections. In September, Amazon CEO Jeff Bezos had

99 Seinfeld, K. (2018, March 5). *Rising Number of Homeless Deaths Reflects Increasing Numbers of People Needing Shelter and Care*. Public Health Insider. Retrieved February 3, 2023, from https://publichealthinsider.com/2018/03/05/rising-number-of-homeless-deaths-reflects-increasing-numbers-of-people-needing-shelter-and-care/

announced the company would begin the search for a second headquarters, "a full equal to Amazon's headquarters in Seattle," triggering a bidding frenzy by 238 cities in the US, Mexico, and Canada.[100] City and state governments offered billions in tax breaks, expedited construction schedules, special treatment, and sometimes straight-up cash in a desperate bid to woo the company, already one of the richest in history. Members of Seattle's political establishment expressed shock and disappointment that Amazon was abandoning the city. But Amazon wasn't leaving. With more than 50,000 employees in the region plus more than 3,000 advertised Seattle job openings and growing by leaps and bounds, Amazon was running out of room for expansion. And company executives recognized that by instigating a bidding war they could leverage unprecedented local and state government concessions.

City Council Democrats saw it otherwise, penning a groveling letter to Bezos that five of them signed along with 20 other local and state elected officials. "We understand there are many reasons for your decision to potentially site HQ2 in a different city," the letter began. "To the extent that this decision was based on Amazon feeling unwelcome in Seattle, or not being included in some of our regional decisions, we would like to hit the refresh button. You have heard mixed messages from our community, whether

---

100 (2017, September 7). *Amazon Opens Search for Amazon HQ2 – A Second Headquarters City in North America*. BusinessWire.com. Retrieved February 13, 2023, from https://www.businesswire.com/news/home/20170907005717/en/Amazon-Opens-Search-Amazon-HQ2-%E2%80%93-Headquarters and Wingfield, N. (2017, October 23). *Amazon Counts Its Suitors: 238 Want to Be Home for 2nd Headquarters*. The New York Times. Retrieved February 13, 2023, from https://www.nytimes.com/2017/10/23/technology/amazon-headquarters.html

it stems from comments in our local newspapers or comments from elected officials who have differing views and positions that are less than collaborative," they wrote, all but uttering Sawant's name. "This does not leave a good taste in anyone's mouth. Those of us who are signing onto this letter want you to know we have heard you. We also want you to stay with us and grow with us, both in Seattle and with our sister cities across the state."[101] It was a nauseating display of public sycophancy. To the political establishment, pleasing Amazon executives was more important than addressing working class needs.

The second 2017 event was the November election of Jenny Durkan as Seattle's new mayor. Durkan had the ideal resume for Seattle's corporate leaders. Reliably pro-business and a former "tough on crime" federal prosecutor, Durkan was deeply entrenched in establishment circles. She collected endorsements across the political establishment spectrum from the Chamber of Commerce to the local labor council. Durkan also was helped by a $350,000 campaign donation from Amazon, at the time the company's biggest local political donation ever and a not-too-subtle statement that it intended to protect its tax-free status in the city. Durkan cruised to victory over a candidate who ran to her left.

Going into 2018, the Democrats outwardly were optimistic they could craft a tax plan that would avoid inflaming big business. Celebrating the unanimous City Council vote to create the task force, Councilmember M. Lorena Gonzalez declared that "we

---

101 (2017, October 13). Seattle City Council letter to Amazon. Seattle.gov. Retrieved July 12, 2023, from https://www.seattle.gov/Documents/Departments/Council/letters/Amazon-Letter.pdf

must deploy bold actions that will meet the reality of the needs in our City."[102] Even the new mayor agreed, though she studiously avoided endorsing a tax on the same businesses that boosted her into office. Seattle's top priority "must be to build a more affordable Seattle," Durkan said. "It's the moral challenge of our time," she intoned.[103]

Yet six months later the tax-for-housing plan lay in ruins. The housing crisis continued unabated, while progressive advocates lay beaten, demoralized, and scattered. What transpired in Seattle that year was a textbook lesson in what happens when progressive forces reject the class struggle approach advocated by Sawant's movement and instead rely on an inside strategy. It was a repeat of the 150-year-old clash between reformist and revolutionary politics.

Washington state restricts the taxing authority of municipalities, so when the task force began work in January 2018, members settled on the Employee Hours Tax (EHT) framework that Sawant had previously proposed. The group proposed a tax rate that would bring in $75 million a year for housing and services—half of what Sawant had called for in the fall – even though their final report acknowledged that to meet the need for affordable housing, the city would require seven times that revenue, every year, for at least a decade.

---

102 Seattle City Council (2017, December 19). *Council Announces Progressive Revenue Task Force Co-Chairs, Members*. Council Connection. Retrieved February 13, 2023, from https://council.seattle.gov/2017/12/19/council-announces-progressive-revenue-task-force-co-chairs-members/

103 (2018, February 20). *Mayor Jenny A. Durkan's 2018 State of the City Address*. City of Seattle Mayor's Office. Retrieved February 13, 2023, from https://durkan.seattle.gov/2018/02/state-of-the-city-2018/

Additionally, not wanting to alienate big business, members of the task force proposed to tax virtually all companies, from Amazon to small and medium sized companies, because, they argued, all businesses should have "skin in the game." The task force's final report in March 2018 waxed on at length about the problems of homelessness and a lack of affordable housing but failed to point the finger at the source of the problem. Nowhere in the 8,900-word report was Amazon mentioned by name, nor did the report point out the big landlords and profiteering developers who were responsible for the systemic destruction of affordable housing and the economic eviction of working-class households. It was as if the housing crisis had magically dropped out of the sky, cause unknown.

Rather than allay big business concerns as task force members intended, the report's conclusions handed powerful weapons to opponents. The "skin in the game" argument allowed the Chamber to put forward small business owners as the face of the no-tax campaign. And by failing to cite the reasons for the housing crisis, the task force allowed opponents to define the problem. Big business had a ready answer: The problem was not Amazon, nor was it the insatiable corporate developer lobby, but a profligate City Council that simply wanted to impose "a new tax on jobs."[104]

"Big business and the political establishment are carrying out a cynical strategy," Sawant said. "If the proposed EHT is extended to cover small or medium sized businesses, it allows them to play small business owners against any EHT tax. As such, 'skin in the

104 Strickland, M., Scholes, J., & Chernin, L. (2018, March 22). *No to jobs tax: Seattle's approach to homelessness is not working*. The Seattle Times. Retrieved February 13, 2023, from https://www.seattletimes.com/opinion/no-to-jobs-tax-seattles-approach-to-homelessness-is-not-working/

game' is a Trojan horse. Big business cannot make a compelling argument for why they should be allowed to evade paying taxes yet again, so they have a desperate need to reframe the debate."[105]

By the time the City Council translated the task force's recommendations into a bill in the spring of 2018, the business tax was under withering assault. Talk radio and online news sites were awash with criticism of the "tax on jobs." Media referred to the proposal as a "head tax," implying that the tax would fall on employees—or worse, conjuring up memories of the racist head tax levied by West Coast governments against immigrant Chinese laborers more than a century earlier. Outraged small business owners started taping "No Tax on Jobs!" signs on their windows. Nominally, the labor movement was on board—the Martin Luther King County Labor Council had endorsed the task force proposal—but most union leaders ducked out of visibly promoting the measure.

Sawant and community activists worked to shift the focus back to Amazon with town halls, a petition, and public speak-outs at City Council meetings. A spirited Tax Amazon rally outside the Spheres in April drew 200 people, who heard from union members, people living on the streets, and housing advocates. The ironworker Logan Swan brought a delegation of construction workers who held up signs. "Can't afford to live in the city I risk my life to build," read one.

They also continued calling for $150 million in new revenues and not flinching from calling it a tax on Amazon. But now the movement was facing headwinds from both the task force and progressive

105 Sawant, K. (2018, March 10). Tax Amazon - Build Affordable Housing [Unpublished speech at City Council; in author's possession].

activists. The task force's $75 million EHT proposal in effect set the political high-bar. Several progressive community activists also began to call on Sawant and the movement to drop the $150 million demand. Sawant demurred, "Not because I don't think $75 million would also represent an important victory—it would—but because cutting our demand in half is a form of the movement negotiating with itself, and because working people and homeless people need the full $150 million, and more. We should fight boldly to win the largest tax on Amazon by building the strongest possible movement, because they can afford to pay for housing security in Seattle, while increasingly our neighbors cannot."

But citywide momentum had swung the other way. Sawant and the community members had lost control of the unfolding narrative. That had been shaped by the task force and the council Democrats, who had determined to tiptoe around the cause of the problem and lower their sights. The other side's message—"No Tax on Jobs"—resonated clearly and attracted increasing support from small businesses, the media, and anyone with an ax to grind against city government.

On May 3, two weeks after Sawant's rally at the Amazon Spheres, the task force held a town hall at a church in Ballard, an older, whiter neighborhood in the northwestern quadrant of the city. It was ripe for sabotage. Anti-tax activists set up a faux homeless encampment outside the church, complete with trash, a shopping cart, and a container holding a yellow liquid meant to be urine. They shouted down the pastor when she opened the meeting. Some loudly swore at the task force members on the stage. They demanded an open mic when City Councilmember Mike O'Brien, whose district included Ballard, tactlessly announced the panel would field written comments. The mood turned sour. "Resign now!" several people screamed. A homeless woman who rose to speak was heckled. Another speaker suggested organizing "a highly publicized event where we round up some of them."

"What was supposed to be a panel discussion, with a moderated Q&A, on a proposed business tax to pay for homeless services, was not just a crowd of angry neighbors wanting to be heard by their elected representatives," reported Erica C. Barnett, an independent journalist. "It was an organized mob that showed up with a single goal: To shut down dialogue, create chaos, and prevent people with opposing views from having a voice."[106]

Not all the attendees were against the EHT. Barbara Phinney, a union nurse at the local Veterans Administration (VA) hospital, lived near Ballard. A regular at Tax Amazon events, she wanted to show her support for the tax. Phinney was no stranger to tough environments. As a young adult in the steel town of Lorain, Ohio in the 1970s, Phinney was one of the first women to be hired to work on the Great Lakes iron ore boats that transited from the northern mines to smelters outside Cleveland and Chicago. Years later she drove west to Seattle in an old Chevy Impala with her dog and a few belongings, couch-surfed until she found stable housing, and eventually went back to school for nursing and became head of her local union at the VA. Phinney had first gotten connected to Sawant during the Block the Bunker fight, as the proposed police precinct was only a few blocks from her north

106 Barnett, E. C. (2018, May 3). *Tonight In Ballard: Two Hours Hate*. Publicola. Retrieved February 14, 2023, from https://publicola.com/2018/05/03/tonight-in-ballard-two-hours-hate/

Seattle home. Recently retired from hospital nursing, she found her political home through that fight. After the victory, "I was thinking, 'Oh, I want to be part of this. I know where I stand here,'" Phinney recalled.

But the pure hatred at the Ballard meeting astonished even Phinney. "There was a palpable feeling of violence ready to erupt at the church meeting. Just anger. That they aren't going to stand for homeless encampments, people sleeping on the streets, that they will not tolerate it, and they don't want big business taxed, they didn't think that people deserved more money for services. And of course, they didn't say anything about the need for more housing, you know, no solution," she said.

"For me, it was a watershed moment because the task force members were so frightened by the anger, the hatred being spewed at them. In my opinion, that's when Councilmember Lisa Herbold lost her ability to stand up for anything. And Mike O'Brien, I saw that as the end of his political career."

Task force Democrats had been further traumatized by a development the previous day. On May 2, Amazon executives had announced that "pending the outcome of the head-tax vote by City Council," the company was pausing construction planning on one of several new downtown tower projects and threatening to sublease space in another building they previously had committed to occupy.[107] Union workers recognize the disruptive power they have in striking. By collectively withholding their labor, they aim to

107 Day, M., & Beekman, D. (2018, May 2). *Amazon issues threat over Seattle head-tax plan, halts tower construction planning*. The Seattle Times. Retrieved February 14, 2023, from https://www.seattletimes.com/business/

force a crisis that an employer or political body can resolve only by making concessions. This move by Amazon was the reverse, a strike by capital. It was designed to whip up fear, divide the community, and send a warning shot to the political establishment. It was tremendously effective.

"I'm deeply concerned about the impact this could have on a whole range of issues," Mayor Durkan said. "My read is they're serious," echoed Bob McCleskey, CEO of construction giant Sellen, saying that halting the project could cost 350 to 400 jobs. Worse yet, "We have a couple other projects teed up for other clients who may not have signed leases with Amazon but are counting on that," he said. "I wouldn't be surprised if those projects hit the brakes and these high-rise residential projects—several are slated—those could stop as well."

Amazon's capital strike provided tangible proof to the political establishment and business leaders that the EHT was a tax on jobs. It also aimed to draw construction unions into the fray. Politics among construction union members run the full gamut from far left to far right. But over the years, most construction union leaders have grown cozy with big business. Controlling hiring halls that provide skilled labor to big construction projects, the union leaders increasingly saw their fates intertwined with industry's. Any project that produced more jobs was good; it kept members working and increased the union's dues revenue. Any disruption was bad. When members were out of work, they were unhappy. They had bills to pay and got restless. Often they'd direct their frustrations

amazon/amazon-pauses-plans-for-seattle-office-towers-while-city-council-considers-business-tax/

at the union leaders. Outwardly, many of these construction union leaders, who carried the job title of "business manager," seemed more comfortable acting as labor brokers than worker advocates. Even in the booming Seattle construction market, where the labor shortage was so bad that workers were being recruited from several states away, giving workers enormous collective power over the industry, union leaders kept up the mantra that the only thing that mattered was jobs. A "tax on jobs" had to be bad.

This business union dogma put the construction union leadership on a collision course with the Sawant's Tax Amazon movement, and in particular with the ironworker Logan Swan and the construction workers who had joined him.

In late April, Swan had penned an article in *The Stranger*, the local alternative newspaper. "My workday starts on an unfinished floor with no windows, 40 stories up. I scan Seattle's skyline, watching the endless headlights stream along I-5 and Highway 99. As the sun comes up, I can see people coming and going from the buildings that I helped build. I am part of the pulse of life and industry, knowing that none of this glass and steel would be here if it wasn't for me and thousands of other construction workers."

But, Swan continued, "I also see the human toll of our housing crisis. I look down on the flimsy canopies of people coughed up by this crisis, while the working class grinds along the choked highways to staff a city that's off limits when you're off the clock."

"Enough time has been wasted debating band-aids," he wrote. "We need solutions to the housing crisis, ones that put the needs of the people over the profits of a few to provide permanent housing. Taxing the enormous private wealth hoarded in this city at a modest rate of $150 million per year and using it to fund 750 units of new public housing construction every year is the best proposal I've heard. . . . We need housing now in Seattle. And my union sisters and brothers are ready to start building it."

Swan was already on the union leaders' watchlist. Earlier in the year, he had convened meetings with fellow rank-and-file ironworkers to talk about labor history and contemporary struggles, like the burgeoning Red for Ed educators strikes in West Virginia, Oklahoma, and Arizona. His union leaders were not happy. "I was told, 'We think this could be dangerous. We don't want members getting fired up. It used to be that it was the union against the contractors and it was very difficult. Now we're in a partnership and everything's so much better,'" Swan recalled being told.

Swan had successfully recruited a half dozen other construction workers to attend March and April Tax Amazon rallies. He later heard that afterwards his Ironworkers Local 86 Business Manager, Chris McClain, and other leaders had approached these new activists. "They never talked to me, but they went to them and said, 'Be careful, shit's about to hit the fan.'" McClain also knew that I worked in Sawant's office. After Swan's article in *The Stranger* appeared, he called to warn me that, in his estimation, the socialist was playing with fire.

The day after Amazon's capital strike announcement, Sawant had scheduled a lunchtime press conference outside The Spheres to denounce the company's extortion threat. She was joined by a dozen community activists, including Swan, who took his lunch break from a nearby worksite. With TV cameras filming, as Sawant prepared to open the event, about 25 ironworkers—large men dressed in reflective vests and hardhats, led by McClain—barged into the press conference chanting "No head tax!"[108]

Their cacophony drowned out Sawant. Swan gamely tried to speak. "Is it worth it to fight one another for the benefit of big companies like Amazon that are paying zero in taxes?" he asked before being overwhelmed by more shouts and jeers from his union brothers. Giving up, Swan stepped away from the mic. At McClain's signal, the ironworkers in unison turned their backs on him.

Sawant tried to speak again but was stymied by the ironworkers' renewed chants. The ironworkers turned to face her and stepped forward, many of them physically towering over the community members gathered around the mic. With TV cameras recording every second of the conflict, Sawant huddled briefly with her Council office staff, who agreed that the most effective response to McClain's truculence would be an invitation to dialogue. Sawant was not afraid of a debate.

One of the Council staff, Ted Virdone, took the mic and handed it to McClain. "Don't you want to speak?" he asked McClain, who appeared surprised to be offered the mic. Gesturing toward the media, Virdone asked, "Don't you want to tell all of these people your reasons?"

"Please speak, and then we'll speak," Sawant said.

---

108 This and following dialogue from [GeekWire]. (2018, May 3). *Raw Video: Clash at Amazon HQ over Seattle tax plan* [Video]. YouTube.com. https://www.youtube.com/watch?v=ycEa1l01_A0&t=261s

"Amazon is a responsible developer that pays living wages," began McClain. "They don't have a requirement to pay prevailing wage, but they do. They provide health insurance and retirement for ironworkers. . . .Homelessness is an enormous issue, not just an Amazon issue. It needs to have a regional approach that is fair and reasonable, something that this is not." He returned the mic.

"There is a legitimate concern about construction jobs because Amazon has issued this extortionary threat against construction jobs," Sawant acknowledged. McClain, having been given the opportunity to air his views, was not in a position to drown out the socialist. He and the ironworkers stood back, lingered for a bit, and then peeled off as Sawant continued to address the media and supporters. "We stand in solidarity with the entirety of the labor movement that demands union rights for all workers, decent standards of living," Sawant said. "And we will continue to work together even when we disagree. . . . Because the reality is, that this is classic divide and rule. When we fight against each other as workers, the only people that win are the bosses. The capitalist class.

"So, what should we do in the face of Amazon's threat?" Sawant continued, addressing both the media and the ironworkers. "Should we say, 'Okay, we can't pass this tax law because Amazon is going to take away jobs?' But what would the consequence of that be?"

Sawant continued: "If we don't tax big business in our region to massively fund publicly owned affordable housing, the only consequence of that will be an exacerbation of the already massively acute housing, affordable housing crisis, the skyrocketing rents, and the exploding homelessness. . . . The housing crisis is being faced by every single metropolitan area in the United States. So, the only conclusion of backing down and accepting Amazon's extortionary threat will be a continuation and an intensification of the race to the bottom, not just in Seattle, but nationwide."

"We have to recognize that what Amazon has done is not stand with construction workers," she added. "They are, in fact, yet another big corporation in the history of US capitalism who have resorted to bullying and extortion in the face of a courageous movement of working people who are fed up with inequality, acute housing shortage, skyrocketing rents and exploding homelessness around the country."

That was true—Amazon executives were increasingly wary of the Tax Amazon movement's staying power. But also true was that the ironworkers' disruption was an impressive power move by the anti-tax coalition. For the next several news cycles, TV news and online media played and replayed the dramatic images of the ironworkers towering over and drowning out Sawant's press conference with their "No head tax" chants. Jeff Bezos and the Chamber of Commerce didn't need to lift a finger when confused members of the working class would do the work for them.

Two weeks later the Democrats took up the tax measure, now lowered by Mayor Durkan from $75 million to $48 million annually, and set to expire after five years. It was unanimously adopted. As a first-ever tax on big business in Seattle, it represented a breakthrough. But it was a shell of the original design.

It also was extremely short-lived. Less than 72 hours after the City Council adopted the EHT, the Chamber of Commerce convened a meeting of the top Seattle businesses. They immediately formed a No Tax on Jobs committee, filed campaign papers, and wrote checks totaling $350,000 to launch a repeal referendum. The initial donors were a who's who of the corporate power structure: Starbucks, Amazon, major developers and construction firms, cruise ship and maritime companies.[109] They hired the national consulting firm Morning in America, renowned for helping Donald Trump win his upset 2016 election.[110] The No Tax on Jobs Committee would need just 18,000 signatures to put a tax repeal measure on the November ballot. Taking no chances, they flew in canvassers from out of state and paid them up to $6 a signature. They flooded local internet sites with ads condemning the "Tax on Jobs" and lit up the airwaves with attacks on the measure. Editorials blasted the tax. The two-to-one polling support that the EHT enjoyed in April had completely vanished. In early June, the No Tax on Jobs Committee announced they had collected 45,000 signatures and were prepared to file their ballot measure.

Panicked about the prospect of a tax repeal on the November ballot, on the weekend of June 9 the council Democrats huddled with Mayor Durkan in a series of private meetings. It was by all appearances a violation of the state's Open Meetings Law—the City would later pay out fines stemming from two open government

---

109 (2018, May 22). *No Tax on Jobs C4 Filing*. Washington State Public Disclosure Commission. Retrieved February 15, 2023, from https://www.documentcloud.org/documents/4482175-No-Tax-on-Jobs-Filing.html

110 Hsieh, S. (2018, June 12). *Amazon Wins: Seattle City Council Votes to Repeal Head Tax*. The Stranger. Retrieved February 22, 2023, from https://www.thestranger.com/news/2018/06/12/27509559/seattle-city-council-votes-to-repeal-head-tax

advocate lawsuits[111]—but to the political establishment any legal misdemeanors were trivial compared to their absolute commitment to stop the referendum. On Monday morning, June 11, City Council Democrats introduced a tax repeal measure they had hastily drafted and reviewed in secrecy over the weekend. They announced an extraordinary emergency meeting the following day, June 12, to vote on it. Not surprisingly, Sawant had been excluded from the secret weekend deliberations. Her council office was the last to be informed that Democrats were placing the bill on the Monday City Council agenda, and that a special meeting was being arranged for the following day.

Council chambers were packed for the June 12 emergency meeting—mostly by tax advocates but also a number of people supporting the repeal. The result was a foregone conclusion. Before the meeting, Durkan and seven of the eight Democrats issued a public statement in support of the repeal, with only Councilmember Teresa Mosqueda declining to side with her fellow Democrats. The mayor had insisted that council Democrats issue the public statement preceding the vote, a deft way of whipping the council Democrats into line.

But before the official voting the councilmembers had to endure public comment. Movement activists were not about to pass up the opportunity to confront the political establishment. As Marxists leading the movement, Sawant and Socialist Alternative were

---

111 Kamb, L. (2020, October 19). *Seattle agrees to pay $35,000 to settle lawsuit alleging city council broke open meetings law over head tax repeal.* The Seattle Times. Retrieved February 17, 2023, from https://www.seattletimes.com/seattle-news/politics/seattle-agrees-to-pay-35000-to-settle-lawsuit-alleging-city-council-broke-open-meetings-law-over-head-tax-repeal/

determined to use the opportunity to expose the Democrats' perfidy and illustrate the need for independent working-class politics.

First up to speak was Emerson Johnson, a restaurant worker who had joined Socialist Alternative two years prior, during the 2016 presidential election. "I was so demoralized in the beginning, when Trump was running for office, and it was just him versus Hillary. And when I got involved in SA, that demoralization shifted into anger and action," he recalled. On the day of Trump's election, Johnson headed downtown to a protest organized by Sawant and Socialist Alternative. Thousands of people turned out. Johnson approached Emily McArthur, an SA organizer.

"What do I do?" he asked her.

"Take a clipboard, sign people up," she replied.

"I was like, cool. That catapulted me into getting more involved, and then I ended up organizing a rally at Seattle Central [College] the day of Trump's inauguration. And it was just so clear to me – these people are actually doing something."

Johnson had avidly organized for the Amazon tax. He had been at the chaotic press conference that was disrupted by the ironworkers. Now it was his turn to stir things up in the council chambers. "I'm angry," he began, holding up a Tax Amazon sign. "Less than a month ago, the Seattle City Council made history in passing the the first progressive tax of its kind."

The measure "has inspired working people across the country," he noted. "And now, less than a month later, seven self-proclaimed progressive Democratic City Councilmembers are going to repeal this tax without even providing an alternative.

"So I have to ask these Democrats: What has changed so drastically in the past month about our housing crisis and the tax structure that you are willing to break all the promises you made to us about finding a solution just a few weeks ago? The thing is, nothing has changed. What the council is doing is what they have always done: Putting profit over people. That's why we have the housing crisis and the most regressive tax structure in the nation."

"Thank you, Emerson," said Council President Bruce Harrell, signaling that Johnson's speaking time was up.

But Johnson was not done. "You oppose this as progressives, but put to the test, you've chosen the route of capitulation and cowardice!"

"Will you please wrap up, Emerson?" Harrell asked.

Johnson ignored the council president. "And for that, we will vote you out in 2019!"[112]

"I'm going to ask you to stop one more time," said Harrell, as the clerk shut off Johnson's mic.

Johnson turned from Harrell to face the audience. "We are ready to fight! Housing is a human right!" he shouted, and the community

---

112 This and following quotes from the June 12, 2018 City Council meeting are from: [Seattle Channel]. (2018, June 12). *Full Council Special Meeting 6/12/2018* [Video]. Seattle Channel. https://seattlechannel.org/FullCouncil?videoid=x92047

members picked up the chant, drowning out the council president for 30 seconds.

"If I can't restore order in the Council chambers, we will reconvene and meet somewhere else and proceed," Harrell warned. It was unclear how Harrell would carry out his threat to move the meeting without breaking the state's Open Meetings Law. But given that he and the other Democrats had just ignored the law in organizing the repeal vote, perhaps he was less concerned about such legal details.

Rev. Cecilia Kingman, a Unitarian minister active in the local Poor People's Campaign, told the council, "In my congregation, we have homeless families sleeping in the parking lot every night. We have children sleeping in the parking lot. This is a sin in such a rich area as ours, and I believe we have a moral imperative to give all our families a home, all our children homes." Shaking her finger at the councilmembers, Kingman said, "Housing is a human right, and I demand in the name of the poor and the Poor People's Campaign and all that is holy, that you do not only not repeal, but strengthen this plan."

Kingman paused as the crowd applauded.

"Thank you Councilmember Sawant and Mosqueda for standing up and shame, shame on the rest of you, for caving to corporate interests," she said.

"Rent and home prices keep rising," noted Pam Keeley, a union nurse. "Is it any wonder that the number of people living in cars, tents, and on the streets is also rising? The employee head tax meant real money for real services and new housing, paid for by top-tier companies whose employees live in those $800,000 bungalows. We are a society in grave trouble when, in spite of such wealth, thousands go unsheltered as fake progressives dither and wilt in the face of corporate tyranny," she said. Noting that council Democrats had no qualms railing against President Trump's immigration crackdown, Keeley concluded, "You elected officials, seemingly outraged over children ripped from parents at the border, have no trouble sleeping at night while hundreds of kids in your own city go homeless and hungry."

After more than an hour of public comment, it was the councilmembers' turn.

Explaining her rapid about-face, Councilmember Lisa Herbold said, "This is not a winnable battle at this time with this particular measure. The opposition has unlimited resources." She noted she had been in close consultation with Bring Seattle Home, the pro-tax group organized by local labor leaders and the Transit Riders Union. Bring Seattle Home had conducted a poll that showed sinking support for the measure. The group had been campaigning in coordination with Sawant's Socialist Alternative forces but had a much more moderate orientation. They had advocated for more modest taxes than Sawant and movement organizers had called for and had conceded to the mayor's last-minute downward ratcheting of the tax revenues. They had always counted on the Democrats holding firm against corporate pressure. Now that line of defense had utterly crumbled.

"The margin is simply too great to overcome again, especially when one side has unlimited options," Herbold said. "People who are saying that we are bowing to political pressure, nothing could be further from the truth," she insisted.

Derisive laughter and shouts broke out in the audience.

Mosqueda, the sole Democrat to refuse the mayor's recall demand, decried the right-wing political assault on the tax. "The people who have won today by running this campaign are the large firms like Morning in America, that worked with the Trump campaign. . . .The folks who are winning today are the people who said that they were going to do a 'shock and awe' campaign against this city." But, Mosqueda continued, in a rebuke of the Tax Amazon signs in the audience, "I don't think this was about one corporation. This was about shared responsibility so we can have greater shared prosperity."

"I do not see a path where we can move forward where six months from now, eight months from now, we will actually have the revenue to do what we need," Councilmember O'Brien said. "And I can't tell you how hard it is for me to say that publicly. And so I'm in a position where I'm going to vote to repeal this and I do not have a replacement for you."

Boos and calls of "shame" rang out from the crowd.

"I, like Councilmember O'Brien and Councilmember Herbold, have been unable to find a path forward in which we would be able to out-fund and out-resource and win this campaign in November," said Councilmember Lorena Gonzalez. "And that saddens me, that saddens me," she said, pledging along with her fellow Democrats to "fight for solutions that make sense."

The councilmembers' hollow rhetoric and excuses set the stage for the final speaker in the debate, Sawant. "The Democratic party establishment, which controls this city, has presided over this crisis over decades. This is not a crisis that happened in a day or a month or a year. This has been decades in the making," she said. "They have let it worsen with no real solutions. And we know not only from our knowledge of economics, but we know from common sense, from the status quo that the only solution to address the affordable housing crisis is for the city to build social housing, which is publicly owned, permanently affordable housing. And we also know that it is completely rational. And the only idea to raise revenues is to go to those who have not paid anything close to their fair share, which is big business.

"While councilmembers were meeting behind closed doors last week, I wasn't among them to plan this repeal," Sawant continued. "What was our movement doing? Our movement was gearing up to begin building that campaign so that we could knock on the doors of tens of thousands of voters throughout the summer and fall so that we can push back against the referendum. Is there a guarantee that we would've won despite that? No, of course, there's no guarantee, but there was a chance of winning. And I can tell you something with this capitulation there is a guarantee that this will be a massive setback for the movement."

Other councilmembers had asserted that repeal "is the sober, responsible thing to do," Sawant noted. "Well, I stand before you as a councilmember, as an elected representative, who is completely disagreeing that that is a sober, responsible thing to do. No, this is a cowardly betrayal of the needs of working people," she said.

Mosqueda might have been voting along with the movement, but her earlier reproach of the activists for singling out Amazon was too repugnant for the socialist to gloss over. "It is magical thinking," Sawant said, "to believe that somehow you will be able to win attacks like this without making enemies out of Jeff Bezos. No, Jeff Bezos is our enemy. He is our enemy, and we have to fight big business. The question is, will we have elected representatives who will fight with us or not?"

As Sawant sat down, the activists stood up and began chanting loudly, "No tax repeal" and "We are ready to fight—housing is a human right!"

Above the din, Council President Harrell tried to move the vote. "I'm going to ask my colleagues to try to hear what I'm saying. Do you now hear what I'm saying? It's been moved and seconded, it's been moved and seconded on the passage of the bill," he said.

The clerk began the roll call of the councilmembers' names, but it was impossible to hear the ayes and nays above the hubbub.

Sawant stood up and the crowd quieted. "I just want everybody to know the vote is happening. My name has been called and I haven't voted yet, but I can't vote without the public actually being engaged on this."

The repeal was the only item on the agenda for this emergency meeting, and the Democrats were eager to escape this unpleasantness as quickly as possible. But with the clerk calling Sawant's name in the roll call, the meeting could not end until her voice vote was recorded. And Sawant was determined to use the vote for one final, collective denunciation of the Democrats.

The chanting resumed.

"Did everybody vote except Councilmember Sawant?" Harrell asked the clerk. "Sawant, do you want to vote? I can't speak over them. We're can't wait for it to die down."

The other councilmembers shifted uncomfortably in their seats.

"Adjourn the meeting. Just adjourn," Herbold insisted to Harrell.

The chanting continued.

"I need one more vote," Harrell again said above the noise, frustrated that Sawant's refusal to cast her vote was keeping the meeting from adjourning. "Councilmember Sawant, I'm going to ask that you vote because I can't restore order, but we can still proceed."

Facing the crowd, Sawant said, "Council President Harrell is urging me to cast my vote on this legislation, but I don't feel comfortable doing that when members of the public can't hear. I mean, did you hear other Councilmembers vote on that?"

"No!" a chorus shouted back.

"This is unbelievable," Gonzalez muttered.

"So Councilmember Sawant, the vote is yours," Harrell said. "The vote has been cast by the other councilmembers. So, how do you vote?

"Well, I think they need to hear other votes," Sawant replied.

Herbold's impatience was overflowing. "There's got to be some rules about this."

"Let's just call it again. Couldn't we just call it again?" suggested the clerk.

No, Harrell responded, "we've already voted." He asked the clerk to read the roll call back, "but first of all, Councilmember Sawant will like to get her vote on the record, and then we will have the votes read out loud. Councilmember Sawant?"

Sawant stood again, and the crowd quieted. She was determined to make this not just her personal vote, but a vote cast by the movement. "I am the only Councilmember left to vote on this. What does our movement want to do here?" she asked.

"Stop the repeal!" the crowd shouted back.

"On behalf of the movement, "I will register the 'no' vote," Sawant announced.

"She voted no. Record the no," Harrell directed the clerk as the chanting resumed, this time with anti-tax audience members rising with their competing shouts.

Harrell hastily adjourned the meeting. It was a tumultuous finale. The political establishment accomplished their repeal goal, but not before the community movement had exposed their shameful about-face with a disruptive display of collective anger.

Most of the Democrats on the council stood up and quickly headed for the exit as the clerk read the votes into the record. Their swift retreat demonstrated how much political winds had shifted. All of the progressive momentum to tax big business and fund housing and social services was replaced with a pro-business, pro-austerity, law and order backlash that summer. Right-wing pundits railed against and criminalized people living on the streets. The mayor blamed social service workers for "inefficiencies." Everybody in the establishment blamed Sawant.

Movement activists were split, too. Transit Riders Union leader Katie Wilson, a community member of the Progressive Revenue Task Force and a key driver behind the Bring Seattle Home group, concluded that the movement had failed because it did not conciliate with and neutralize opponents. The next time, pro-tax advocates should "prevent or minimize" the antagonism of conservative union leaders by appealing to them earlier, run a stronger public relations campaign, and tailor the tax measure to affect fewer companies, thereby "cultivating more vocal business support," she wrote in the aftermath.[113]

"We expected business opposition, but I don't think we anticipated the degree," Wilson told *The Seattle Times*. "In retrospect, we were very naive."[114]

By "we" Wilson presumably did not include Sawant and the socialists, who took issue with her reformist perspective. They recognized that winning would take a powerful movement, not negotiation and conciliation. "This was never going to be easy. It is no surprise in any way whatsoever that big business has launched a campaign of lies and distortion. This is what they will do," Sawant said.[115]

---

113 Alimahomed-Wilson, J., & Reese, E. (2020). *The Cost of Free Shipping: Amazon in the Global Economy* (p.156). Pluto Press.

114 Beekman, D. (2018, June 24). *With Seattle's head tax dead, business lobbyists set sights on City Council elections*. The Seattle Times. Retrieved February 17, 2023, from https://www.seattletimes.com/seattle-news/politics/seattles-head-tax-is-dead-but-political-debate-may-reverberate/

115 [Seattle Channel]. (218, June 12). *Full Council Special Meeting 6/12/2018* [Video].Seattlechannel.org.https://seattlechannel.org/FullCouncil?videoid=x92047

The Bring Seattle Home activists had wanted—earnestly—for the Democrats to adopt an obviously needed social redistributive policy: a tiny amount of wealth from the ultra-rich to fund housing for those in dire need. But they had failed to understand what was at play. They thought they were involved in a contest over a policy idea. In fact the fight was about class interests and power. When push came to shove, the political establishment lined up not with workers and renters, but with the corporations and developers who had made the city a playground for the rich, and who had every intention of keeping it that way.

Sawant challenged political activists to take three lessons from the fight: "Number one, our movement should not negotiate against ourselves. Our original demand was $150 million but many reduced that demand to $75 million to compromise with what council members were comfortable with. Of course, the minute some in the movement made that compromise, big business demanded more compromise." Task force members proposed the divisive "skin in the game" argument, and Bring Seattle Home members went along with the ratcheting-down of the tax rate, thinking that those concessions would tamp down opposition. But, in fact, compromises only showed weakness and whetted the appetite of big business to fight harder.

The second lesson was to not rely on the Democrats. "The movement needs its own representatives rooted in the strength of the movement and in the struggle of working-class people rather than what is possible to achieve in negotiations with the political establishment and big business," Sawant said. Bring Seattle Home members relied on their relations with Democrats, she noted. When the political establishment caved, the Bring Seattle Home strategy fell apart.

The third lesson, Sawant said, was the need to build greater working-class unity—not by conciliating with construction union leaders, but by calling for common struggle around the material needs of working people. "When there are divisions in the workers movement in general or the labor movement in particular, it weakens the political power of workers everywhere and only bosses gain from that," Sawant observed. "When Amazon threatened our construction sisters' and brothers' jobs, some in the labor movement were correctly very concerned. We were concerned. We take Amazon's threat seriously because we know that they have the incomprehensible power and wealth to follow through on their threat if they so choose to.

"In history there are countless examples of corporations threatening to or actually attacking jobs to try and undercut the workers movement," she said. "When the labor movement has been strongest is when it's been united and those threats have been defeated with mass demonstrations, occupations, strike actions and sometimes even taking the businesses under democratic public ownership."

Following the repeal debacle, the Democrats acted as if the tax proposal had never happened. Despite their loud pledges at the June 12 emergency meeting that they would redouble efforts to find a new progressive tax, the Democrats submitted no housing proposals when the fall budget debate got underway. Sawant offered several different options for raising $48 million in the budget for housing, but Democrats rejected every one of them. The mayor proposed to devote a scant 0.8 percent of the budget on new housing.[116] Instead of a stirring call-to-arms about "the crisis of affordability," the mayor preached austerity for working people, lecturing that "we have to live within our means."[117]

The seismic shift in the political environment was an impressive display of brute power by the local business elites. It was a vivid illustration of the assertion by Marx and Engels in *The Communist Manifesto* that "The executive of the modern state is but a committee for managing the common affairs of the whole bourgeoisie." Amazon and other big businesses had whipped the Democrats into line and reasserted their political hegemony. It augured poorly for Sawant as she headed into a challenging 2019 reelection fight.

---

116 Derrick, A. (2018, September 24). *Mayor Jenny A. Durkan's 2019-2020 Biennium Budget*. Seattle Office of the Mayor. Retrieved February 19, 2023, from https://durkan.seattle.gov/2018/09/mayor-jenny-durkans-2019-2020-biennium-budget/

117 Beekman, D. (2018, September 24). Seattle Mayor Jenny Durkan unveils $5.9 billion budget proposal. *The Seattle Times*. https://www.seattletimes.com/seattle-news/politics/seattle-mayor-jenny-durkan-unveils-5-9-billion-budget-proposal/

5

Socialist Phoenix

In the union anthem "Solidarity Forever," workers pledge to "bring to birth a new world from the ashes of the old." From the wreckage of the 2018 Amazon tax debacle, Sawant's movement clawed back over the next two years and won a new Amazon tax—one that was more than four times bigger than the original bill. It was a stunning comeback. But it didn't just materialize out of the blue, just as political revolutions don't burst out spontaneously. Their victory was the product of persistent, relentless organizing, starting with thousands of conversations—workers talking with one another, pressing issues forward, challenging myths, raising expectations, and patiently rebuilding the movement one step at a time.

Far outside the limelight, workers started the painstaking work that would set the stage for a showdown between the socialists and one of the most powerful companies in the world, a rematch that would culminate in a spectacular, historic tax victory.

The ironworker Logan Swan faced continual harassment from his union leadership for supporting the 2018 Amazon tax. He worked daily with construction workers, many of whom had seen the televised press conference confrontation and were taken in by the No Tax on Jobs message. One day after work, Swan was at a bar with a crane operator from his jobsite. "I saw you on the news," the operator said. "Yeah, giving that bitch some motherfucking," he said, assuming that Swan had been part of McClain's disruptive crew.

"I was like, hmm, actually I was the guy," Logan recalled replying. "And he looks at me and goes, 'Why?' and I brought out all the talking points. That Amazon paid zero taxes. You look at the cost of living here, it used to be cheaper. How long's your commute, bro? And how do you like paying all the taxes we do? Well, someone has to pay for the roads and bridges and hospitals and schools. And if Amazon doesn't pay taxes, that means we do, we got to make up that difference. So this is to make them pay taxes to create jobs for us building the stuff that we need.

"And he said, 'Well, that makes a lot of sense.'"

Swan's unabashed focus on working class interests created the seeds of a new relationship. Two months after the Tax Amazon repeal debacle, the operating engineers union went on strike, and the crane operator reached out to the ironworker for advice and solidarity.

Then later that summer, Swan's high-rise job ended and he got assigned to a building retrofit project. The crew was new to him.

They were chatting at work one day when one of the ironworkers said, “I know why you look familiar. You’re that fucking guy!”

Swan recalled, “I was like, ‘Alright, here we go.’ All of a sudden I’m surrounded by half a dozen to a dozen ironworkers having this discussion about this whole thing that happened.” After going through his arguments, Swan said, “I did not have a single person who had a negative response to it, just a lot of questions. And at the end of it, people were like, ‘That’s bullshit. They did you dirty.’ The mix of response was anywhere from political agreement to at least appreciating defiance to our rotten leadership. And there wasn’t a single person who was hostile.” One of the ironworkers in Swan’s new crew ended up volunteering on Sawant’s reelection campaign.

Also outside the immediate limelight, the raging fever of gentrification and displacement that the Amazon tax was meant to quell was forcing working class residents like Renee Gordon off the sidelines and into the fight. In 2014, Gordon had returned to her birth home of Seattle to care for her 84-year-old aunt. For three decades Mother Gordon, as Renee affectionately called her, had lived at the Chateau Apartments, a modest L-shaped complex in the heart of the historically African American Central District. Mother Gordon and her family had been sharecroppers in Tyronza, Arkansas, in the 1940s. As part of the Great Migration, they traded the dirt floors and backbreaking cotton field work for modern amenities in Seattle’s Central District. The Central District was, at the time, the only part of town where racist redlining practices permitted Black people to live. Once settled, Mother Gordon married a pastor and raised her niece, Renee, as her own. The Pentecostal church, where the elder Gordon played piano and sang, was their second home.

Fast forward to 2014: Renee had left Seattle to work for a mortgage loan company in southern California when she got a call that Mother Gordon had advanced cancer. Renee packed up her life's belongings and moved back to Seattle. The doctors estimated that Mother Gordon likely had six months to live, but she defied their prediction. Following hospital treatment, Mother Gordon returned to the Chateau, and Renee became her live-in caregiver. She took Mother Gordon out to restaurants her aunt had never had the opportunity to sample – Red Robin, the Cheesecake Factory, and the Blue Water Bistro. Together, they strolled down the sidewalks, visited the grocery around the corner where the clerks greeted Mother Gordon as an old friend, watched the city rabbits dart in and out of the bushes, and chatted with neighbors, "just loving each other and making up for lost time," Renee said.

Mother Gordon's Chateau neighbors included an East African mother who had been homeless and was now working at an Amazon warehouse while studying to become a surgical assistant; a union sanitation truck driver; a recently-homeless family with two toddlers and another child on the way; a double-amputee from Laos, who'd called the Chateau his home for 39 years; a union nurse at the nearby Swedish Medical Center; a couple from China, 93 and 88 years old; and a postal worker who also drove for Uber to make ends meet. Renee and her aunt hoped that when it was time for—in the church's term—Mother Gordon's homegoing, she would go peacefully at the Chateau, in the loving embrace of her church, her neighbors, and her community.

Chris Garvin and Barrett Johnston, the founders of Cadence Real Estate, had a very different plan in mind. In 2018, Cadence, which boasted online of buying and flipping apartments for "above market returns," purchased the Chateau Apartments from a family owner. They filed papers with the city to demolish the building and replace the 21 family-sized apartments with 73 market-rate studios, more suitable for tech professionals with cash to spend on upscale urban living. In February 2019, Cadence told Mother Gordon and the other tenants that they would have to leave by the end of the year. It did not appear to concern Garvin and Johnston that Mother Gordon might not, as a consequence, be given her homegoing wish, or that her elderly and immigrant neighbors, cast into the tempest of the Seattle housing market, might not survive the storm. For Cadence and its investors, there was big money to be made.

I first met Renee and Mother Gordon on a snowy afternoon in February 2019, when a fellow Sawant office organizer, Sasha Somer, and I door-knocked the building. Sawant's City Council office had caught wind of the Cadence demolition plan from a local anti-displacement activist. We first encountered two other tenants who had not heard yet of Cadence's plan to demolish the building. Did they want to organize and fight back? Yes, they did. Talk to Renee, they said—she knows everyone.

It was just as they said: Renee knew everyone. She took us around to meet her neighbors, and before long we—the residents, Sawant, Somer and I, and Renee's pastor—were meeting as a group at the Gordons' church, Gods Pentecostal Temple, three blocks down from the Chateau. The group drafted a set of demands: a long delay in the eviction, relocation money, and a commitment that the developer would re-house everyone in the neighborhood if they wanted, including the residents who were on Section 8 housing vouchers. They sent Cadence a letter demanding to meet.

Renee helped collect signatures from 19 of her 21 neighbors on a letter listing the Chateau residents' demands. When the Cadence developers visited the Chateau, a delegation of residents handed the letter directly to Garvin and Johnston.

The campaign ramped up from there. Hundreds of community members signed a Sawant petition demanding that Cadence honor the residents' demands. Sawant organized a press conference at a nearby café, where the residents publicized their demands to a crowd of union members, tenants' rights activists, and clergy. She also announced a special Saturday meeting of the City Council's Renters Rights Committee, at a church one block away from the apartment building. This would give Chateau tenants an organizing platform in the neighborhood to fight for their homes. As chair of the committee, Sawant had the authority to set committee meeting agendas, along with scheduling special meetings outside the normal weekday committee time.

More than 130 people filled the pews of New Hope Missionary Baptist Church for the City Council committee meeting. Mandarin and Vietnamese interpreters hired by the city at Sawant's direction set out their translation headset gear. Media crews set up their cameras. Missing in action: the four Democrats who served on the committee. It was not unusual for the other City Council members to skip Sawant's committee meetings, and the weekend scheduling gave them a ready-made excuse. But their absence had no impact—this was a public hearing on Cadence's planned displacement of working-class residents. Since no committee votes were going to be taken, a quorum was not needed.

Sawant first called up a parade of community supporters—African American and Vietnamese community members, small business owners, low-wage workers, union members, and neighbors, all praising the bravery of the Chateau tenants and pledging to support them.

Then it was the Chateau residents' turn. Testifying at the front of the church sanctuary, Roselle Johnson described how she had moved to the Chateau a decade earlier. She and her husband were living north of the city when, walking down the street one day, they were struck by a car. He was killed, and she was hospitalized for two weeks with a severe brain injury. She moved into the Chateau to recover from the double trauma of constant physical pain and suddenly losing her partner. Her parents, who lived close by, could care for her there.

What started out for Johnson as a temporary exigency became a permanent home. In 2015, she told the crowd, "I married my best friend, Warren. We live in Apartment 309 at the Chateau and love our neighbors. It's very quiet here, and close by to the store. It's close by to my medical care. And it's close to my parents. We all love our parents."

Now, Roselle's parents needed her caregiving. "My dad was recently diagnosed with stage four lung cancer," she said. "He undergoes chemotherapy all the time. My mom, she just had knee surgery. They depend on me," she said. While Roselle remained disabled from the car accident, she still found a way to take her dad to his weekly chemo sessions. She paused. Tears began to trickle down her cheeks. Renee Gordon, sitting next to her at the committee table, put an arm around her. Someone handed her a pack of tissues. Johnson continued, her voice quavering. "If Cadence is going to move us out, I don't know where I'm going to live. Who is going to help my parents?. . . Some of the tenants have lived here for decades. We organized at the Chateau to stand up for our rights against Cadence. And we're glad to see so many other people, friends, tenants, and neighbors supporting our cause," she said, scanning the crowd. Her tone shifted from pleading to defiant. "This is our city, our neighborhood, and we will fight for the right to live here!"

The crowd applauded. Renee took her turn at the mic, and told the crowd about Mother Gordon's 30 years in the neighborhood. "We just want to stay in our neighborhood. It's sad that so many of us have already been pushed out. The developers seem to just care about profits. But what about us, the people?" she asked.

Gordon read out the residents' demands and announced that she and her neighbors also had filed a slew of complaints against Cadence for failing to maintain the Chateau Apartments up to city code—exposed wiring, missing handrails, flooring that came loose, an inoperative wheelchair lift, missing smoke detectors, crumbling stairs and broken appliances. Sawant urged the public to sign and circulate the community petition before she adjourned the meeting.

The committee meeting galvanized a disparate range of forces—much broader than just the socialist left—with the Chateau residents and their cause. Here, Sawant was employing "the parliamentary rostrum" to advance working class fights: While the hearing focused on one apartment building, it put human faces on and universalized the fight against racist gentrification. The hearing also boosted the confidence of the Chateau residents and served as a platform for broader community organizing.

The absence of the Democratic City Council members plainly revealed the political lines in the battle. Notwithstanding

Democratic rhetoric about fighting racism and supporting affordable housing, when the community called for tangible support, the political establishment ducked out.

Two weeks after the committee hearing, Cadence made two notable concessions. They agreed to give each household $5,000 in relocation aid, on top of the $3,900 that tenants were entitled to under city law. Additionally, the developers said they were delaying redevelopment for at least three years. The residents could stay for the time being.

Sawant and the residents celebrated these landlord concessions at a press conference outside Chateau, during which they also announced that city housing inspectors, following complaints that Gordon and her neighbors filed, had ordered Cadence to make prompt repairs on 63 different building code violations. As if on cue, as the press conference wrapped up four city inspectors arrived to scrutinize the company's ongoing work.

Two of the residents' three core demands had been met, but the third—Cadence's commitment to re-house everyone in the neighborhood if they wanted—was more complicated. Over the next six months, the residents and Sawant's office ratcheted up the pressure, petitioning at community festivals, writing op-eds, speaking at local churches, and postering their cause throughout the neighborhood.

The Chateau residents also disrupted Cadence's development plans. To get the green light for construction, the company had to win architectural approval from a local design review board. The design review process was normally a dull, highly technical affair, reviewing things like setback measurements, exterior materials, color tones, landscaping, and the structure's relationship to adjacent buildings. The Chateau residents gummed up the works by showing up and speaking out at the board's public meetings about their pending displacement. Design review board members—architects, civil engineers, and planners not used to public controversy—at first tried to argue that the residents' concerns were beyond the scope of their review. That didn't stop Gordon and the other residents, who kept showing up and demanding to testify.

Their persistence paid off: Eight months into the Chateau struggle, the design review board shocked Cadence by rejecting their building design proposal, forcing the company to go back to the architectural drawing board. It might have been only a temporary setback for Cadence, but the residents' resilience, and their determination to take the fight to every possible arena, was apparently too much for the company. After the design board rejection, Cadence announced that they had reached an agreement with a local non-profit housing developer to relocate all the Chateau residents in nearby affordable housing. In the meantime, Mother Gordon and her neighbors could stay in their Chateau homes for at least three years. A powerful development company had been stopped in its tracks by a scrappy group of tenants and a socialist councilmember practiced in the art of Marxist insurgent politics.

The Chateau wasn't the only site of struggle in 2019 for area working class residents confronting displacement threats. Sawant organized and staged a press conference with union members and faith groups to fend off evictions for immigrant tenants south of Seattle. She joined a group of Carl Haglund's tenants to block evictions and rent increases. To the north, she helped the 85 senior community residents at Halcyon Mobile Home

Park beat a for-profit developer's attempt to buy and demolish the homes. Sawant helped the community organize, confront the park's trustee, and win a city ordinance, introduced by the socialist, that blocked the sale. In central Seattle, tenants at the Kenton Apartments contacted Sawant's office to contest notices of rent hikes up to 69 percent. The tenants signed a joint letter demanding talks with the landlord, a local real estate company with more than $65 million in holdings. After a week of no response from the landlord, eight tenants joined me one evening to deliver their petition to the landlord's sprawling lakefront estate. No one answered the mansion door; the tenants clipped the written demands to it. The next day the landlord sent each of the Kenton residents letters notifying them—in oversized red letters—that the rent increases were "Rescinded Immediately" and would be replaced later in the year with much more modest changes in rent and utility charges.

These flareups underlined the general crisis that tenants faced, particularly in low-income neighborhoods. With landlords continuing to raise rents, nearly half of all Seattle tenants were "rent burdened" by federal standards—paying at least 30 percent of their income on rent and forced to give up basic necessities of life.[118]

At a press conference in spring of 2019, Sawant and Socialist Alternative revived the push for rent control. Flanked by tenants, union members, and socialist activists, Sawant announced that she was launching a community petition and planning a citywide renters' summit in advance of introducing a rent control ordinance

---

118 Lloyd, S. A. (2018, June 25). *One-third of Seattle-area households are burdened by housing costs*. Curbed Seattle. Retrieved March 15, 2023, from https://seattle.curbed.com/2018/6/25/17501872/seattle-area-housing-cost-burden

in the fall. Sawant announced that her legislation would be universal, without exceptions for landlords to exploit. She noted that other rent control laws, such as those in California, New York, and Oregon, were riddled with pro-landlord loopholes: exempting newer buildings, allowing landlords to raise rents as much as they liked when tenants left, and permitting rent hikes well above the inflation rate. This Swiss cheese approach to rent control fails renters, she said.

Placing rent control back on the Seattle political agenda was a textbook illustration of Sawant's second pillar of Marxist insurgent politics: Independent movement-building with bold demands that underscore the need for broader societal change. No other councilmember supported rent control, but counting votes wasn't the point. The rent control demand excited tenants, addressing the leading economic stressor facing working class community members while encouraging people to question landlords' iron grip over the housing market.

In 1980, the Washington state landlord lobby had succeeded in getting the state Legislature to ban local rent control laws, so Sawant's campaign would need to both win a local ordinance and fight to get the state ban overturned. Landlords and developers would be sure to fight it tooth and nail, but the movement also would need to take on the state Democratic political establishment, which held close to monopoly power at the state capitol.

For all the previous 18 years, Democrats had controlled the governor's mansion and the state House in Olympia, and for 11 of those 18 years, they'd also controlled the state Senate. That meant Democrats ran the legislative committees and decided which bills got hearings and were brought to a vote. Democrats routinely campaigned as tenants' allies but, not wanting to alienate landlords, worked assiduously to ensure that nothing close to overturning the rent control ban came up. Bills for rent control and even more modest housing justice measures typically died in committee or didn't get hearings at all. The more liberal state legislators from Seattle claimed they had simply run out of time, or that conservative Democrats or Republicans blocked the effort. "Wait 'til next year," became a common refrain that housing activists heard. Then the same excuses were dredged up the following year.

As with the fight for a $15 minimum wage, Democrats in fact did not want to see rent control come up for a vote. Many of them were dependent on the developer lobby for financial and political support, and the party overall benefited from a longstanding détente with big business. The socialists recognized that it would take a powerful grassroots movement to move the City Council and then the state Legislature.

Council office staff circulated Sawant's community petition demanding that the City Council enact rent control that would be triggered automatically by the state Legislature lifting the ban. Over the spring and summer, union members, renters rights activists, and tenants from the recent fights at the Chateau, the Kenton, and other apartments collected signatures at community tables, farmers markets, and door-to-door.

Sawant's political enemies likely didn't feel a need to directly counter the socialist's rent control push. Energized by their 2018 defeat of the Amazon tax, they fully intended to sweep away their Marxist political problem in the 2019 municipal election, and with it, dispatch any concerns about rent control or the specter of taxing the rich. Their campaign template was the scorched-earth strategy that had worked so well for them in reversing the tax. Through that fight, the political and business establishment had built a powerful alliance: downtown businesses, conservative building trades union leaders, Mayor Durkan, and a large swath of Democratic Party officials. They all agreed that it was time for Sawant to go.

In addition to Sawant's race, six other City Council district seats were up. "This is a change election," crowed local Chamber of Commerce President Marilyn Strickland. The chamber recruited candidates to run in all the races, even where incumbents ultimately had voted to repeal the tax; to big business, they were no longer considered reliable votes. Councilmember Mike O'Brien, after enduring a withering right-wing assault in the Amazon tax fight the previous year, opted to retire.

The chamber's basic electoral strategy entailed blitzing the airwaves and social media with attack ads, flooding the mail daily, enlisting mainstream media allies, deploying biased polling, and hiring armies of paid canvassers. The chamber's goal was not to win hearts and minds, but to display such overwhelming force as to make resistance seem futile.

Sawant was of course on the ballot for just one of the seven city council seats, but the chamber intended to make every race about the socialist. Their literature outside of Sawant's district featured her face and name prominently. "If you like extremist Kshama Sawant, then you'll love Emily Myers," declared a mailer in northeast Seattle, the words set over a backdrop of homeless encampments. The chamber's attack on Myers, a Democrat, knocked her out of the primary, enabling the favored business candidate in that race to face off in the general election against an opponent whom the chamber deemed more beatable.

For key spokespeople, the business forces recruited community messengers, such as prominent small business owners, who could claim progressive bona fides. Leaders of some of the building trades and the more conservative-led unions attacked Sawant, a rank-and-file member of the teachers' union, for her leadership on the Amazon tax. They said that while they supported her in the past, her district deserved a "more effective" council member.

Other messengers served as attack dogs. "Kshama Sawant must go," demanded *The Seattle Times* editorial board. Democratic Seattle State Senator Jamie Pedersen called Sawant a "mirror image of Donald Trump."[119] Talk radio and online hosts blamed her for every ill in the city, and avidly replayed clips of the ironworkers' disruption of her press conference the previous year.

The chamber also recognized that, just as with the Amazon tax fight, it needed to shift the narrative away from social needs like housing. For this strategy, they pulled a page from the Trump playbook: divert attention away from the billionaires and their political friends by condemning and criminalizing the city's most vulnerable.

---

119 (2019, October 11). *The Times recommends: Kshama Sawant must go — Elect Egan Orion for Seattle City Council, District 3.* The Seattle Times. Retrieved March 16, 2023, from https://www.seattletimes.com/opinion/editorials/the-times-recommends-egan-orion-for-seattle-city-council-district-3-dont-waste-your-vote-on-kshama-sawant/

In March, KOMO-TV, the Seattle station owned by right-wing Sinclair Broadcast Group, aired "Seattle Is Dying," a melodramatic hour-long documentary that blamed Seattle's ills on drug addicts and people experiencing homelessness. Sensationalized scenes of homeless encampments, piles of garbage, and people struggling with drugs filled TV screens across the city.[120] The ensuing media echo chamber amplified KOMO's hit piece. Newspapers ran articles, pundits hosted debates, and talk radio dedicated programming to the question of whether homeless people were, indeed, killing this beautiful city. Editorialists pointed to polls following the documentary's release, claiming they showed that Seattle voters were blaming the homelessness crisis not on capitalist greed but on Sawant, other housing advocates, people with substance abuse problems, and "wasteful" social service workers.

The anti-Sawant forces also benefited from a split within the labor movement that had developed the previous year, just four months after the tax debacle. The Seattle Police Officers Guild (SPOG) completed negotiations for a new contract with the city in 2018, and in November of that year the contract came before the City Council for ratification. The police won new raises in the contract while also negotiating rollbacks of modest accountability measures that the City Council had passed into law just the previous year. Half a dozen years earlier, the US Justice Department had placed the city police department under federal oversight because of a brutal history of police violence and abuse disproportionately directed at people of color. The accountability measures were a small effort by the city to provide more transparency

---

120 [KOMO-TV]. (219, March 14). *Seattle Is Dying: A KOMO News Documentary* [Video]. Youtube.com. https://www.youtube.com/watch?v=bpAi7OWWBlw

into investigations of police abuse. But this intrusion into police affairs was too much for SPOG. The guild insisted that the city overrule the law in the collective bargaining agreement, and Mayor Durkan agreed.

The leaders of two dozen community organizations, including the NAACP, the Church Council of Greater Seattle, the American Civil Liberties Union, and a slew of immigrant rights groups protested the city's sellout to SPOG. They urged councilmembers to vote the contract down.

Labor leaders, however, declared that the City Council's vote on the police contract would be a litmus test of labor solidarity. SPOG was a member of the Martin Luther King County Labor Council, the local federation of labor unions. The labor leaders lobbied the Democrats aggressively for ratification. On the day of the vote, I was standing in the back of the council chambers as City Council debate was about to get underway when Dustin Lambro approached me. The political director of a big local Teamsters union, Lambro also had recently been elected president of the labor council. "I just want you to know," he told me, "if Kshama votes against the contract, we will never support her again and we'll run someone against her." Lambro was not bluffing. But it was foolish for him to think that the socialist office would surrender to his blunt threats or play into his transactional politics.

In Sawant's remarks before the vote, she pointed out that SPOG and the labor leaders did not represent the unanimous sentiments of workers. Indeed, more than 40 prominent union members—urged on by Sawant's Council office—had just that morning penned a letter urging that City Council side with marginalized communities and reject the SPOG contract. "The labor movement has a proud history of standing with working people facing racism and oppression," she noted. "In its best traditions, the labor movement has fought against how the ruling class uses the police to oppress and divide sections of the working class, against Black and Brown workers in particular, but also against the queer community, homeless community members, impoverished people, and against protests and picket lines," she said.

"It is with this proud tradition, and with my fellow union members in Seattle who are opposing this contract in its current form, that I stand in calling for the contract to be renegotiated and all police accountability measures restored," she said.

Alluding to the political threat made by Lambro, which was now beginning to circulate in the media, Sawant added, "Some have said that voting against this contract would lose me their support in the next election. However, at the end of the day, I am not a career politician. I am here to fight for all those who are left out of the corporate politics of City Hall and its backroom deals. If I wasn't going to consistently stand up for working people and oppressed communities, there would be no point in my being here."[121]

The City Council voted 8 to 1 to adopt the contract, with only Sawant dissenting.

The 2018 SPOG vote sealed Sawant's political fate in the eyes of leaders from several of the area's larger unions. Lambro's

---

121 (2018, November 13). *My Speech while Voting 'NO' on the Seattle Police Officers Guild Contract*. Office of Councilmember Kshama Sawant. Retrieved March 16, 2023, from https://sawant.seattle.gov/my-speech-while-voting-no-on-the-seattle-police-officers-guild-contract-tues-nov-13-2018/

Teamsters union, construction and transit unions, and SEIU 775—the large homecare union that had backed Sawant in 2015—lined up with candidates running against Sawant.

Against the "Seattle Is Dying" drumbeat, and with two independent expenditure Political Action Committees (PACs) joining the chamber's own efforts, the anti-Sawant forces predicted that the August primary election would reveal her weaknesses. Sawant won the endorsement of a dozen unions before the primary, but the SPOG vote had sharply split a key base. "People are just over the Kshama thing," Lambro told *The Seattle Times*. "She acts like she knows better than our workers."[122]

The August primary must have confirmed the chamber's belief that their strategy was on track. In all seven of the city council races, their chosen candidates came through in either first or second place. Sawant emerged from a crowded field with 37 percent of the vote—first place among six candidates by a 15-point margin, but widely considered a "vulnerable showing" for an incumbent. Second place went to Egan Orion, a small business owner and the chamber's favored candidate.

Plenty of political consultants would instruct an incumbent scoring that poorly in the primary to tone down their rhetoric for the general election. Indeed, in the other districts several self-described progressive candidates had tacked to the right, boasting about how they supported the mayor's anti-homeless crusade and

122 Beekman, D. (2019, July 1). *Socialism faces a key test in Seattle City Council elections*. The Seattle Times. Retrieved March 16, 2023, from https://www.seattletimes.com/seattle-news/politics/socialism-faces-a-key-test-in-seattle-city-council-elections/

promising not to bring back the failed 2018 big business tax. They made it through the primary with better numbers than Sawant.

But Sawant maintained a clear emphasis on the movement's core demands: rent control, taxing Amazon to build social housing, and local funding for Green New Deal projects. And as with her previous campaigns, she never hesitated to remind voters that this was a socialist campaign going up against a corporate-funded candidate. In late September, Sawant convened a packed City Council committee meeting to unveil her draft rent-control legislation, applauding activists who had collected more than 13,000 rent-control petition signatures in the preceding months.

Every day from Labor Day onward, several Socialist Alternative staff and even greater numbers of volunteers—rank-and-file union members, tenants, students, seniors, members of the LGBTQ community, and people of color—fanned out through Sawant's district to knock on doors, table, put up posters, and leaflet at public transit stations, urging voters to support the socialist's program.

All told, 1,000 Sawant campaigners knocked on 225,000 doors between May and November, an average of more than three door knocks for every eligible voter in the district. The campaign created three zone teams focused on neighborhoods where most working-class people, people of color, and young people lived. Socialist Alternative staff organizers in each zone were assigned "perma-turf"—precincts that they walked consistently over months, getting to know and building trust with residents, and successfully recruiting many to be campaign activists.

More than 7,900 people—including one of every twenty voters in Sawant's 74,000-voter district—donated to the campaign, with a median contribution of $20. The campaign also built strong organizational support, eventually garnering endorsements from 22 local unions, plus immigrant rights, environmental, and LGBTQ groups, along with key leaders, clergy, and activists in communities of color.

In the months leading up to the election, Amazon, Starbucks, Comcast, Expedia, Lyft, Boeing, private equity firms, and major real-estate developers had anted up to support Sawant's opponent and three anti-Sawant PACs. Leaving nothing to chance, however, with ballots about to be mailed out in mid-October, Amazon—which had already given the chamber PAC a record $400,000—dropped an astounding million-dollar money bomb into the campaign. Starbucks, Vulcan, and other major landlords wrote additional checks, giving the chamber and allied PACs more than $4 million in total anti-Sawant funds.

These massive contributions were intended to obliterate the Marxist. But the donations did the opposite. For voters, it confirmed what Sawant campaigners had been saying all along about the election. News about Amazon's money bomb dramatically changed the political discourse on the street and at the doors from "Seattle is dying" to "Seattle is not for sale!"

It didn't take long for the establishment media to realize Amazon's colossal mistake. Sawant staged protests at Amazon's headquarters. Some local Democrats who had remained steadfastly on the sidelines joined her, sensing the shift in political winds. Nationally, presidential candidates Bernie Sanders and Elizabeth Warren assailed the company and urged voters to support Sawant and the more progressive candidates in the other districts.

"I doubt this was a smart play by Amazon," bemoaned *Seattle Times* columnist Danny Westneat, normally a reliable soldier in the anti-Sawant media army. "The election was playing out as a referendum on the performance of the City Council. Now it could well be a referendum on Amazon and corporate power."[123]

Westneat was prescient in this case. Amazon's political gambit confirmed to voters what Sawant had been saying all along: "What's at stake this year is who runs Seattle—Amazon and big business, or working people." It polarized voters against the company and their chosen candidates in the other districts.

"When the money bomb happened, everyone was so much more serious about the election. The stakes just became very real for people," recalled SA's Emerson Johnson. "People were like, 'What the fuck? Why do these people just drop a million dollars on a City Council race?' They drew the battle lines for us in an extremely helpful way. And then when we talked about the Amazon tax, it was like, 'Yeah, sure we should tax them.' People were just angry at Amazon. They were frustrated and they saw Kshama Sawant as the most effective fighter against Amazon."

Amazon's money exposed the true nature of the political enemy, and at the doors and at community campaign tables Sawant's movement embraced the class struggle framework. "We said Amazon wants Seattle to remain a corporate tax haven, where they can run amok and build a playground for the rich. This is

---

123 Westneat, D. (2019, October 23). *Backfire? Amazon may have just made this election about itself.* The Seattle Times. Retrieved March 16, 2023, from https://www.seattletimes.com/seattle-news/politics/backfire-amazon-may-have-just-made-this-election-about-itself/

an example of them attempting to do that," Johnson said. "If you don't want Seattle to be a playground for Jeff Bezos, and a test subject for every other tech startup that wants to buy a city, you should vote for the socialist, who's going to fight Amazon, who's going to tax them to build public revenue for housing, for schools, for public services. And I think that it made the money bomb not just a defeat, it turned it into a political moment for us."

When the November ballots were tabulated, Sawant prevailed over Orion by 52 to 48 percent. In the other districts, Chamber-backed candidates lost five out of the six races.

Much of the mainstream media credited Sawant's win to the profound miscalculation by Amazon CEO Jeff Bezos and his executive team. "How Amazon's Klutzy Politicking Backfired in Seattle," read one typical headline.[124]

But leaving the analysis on that note misses the real lesson. It fails to properly credit the revolutionary socialist movement that Sawant and Socialist Alternative had built over the previous six years. The movement prevailed over Amazon because it applied the Marxist principles of insurgent politics that Sawant had been practicing since taking office in 2014: bold demands for change that resonated with working people; a combative, class-based struggle; and deep organizing and engagement of rank-and-file workers and tenants.

124 Balter, J. (2019, November 14). *How Amazon's Klutzy Politicking Backfired in Seattle*. Bloomberg. Retrieved March 16, 2023, from https://www.bloomberg.com/opinion/articles/2019-11-14/how-amazon-s-klutzy-politicking-backfired-in-seattle#xj4y7vzkg

The movement's resiliency grew out of seven years of community organizing, with a strong emphasis on developing organic leaders in the neighborhoods. Many of the campaign's neighborhood leaders already had significant organizing experience—collecting rent-control petition signatures, uniting with tenants to stop a rent increase, fighting the displacement of immigrant-owned small businesses, winning a new neighborhood post office, or saving the local African American senior center. These were people like Renee Gordon, not those with organizational titles and status. Many of these leaders played critical roles in the 2019 election: educating neighbors, registering them to vote, and making sure they cast their ballots.

Some of those activists became apartment captains, leveraging personal relationships and easy access to neighbors—a crucial factor in getting face-to-face with voters in secure apartment buildings. C. C. Reuge, a Transit Riders Union activist, knocked on the doors of most of her 150 building-mates, showing up with banana bread and campaign literature. She and her partner covered the building twice over, making sure Sawant's votes got out and persuading several of her undecided neighbors to cast ballots for the socialist.

By the time mail-in ballots arrived, the campaign had collected 23,900 voter IDs—one-third of all registered voters. They also had registered more than 1,000 new voters. The get-out-the-vote operation supplemented staff with hundreds of volunteers, saturating key neighborhoods and generating a district voter turnout of 60 percent—far above the 50 percent turnout in the previous election cycle.

Because of the depth of community relationships, Sawant's campaign was able to effectively inoculate voters against the Amazon attack. In a union campaign, workers, if properly educated about what to anticipate in advance of the boss's attacks, will grow stronger, not weaker, when the assault comes, because they have been immunized to expect it. The anti-union attack fails to intimidate but rather confirms to workers that the boss is assailing the union precisely because workers have power and are threatening his fundamental interests.

That is what happened in Seattle in 2019—not in a single workplace, but on a citywide basis. Amazon's massive donation against Sawant reinforced to voters what they had been hearing all along from the socialists: Company executives intended a hostile takeover of City Hall. The gambit failed not simply because it was ham-handed, but because years of grassroots organizing had built political consciousness and movement resiliency. The socialists had inoculated the working class electorate, and Amazon's money bomb blew up in the company's face.

Election Day—the final day to mail in ballots in this all-mail election—dawned foggy and dank, a Seattle harbinger of the coming winter. Campaigning with Chateau leader Renee Gordon at a busy Central District intersection, I asked her how the get-out-the-vote effort was going in her building. She proceeded to whip out a paper from her purse and tick off the names of each tenant in her building and when they had turned their ballots in. Just a year earlier, Gordon hadn't even been a registered voter. But the threat of the Chateau evictions had brought her off the sidelines, and now she was a neighborhood leader in the struggle, not just against her gentrifying landlord but also against one of the most powerful companies in the world.

Sawant trailed Orion on election night, but as late votes—typically more left-leaning—were tallied in subsequent days, she surged into the lead. In the days following Election Day, as Sawant's deficit narrowed and then disappeared, the activists swung from exhaustion to shock to astonishment before settling on jubilation. The Saturday morning after Election Day, Sawant declared victory in front of 250 supporters, with a 1,700 vote lead out of 44,000 votes. "Our successful socialist reelection campaign was a repudiation of the billionaire class, of the richest man in the world, of the real estate tycoons and the political establishment," Sawant declared. "The biggest mistake we could make right now," she said, "is underestimating what we've accomplished. We've won by building the most powerful grassroots campaign Seattle has ever seen."

The ironworker Logan Swan, who had persisted through withering attacks by his union leadership and the deep skepticism of his coworkers, offered a visceral reflection. "It showed that at the end of the day, we've won real things for working people. You would go out and door-knock and table and talk to baristas and grocery store workers and just regular working-class people. And you know, they're not reading *The Seattle Times* op-eds looking for political answers," he said. "They have class instinct, and they know this is an institution that's hostile to them and their interests. And so you talk to them, and they're like, 'Oh, yeah, Kshama's my girl, fuck all the haters.'"

Given the herculean obstacles that Sawant faced in 2019—a united business class, a divided union movement, cowardly progressive Democrats, and merciless media assaults—many Sawant campaigners were themselves stunned at the final result. Yes, through months of stress, exhaustion, and unrelenting attacks they had done tremendously hard work. But it seemed impossible, simply beyond imagination, to think that a band of Marxists could beat a united capitalist class. That simply didn't happen, certainly not in 21st century America. There was no precedent. And yet they had done it. They had emerged from the ashes of 2018's resounding tax defeat, they had fought back, and they had won.

Swan later recounted: "It felt like a victory against these garbage union leaders. It felt like a victory against the richest man in the world. It felt like a victory for working families. And it felt like a victory for the homeless guy who came up to me when we were doing a huddle before going out canvassing, who gave me probably all of the money he had. It was a fist-full of change and a crumpled-up dollar, and he said, 'I want to give this to the campaign.' It was a victory for *that* guy. It was hard-fought and it was against all odds. And it felt fucking great."

6

The Amazon Tax Makes History

Sawant's improbable 2019 re-election assured that the region's main political event in the new year would be round two of the Amazon tax fight.

Not everyone was happy about that. "Political revenge in Seattle," blared a post-election *Wall Street Journal* editorial headline. "Socialists on the City Council aim to punish Amazon and landlords," it read, overlooking that there was only one socialist on the council. From 3,000 miles away, the editorial board complained that, in addition to taxing Amazon, Sawant was aiming to ban winter evictions—which homeless activists and Sawant would win one month into the socialist's new term—and "also wants to impose city-wide rent control and build more public housing in Seattle."[125]

The Wall Street Journal editorial board understood that Sawant's city council election had national consequences. A successful Tax Amazon movement in one city would embolden activists everywhere to take on big business. The editorialists also were doubtless horrified at the prospect of unabashed socialists leading the charge, activists who were unafraid to point fingers, name enemies, and disrupt politics-as-usual.

In early January 2020, Sawant took her oath of office at Washington Hall in the heart of Seattle's Central District, with more than 500 people packed into the historic building's auditorium. It was an opportunity to prefigure the looming battle. "In a sense, *The Wall Street Journal* is right, we have seen political revenge in Seattle," Sawant told the crowd. "Big business and the wealthy attempted to take revenge against working people in our city during last year's city council election. It was the attempted revenge by Jeff Bezos and Amazon executives who are angry that our city's ordinary people have the temerity to demand a big business tax to fund housing and services. It was the attempted revenge by corporate real estate who are angry that our movement has won landmark renter's rights victories and is building serious momentum for rent control.

"For us, for the working people and the majority struggling in our city, it is not about revenge, it is about our right to our city," she

---

125 Editorial Board (2019, December 26). Political revenge in Seattle. *The Wall Street Journal*. https://www.wsj.com/articles/political-revenge-in-seattle-11577404431

added. “It is about a for-profit market that . . . has not only utterly failed to address the housing crisis but has exacerbated it. It is about climate crisis and the complete failure of capitalism and its representatives in the political establishment to take any serious steps to avoid catastrophe.”

That’s why, Sawant said, “We need to tax big business to fund a major expansion of social housing that is publicly owned, high quality, affordable, green and energy-efficient homes for working people, built by union labor. And social housing is a linchpin of winning a Green New Deal for Seattle.”

Before delving into next steps in the Tax Amazon fight, Sawant invited up speakers to spotlight recent skirmishes. She congratulated homeless activists for mobilizing with her office the previous month to stave off the mass eviction of the Northlake Tiny House Village, a community of transitional shelters. And she gave the mic to Anzela Niraula, a postdoctoral scholar at the University of Washington, who recounted how she and her colleagues had won union recognition and a first contract through militant action, including occupying the university president’s office. Now they were ready to join the Tax Amazon push. “We workers, we may wear different hats. Some might be construction workers, some are researchers, some are custodians, some are landscapers but we’re all here fighting the same fight for power, the fight to tax Amazon,” she declared.

Next spoke LouDella Bowen from the Brighton Apartments, yet another apartment complex where Sawant had teamed up with low-income tenants. Bowen and her neighbors had just organized, confronted their landlord, and won a one-year rent freeze, saving many elderly residents from having to move out of Seattle.

"We know that it is not over," Bowen, flanked by a delegation of Brighton residents, told the crowd. "I speak to a lot of widows who are still in their own houses, and taxes are so expensive. They're worried about losing their homes," she said. "We think about us as seniors, we paid our dues, we worked hard to live in those houses and make a home. And now we're going be forced out."

Bowen continued: "For far too long, we went along to get along. . . . We listened to their ideas and we said, 'Okay,' trying to keep the peace, but we say now, 'No more. No more.'"

The crowd burst into applause and whistles.

"And looking at this crowd out here tonight I'm even more encouraged to fight on a little bit more. How about you?" she asked.

More wild applause.

"We'll send another message to Amazon and all of these people," Bowen declared. "They have the money, but we have the majority. If we all stick together, we win. Am I right?" she asked the crowd.

"Yes!" hundreds shouted back.

Back on the microphone, Sawant reminded the crowd that it would take a class struggle approach to win this time. Already, just weeks after the stunning election rebuke of Amazon, some progressive activists and Democrats were urging the socialists to tone things down and stop calling out the behemoth corporation. Councilmember Lisa Herbold declined Sawant's invitation to attend the Washington Hall event, pointedly declaring she would not be part of any legislative effort that focused on Amazon and CEO Jeff Bezos.

"It is legitimate to raise these tactical questions," Sawant said, in reference to Herbold's objection, "because fighting the powerful big business elite is no small thing." But, she continued, "at the end of the day, we're not going to fool Jeff Bezos or the Chamber of Commerce and somehow slip a tax under the radar by calling it something other than the Amazon Tax. We could call it the 'Make Seattle Better for Everyone Tax' and they will still fight us tooth and nail."

Movement democracy would be essential this time, Sawant said. The Democrats had controlled the 2018 Amazon tax fight, first with their Progressive Revenue Tax Force, which came up with the $75 million tax proposal, and then with City Council committee hearings. The Democrats worked with "stakeholders"—usually organizational heads—but the effort lacked a strong grassroots movement. Aside from the forces that Sawant had mustered, community members had been observers, not participants, in the fight. When the big business blowback came, the socialist-led forces were not strong enough and the Democrats and their progressive allies had no effective response other than to compromise and ultimately capitulate.

This time, with socialists setting the battle plan, Sawant vowed that things would be different. The movement would pursue a two-track approach: Legislation that she would introduce in City Council, and simultaneous signature-gathering for a grassroots ballot initiative in case City Council failed to act. It was a replica of the successful 2014 minimum wage strategy.

The movement would be based in democracy, not decision-making behind closed doors. Sawant announced two grassroots conferences for the movement to vote on how to proceed. At the first two Tax Amazon conferences, both held within a month of Sawant's inauguration, hundreds of people spent hours in Washington Hall debating the legislation and campaign strategy, in plenary sessions and in small group discussions. They elected a steering committee to set the meeting agendas—but not to replace the plenary's ultimate decision-making authority. Indeed, even on the steering committee, where Sawant and other Socialist Alternative members had been elected, they did not constitute a majority of the seats. The plenary ratified the two-track legislation-plus-initiative approach that Sawant had laid out. And they settled on a payroll tax proposal that would fall entirely on the largest 3 percent of businesses—those with payrolls over $7 million a year. That would exempt the remaining 97 percent, but taxing those top businesses alone would raise $300 million per year. The conference also debated and voted on where the money should go: 75 percent of the revenue toward union-built social housing, and the remaining 25 percent devoted to Green New Deal projects, such as building weatherization, solar energy, and electric home conversion.

Restaurant worker and Socialist Alternative member Emerson Johnson recalled that the packed auditorium "felt momentous. It felt like we were building the kind of democratic movement that would be necessary to win. We had structures in place that we hadn't had previously . . . and we were building the grassroots support necessary for us to move forward on strong footing."

Most of the conference attendees were not SA members, Johnson noted, and many were new to political activism. "It was really inspiring to see all of these people who had gotten involved during the election campaign stick around and not just be done once Kshama was elected," he added. "That's the whole purpose of the office," he said. "Getting Kshama elected isn't enough. She's there to be a megaphone for the movement and the movement has to continue. And it felt like the movement was continuing in those spaces."

For new activist Alycia Roberts, the grassroots energy at the conference confirmed that "it was going to happen. That there was no giving up on the Amazon tax." Roberts, a resident of Northlake Tiny House Village, had just a month earlier experienced the power of collective action when she and her neighbors organized alongside Sawant to block the mayor's attempt to dismantle the village of 19 homes. The Amazon tax fight would be far more difficult, but the fight to save their homes gave Roberts and her neighbors a huge boost of confidence.

To say that Roberts had known difficulty before her Tax Amazon activism would be an understatement. Five years earlier, as Roberts battled drug addiction, her mother had a stroke. Roberts moved in to care for her. Soon after, her father died. Then their landlord served them with eviction papers, and as winter approached, a sheriff hustled them out of the apartment and into the street. Roberts found a couch for her mother to sleep on while she and her four-year-old daughter slept in an often broken-down car, moving nightly to stay one step ahead of the police: WalMart and grocery store parking lots, the streets of well-lit neighborhoods. After dialing up dozens of apartment listings, she found a place that would take her family's Section 8 voucher, but housing authority officials rejected the lease because they thought the landlord was charging $100 a month too much. Then the bureaucrats revoked her housing voucher, saying Roberts had run out of time. As a result, Child Protective Services took her daughter. Then her mom died. Then the police seized her car; actually, stole it is a more accurate description. Beleaguered and distraught, Roberts dove back into drugs. She became suicidal.

Fortunately, Roberts got into treatment. She eventually landed in a tent city run by SHARE, a 30-year-old grassroots organization of homeless and formerly homeless people. There, Roberts and the other residents democratically made decisions and collectively managed daily affairs: security shifts, maintenance work, community meals. The tent city was also a sober camp—no drinking or drugs allowed, with rules enforced by the residents themselves. For Roberts, SHARE was a lifesaver.

Eventually she moved to Northlake Tiny House Village, a self-managed community similar to SHARE, and joined the Nickelodeons, as the residents called themselves. The previous years had been one nightmare after another for Roberts and many of her neighbors. To the system, they were a problem to be managed, contained, subdued, and ultimately, crushed. They were detested by a string of Seattle mayors and administrators. The iron boot of capitalism—the vindictive cops, the petty nit-picking bureaucrats, the ravenous landlords—pressed down on Roberts' neck until she considered surrendering life itself. Northlake gave her shelter, sobriety, dignity, friends, and a community that came together around common struggle.

When Durkan announced in the fall of 2019 that she intended to evict the Northlake residents at the end of December, the Nickelodeons organized a city-wide campaign with Sawant. They collected petition signatures, spoke up at community meetings, staged press events, testified at a committee meeting Sawant convened, and made plans to defend the community with civil disobedience if city officials carried out their threat. The mayor backed off.

This victory was Roberts' first experience in the power of democratic decision-making and collective action. The Tax Amazon conference was similar, but on a much grander scale. When she stood up to speak in front of the conference, she was nervous. "Even with me stumbling all over the place, they still clapped and cheered me," Roberts recalled. In the breakout sessions she was amazed to be part of detailed discussions around how the tax should be spent. She was no policy scholar, but her opinions mattered as much as anyone else's. "I've never done something like that before," Roberts said.

What made the Tax Amazon conferences so exceptional, noted Sharon Crowley, a member of the UAW 4121 graduate workers' union, was that "the people most affected by the housing crisis in Seattle" were in the room making decisions. "How often does that happen, when the people who most need the progressive revenue that's being proposed, that's being developed, are the ones who are driving the bus?" she marveled.

Crowley, Roberts, Johnson, Sawant, and the rest of the conference-goers spilled out of the Washington Hall brimming with excitement. They were ready to bring the fight inside City Hall and into the streets. They couldn't wait to take on Amazon. First, though, they faced a surprise attack. It came from the Democratic political establishment, including progressives who claimed disingenuously to be supporting the movement's goals while they tried to place an insurmountable roadblock in front of Sawant and the movement.

Even after suffering a bruising defeat in the 2019 ballot, Seattle's business and political establishment refused to concede that the Amazon Tax was going to become law. Having failed in their primary strategy—evict the Marxist from City Hall—they fell back to the next line of defense: Outlaw the very idea of a Seattle Amazon Tax. To play a central role in this scheme they recruited a state House member from Seattle with impeccable progressive credentials: Representative Nicole Macri, a social service administrator and affordable housing advocate who had first been elected in 2016 to a state House district that overlapped largely with Sawant's city district.

Before the start of the state Legislature's 2020 session in January, Durkan, former Governor Christine Gregoire, and other leading Democrats worked with Macri to draft a state bill giving King County—the regional municipality encompassing Seattle and three dozen surrounding cities—the authority to impose an excise tax on corporations to fund social services. No one in the movement would object to that. But the Democrats and business lobbyists intended to attach a poison pill, a clause to the legislation banning cities within the county from imposing similar business taxes. It was as brilliant as it was diabolical: With the bill, Democrats could tell social service advocates that they were raising urgently needed funds by taxing big business, while insulating themselves against any threat of a tax on Amazon led by Sawant and the movement. If they couldn't beat the movement, they would outlaw it.

The Democrats' preemption strategy was plucked straight out of the national right-wing playbook. For the previous decade, the corporate-funded American Legislative Exchange Council

(ALEC) had been drafting model preemption bills for right-wing legislators around the country. It was their go-to tactic for undermining local democracy. ALEC and their legislative allies had been exceptionally successful in getting dozens of state laws passed that prevented local governments from raising minimum wages, requiring paid sick days for workers, or regulating guns. They blocked local governments from setting up publicly owned broadband services, enacting rent control, or protecting undocumented immigrants.[126]

At the end of January, right after the first Tax Amazon Action Conference and with little fanfare—and not surprisingly, zero grassroots input—Macri introduced her bill giving King County the authority to impose an excise tax on businesses, collecting up to $121 million a year for social service programs. It was a small fraction of what the region actually needed. A business-funded study had just determined that King County would need between $450 million and $1.1 billion a year to solve the housing crisis.[127] But Democrats were unwilling to advance a bill that taxed big business at a more needed level. Likely they hoped that this lower amount would relieve political pressure on them to act further.

Democrats knew that they couldn't simply put the preemption clause in the first draft of the bill. That would make it politically explosive. Instead, they planned to have the bill advance in the

---

126 (n.d.). *The threat of state preemption*. Local Solutions Support Center. Retrieved March 23, 2023, from https://www.supportdemocracy.org/preemption

127 Martiz, B., & Wagle, D. (2020, January 22). *Why does prosperous King County have a homelessness crisis?* McKinsey & Company. Retrieved March 27, 2023, from https://www.mckinsey.com/industries/public-and-social-sector/our-insights/why-does-prosperous-king-county-have-a-homelessness-crisis#/

legislative process without the preemption clause, knowing that business lobbyists would demand its addition. At the final stages of the legislation, after the conclusion of public hearings, Democrats—who controlled both the House and the Senate—feigning reluctance, would add the preemption clause and submit it for a final vote without further hearings. Indeed, the bill's main architects admitted this was the plan. The cosponsor on Macri's bill had told legislative colleagues that the preemption clause needed to be added. Macri admitted to the media as much, saying that she expected preemption to be "a closing consideration and not an opening consideration."[128]

Per the Washington state constitution, the 2020 legislative session was short—only 60 days—so legislators would have to move fast. But if they were successful, by mid-March they could have cut the legs out from under the Tax Amazon movement.

Business leaders, previously unwavering in their opposition to a single penny of business taxation, understood the Democrat's stratagem and quickly rallied behind Macri's bill. Amazon, Alaska Airlines, Expedia, Microsoft, Starbucks, Zillow, Weyerhaeuser, Costco—a who's who of regional corporate behemoths—jointly signed a letter in support of the legislation. Some 15 of the state's leading unions also urged the legislature to pass it, remaining noticeably silent on preemption in their advocacy letter.[129]

---

128 Kroman, D. (2020, February 3). *King County's largest businesses weigh support for proposed payroll tax*. Crosscut.com. Retrieved March 27, 2023, from https://crosscut.com/2020/02/king-countys-largest-businesses-weigh-support-proposed-payroll-tax

129 Beekman, D. (2020, February 4). *Big businesses like Amazon support tax for King County, but questions about Seattle, suburbs remain*. The Seattle

The Tax Amazon activists fought back. "We welcome any attempt to raise progressive revenues, whether at the city level, the county level or the state level," Sawant told the media in early February. Noting that big business and the Democrats had just tried and failed to boot her from office, Sawant said, "I want us to recognize that the only reason, the sole reason that big business would enter into an agreement of any kind of taxation on themselves would be if they can get the real prize that they want to have, which is the so-called preemption. . .a statewide ban on cities like Seattle raising our own big business taxes."

The legislative plot, she said, "is an anti-democratic state ban on progressive taxation and anti-democratic ban on taxing big business, right at the moment that the Tax Amazon movement is organizing to finally make them pay their fair share."[130]

A few days later, Sawant joined several dozen activists in the 60-mile drive to the state capitol. Their aim was to talk directly to legislators and, in particular, to confront Macri. The activists occupied the hallway outside Macri's legislative office, demanding to talk to the representative. A Macri aide said she was unavailable. We'll wait, the activists replied. Security officers showed up. The activists refused to leave. Finally, Macri passed word through

Times. Retrieved March 27, 2023, from https://www.seattletimes.com/seattle-news/politics/big-businesses-like-amazon-support-tax-for-king-county-but-questions-about-seattle-suburbs-remain/

130 [Seattle Channel]. (2020, February 7). *CM Sawant denounces proposed ban on big business taxes Councilmember Sawant denounces proposed ban on big business taxes* [Video]. City of Seattle. https://www.seattlechannel.org/mayor-and-council/city-council/council-press-conferences?videoid=x111155

her aide that she would meet the group outside the chambers of the House of Representatives. The activists moved to the legislative building, clustering around the giant wooden doors into the House chamber. Lobbyists and legislative staff struggled to maneuver around the Tax Amazon crowd. A few minutes later Macri emerged through the doors.

Amazon cargo worker Matt Smith led off, handing the legislator a letter signed by 1,000 Seattleites against the undemocratic preemption scheme.[131]

“If there is a preemption,” Sawant told Macri, “that will really completely eliminate our ability as working people to fund the needs that we have. And these are miseries inflicted on us by society, by the system, by big businesses. . . . And so we really need to hear from you, that you will oppose preemption. One, that you will speak out publicly, and then second that you will vote against any bill that has such a state ban.”

The activists crowded in to hear Macri's response. “I will say that I am working closely to negotiate many things on this bill,” she said, pointedly not addressing Sawant's request. “For me, the things that are important are that we have a tool that is progressive, that addresses the huge inequality that we have in our region.”

“Preemption would disempower the communities that you're claiming to represent,” an activist responded.

---

131 This and dialogue that follows are from: [Facebook.com]. (2020, February 12). Tax Amazon movement confronts Rep. Macri (transcript in author's possession) [Video]. Tax Amazon Facebook Page. https://www.facebook.com/TaxAmazon/videos/125727908780456

"My bill does not have preemption, as you all know," Macri replied.

Another activist: "Will you oppose it if it does?"

Macri, again dodging: "I'm sure you all read it, nine pages."

Again: "Will you oppose it if it's amended?"

"I will say that it is important for me that all of our elected officials retain the authority that they need to get their job done. I have been fighting hard for that," Macri said.

Kailyn Nicholson, a Socialist Alternative organizer, pressed her directly. "We're here today to say, we welcome this bill. But if it includes preemption, if you or any other legislators vote for a bill that includes preemption, you will be saying that we need to tax ourselves. . .. And that's completely unacceptable. And that's why we're asking you to say publicly today that you will not vote for a bill that includes preemption."

"I am not going to say that publicly today," Macri replied.

The crowd booed.

Smith spoke up again. "As an Amazon worker, I can say not only do we as Amazon workers, as working people, not only do we bear the brunt of the housing crisis in Seattle, we have skyrocketing rents, we have stagnating wages. Not only that, but we also bear the burden of taxation in the state. . . .If this ban on big business taxes goes through, the only option to fund these things that we need is to ask working people to pay even more, on top of what we already can't afford. We cannot have preemption. We cannot have this ban on big business taxation."

"Thank you, super helpful," Macri curtly replied.

"You're throwing us under the bus," someone in the crowd said. "Stand up for us," said another.

"It's a very simple question we're asking," said Calvin Priest, the SA political director. "Will you oppose the state ban? That's all we're asking. A yes or no question, will you oppose the state ban on big business taxation."

"I'm making no absolute statements," Macri responded, provoking another loud chorus of boos.

Macri's non-answer was, of course, a very clear answer. The activists put the yes-or-no question to her multiple times, and every time she evaded or refused to answer. It was clear that if adding preemption was needed to advance the bill, Macri would consent. "Thank you for being here. I have to go," she said before turning to the House chamber doors.

"No state ban! No state ban!" the crowd chanted as she disappeared behind the doors. "From Seattle to Spokane—no preemption, no state ban!" The chanting reverberated through the marble halls as the protesters marched through the legislative building.

Many social service agency lobbyists were shocked at the movement's aggressive tactics. They rallied to defend Macri, whom they considered their champion. "Don't let the perfect become the enemy of the good," one agency advocate warned me privately a few days after the Olympia confrontation. Others claimed that the Tax Amazon movement was standing in the way of needed tax revenue; we trust Macri to negotiate for us, they said. For them, the problem wasn't big business' blatant extortion, the Democrats' cynical game-playing, or the inadequate tax rate being proposed. To them, the problem was socialists who refused to play by the establishment's rules. Their craven willingness to sacrifice democratic principles and the demands of the Tax Amazon movement in exchange for a fraction of the needed funds revealed the depths to which their advocacy had degenerated. It was pure opportunism, seeking to hijack an opening created by grassroots pressure and steer it into the blind alley of insider politics.

Sawant and the Tax Amazon activists knew that the fight over human needs versus corporate profits would be resolved based on the balance of power between the activists on the one hand, and big business, their lobbyists, and the political establishment on the other. The first pillar of Sawant's insurgent politics—a recognition that the fight was based on competing class interests—was on stark display here. Macri's steadfast refusal to commit to fight preemption confirmed the class nature of the conflict. It was imperative to unmask her role. The social service lobbyists were appalled that Tax Amazon activists were besieging one of their favorite legislators. They took it personally. But it wasn't a personal dislike of Macri that drove the socialists to challenge her; they were simply defending working-class interests against the big business interests that Macri supported.

Meanwhile, the balance of power was shifting due to the movement's persistence and also due to cracks emerging on the other side of the political tug-of-war. The statewide big business lobby came out against Macri's bill because it opposed all business taxation on principle. The insurance industry demanded an exemption. So did the biotechnology lobby. Several mayors in the cities surrounding Seattle complained that Macri and the other Democrats had failed to consult with them. Controversy arose about how the funds would be divvied up between the county and more than three dozen cities.

Tax Amazon activists also kept up the pressure, mobilizing for the weekend Town Hall question-and-answer sessions that legislators set up. Two key Democratic senators came out against any bill that contained preemption, narrowing the path to the bill's passage in the Senate. That put House Democrats in a bind: There was no political benefit to taking a controversial vote if the bill wasn't assured of survival in the Senate. At a legislative Town Hall in Macri's district, more than 50 Tax Amazon activists barraged the legislators on the preemption question. Onstage next to Macri, Representative Frank Chopp, the former House speaker and Macri's district seatmate, announced that he was opposed to any bill with preemption. Chopp's announcement drew a rousing applause and embarrassed the bill's sponsor seated next to him. Four area Democratic elected officials joined Sawant in publishing an op-ed in support of Tax Amazon and against the preemption push.

In early March, the bill was scheduled for a House committee vote, but the Democratic chair skipped over it. The legislation had become politically radioactive. A few days later, the bill officially died as the legislative session ended. The political establishment's second line of defense—outlaw a city Amazon Tax—had collapsed due to fractures in the big business community and a plucky movement unafraid to confront and expose Democrats for their hypocrisy.

In early March 2020, having dealt with the preemption threat, Sawant unveiled the new Tax Amazon legislation alongside community activists and newly elected Democratic City Councilmember Tammy Morales, who agreed to cosponsor. “Today, tens of thousands of people are at risk of being pushed out of Seattle by soaring housing costs,” Sawant said at the unveiling. “They are nurses, bus drivers, restaurant workers, baristas, mechanics, construction workers, teachers, and more. These are the people who make our city run. Communities of color, immigrants, and the LGBTQ community are especially feeling the stress of housing displacement.”

As determined at the Tax Amazon conferences, the bill called for an excise tax on the payrolls of the largest 3 percent of businesses in Seattle, raising about $300 million a year beginning in 2021. About 800 businesses would have to pay the tax; 22,000 would be exempt. Seventy-five percent of the revenue would be dedicated toward affordable housing and services, building an estimated 800 new affordable homes per year, more than triple the city’s previous rate of housing production. The bill included a requirement that new housing be built with union labor, with apprenticeship opportunities for young workers from marginalized communities. The remaining 25 percent of funds would be spent on retrofitting, over 10 years, an estimated 47,000 existing homes to meet Green New Deal standards, and on solar panel and weatherization projects. The investments would create or support 34,000 jobs in construction, retrofit work, and social services. Additionally, Sawant directed bill-drafters to ensure ongoing democratic oversight, through an elected Social Housing Board that included renters and homeowners from each district.

"It's clear, through bitter recent experience, that the private market has failed us and will not fill this need," Sawant said. "So as a socialist city councilmember, elected by and accountable to working people, it's my duty to put forward bold policy solutions that match the scale of the problem, and to mobilize our communities to win them."

Right out of the gate, the Tax Amazon bill faced another enormous challenge. This one couldn't be laid at the feet of the political and business establishment. Beginning in late 2019, the SARS-CoV-2 virus began spreading around the globe, slow at first and then with alarming rapidity. Washington state's first case came in January. Cases grew exponentially, seemingly every 24 hours, as more people got sick and more vulnerable victims ended up in the hospital or died. On March 11, 2020, with 118,000 cases reported in 114 countries, and with thousands more every day, the World Health Organization declared a worldwide pandemic.[132] Governments issued lockdown notices, shuttering schools and workplaces, banning gatherings and sports events, halting travel, and closing businesses and public offices. In the first six weeks of the COVID shutdown, more than 30 million Americans filed for unemployment, including 844,000 in Washington state, representing one out of every five workers in the state.[133] Frontline

---

132 (2020, March 11). *WHO Director-General's opening remarks at the media briefing on COVID-19 - 11 March 2020*. World Health Organization. Retrieved March 28, 2023, from https://www.who.int/director-general/speeches/detail/who-director-general-s-opening-remarks-at-the-media-briefing-on-covid-19-11-march-2020

133 Horsley, S. (2020, April 30). *A Staggering Toll: 30 Million Have Filed For Unemployment*. National Public Radio. Retrieved March 28, 2023, from https://www.npr.org/sections/coronavirus-live-updates/2020/04/30/

healthcare, grocery, emergency, transportation, warehouse, delivery, and other workers were pressed into service, often under unsafe circumstances, and began to sicken and die in disproportionate numbers.

With the social and economic crisis deepening sharply, Sawant and Morales updated an accelerated Tax Amazon bill to provide emergency aid to working class households. They proposed to tax the big corporations immediately and not wait to start the tax until the following year. With a slightly higher tax rate, the new proposal would raise $500 million a year for housing and Green New Deal projects, with the first $200 million going immediately to provide direct cash relief to 100,000 Seattle households in the spring and summer of 2020.

The new legislation sent defenders of big business into a fit of apoplexy. "Seattle's war on employers must end now," demanded *The Seattle Times* May Day editorial. The paper declared that rather than bolster life-saving aid, "cities must cut spending." Seeking to rally the region's political establishment, the editorialists implored state leaders to "weigh in to prevent this attack on Washington's recovery."[134] Downtown Seattle businesses launched a petition urging business owners to "tell the City Council to vote NO on

848021681/a-staggering-toll-30-million-have-filed-for-unemployment and Roberts, P. (2020, April 30). *1 in 5 Washington workers have filed unemployment claims as federal coronavirus relief kicks in*. The Seattle Times. Retrieved March 28, 2023, from https://www.seattletimes.com/business/economy/washington-sees-nearly-146000-new-jobless-claims-as-federal-coronavirus-relief-kicks-in/

134 (2020, May 1). *Seattle's war on employers must end now*. The Seattle Times. Retrieved March 28, 2023, from https://www.seattletimes.com/opinion/editorials/seattles-war-on-employers-must-end-now/

Kshama Sawant's job killing new tax."[135] Seattle Mayor Jenny Durkan threw cold water on the legislation. Asked by a local television reporter about the new Tax Amazon bill, she replied, "Yeah, that never is going to happen, and I think it's irresponsible for anyone to say that that's even possible."[136]

National business megaphones weighed in as well, recognizing the broader ruling class interests. "Mindless in Seattle," *The Wall Street Journal* editorial board proclaimed. "The economy is on life support, but that isn't stopping the Seattle City Council from trying to soak employers with a new tax on hiring."[137]

The new legislation put the Democratic establishment in an extraordinarily difficult position. They wanted to appear responsive to the dire public health crisis. Working class people worldwide were worried about how they were going to buy food and necessities. The proposal to provide direct cash assistance was extremely popular; European governments were rolling out cash-aid programs. But Seattle Democrats had not given up on the hope

---

135 (n.d.). *No Tax On Jobs . . . Recovery Now!* Change.org. Retrieved March 28, 2023, from https://www.change.org/p/mayor-jenny-durkan-and-the-seattle-city-council-no-tax-on-jobs-recovery-now?utm_source=share_petition&utm_medium=custom_url&recruited_by_id=8bcf5360-7dbe-11ea-b77a-c91dea797eb3

136 (2020, April 22). *'Irresponsible': Seattle mayor slams proposed payroll tax that's promising to provide stimulus checks.* King 5. Retrieved March 28, 2023, from https://www.king5.com/article/news/local/seattle/seattle-city-council-payroll-tax-legislation-stimulus-checks-coronavirus-recovery/281-b38cb566-c397-4123-885c-a73fa01fb24f

137 (2020, April 30). *Mindless in Seattle.* The Wall Street Journal. Retrieved March 28, 2023, from https://www.wsj.com/articles/mindless-in-seattle-11588288646

that they could defeat the Amazon tax entirely. The sharp editorials and critiques from big business were reminders to the political establishment of their responsibility to hold the line against Tax Amazon. Having failed to unseat Sawant, and then having failed to outlaw her legislation, the Democrats now fell back on a third line of defense: cancel hearings and freeze the bill. Seizing on an emergency pandemic order issued by Washington Governor Jay Inslee, City Council President Lorena Gonzalez announced that the new Amazon tax would not be considered during the COVID public health emergency.

Among the emergency orders issued by Governor Inslee was a proclamation limiting local governments from conducting any business unless it was paying necessary bills or part of the emergency response to the pandemic. Even though the new Tax Amazon bill directly addressed the COVID emergency, Gonzalez and the other Democrats declared the legislation out of bounds.

For two months the political establishment held to this antidemocratic line until finally, at the end of May, facing withering legal critique and growing public pressure, Inslee relented and lifted the restrictions. Inslee's revised emergency order meant that the City Council could take up the Tax Amazon bill in June.

In addition to delaying the legislation, the COVID lockdown shackled the movement's grassroots work. The Tax Amazon strategy, ratified at the winter Tax Amazon conferences, relied on a two-track approach: push the legislation while collecting signatures for a ballot initiative. In the past, activists had great success collecting signatures in busy public places or in door-to-door organizing in working class neighborhoods. But in the initial weeks of the pandemic, people were leery of opening doors and only ventured outside if they needed to work or run essential errands. Online, thousands of Seattle residents signed Sawant's petition, and more than 70 faith leaders wrote a letter to City Council demanding passage of the new bill.

Over the spring as restrictions were loosened, activists began to set up signature-collecting tables, complete with masks, boxes of Clorox wipes, and hundreds of individually sanitized pens. Progress was slow—at least until the explosion of the Black Lives Matter protest movement. On May 25, Minneapolis police murdered George Floyd, and the world rose up in protest against yet another racist police killing. At least 20 million people took to the streets in 2,000 cities across 60 countries in the largest recorded civil uprising in world history. As in other cities, tens of thousands of Seattleites overcame their COVID inhibitions and in late May and June poured out of their homes to join mass protests against police violence. Sawant and Socialist Alternative members had long been involved in local campaigns against police violence, and her 2018 vote against the police guild contract set her apart from other elected officials. Sawant joined the big community marches in nighttime standoffs against the police, who unleashed volleys of tear gas and blast balls.[138] The street protesters eagerly snapped up Tax Amazon petitions and called friends over to the campaign tables to get them signed up as well. Signature-gatherers ran short of clipboards. They could barely keep up with the public demand for petitions.

138 Much more on the Black Lives Matter movement and Sawant's role are in the next chapter.

"There was a tremendous response," recalled ironworker Logan Swan. "I've never petitioned so aggressively. I could just shout at people like 'Hey, have you signed this petition to tax Amazon and big business for union jobs and affordable housing?' And people would hear 'Tax Amazon' and just be like 'fuck yeah.' They would just come up and be like, 'Fuck Jeff Bezos' and start signing their name."

As in other cities, what drew people to the streets was unbridled collective rage over the murder of George Floyd, but also the 1,000-plus US police killings a year, disproportionately of Black and Brown men.[139] Seattle police had killed 29 people in the previous decade: a pregnant mom, a young man holding his baby, a man struggling with his mental health. Once in the streets, the protests expanded beyond demands for stopping police violence as people vented their rage at the economic and social system that pressed down on them, even more so with the pandemic.

Some of the prominent leaders in the marches called on Tax Amazon activists to stand back and allow the movement to focus solely on the police. But community members—including many newly activated people—gravitated to the Tax Amazon struggle in the Black Lives Matter protests. They recognized the connection between the gross inequities in society and the police violence that enforced the system. In Amazon, they saw a concrete manifestation of this inequity—a hegemonic employer responsible for gentrifying and pushing people of color out of their communities, while denying any social responsibility to pay taxes. And they

139 (2023, March 27). *1,082 people have been shot and killed by police in the past 12 months*. The Washington Post. Retrieved March 28, 2023, from https://www.washingtonpost.com/graphics/investigations/police-shootings-database/

experienced the physical violence of police forces who existed to perpetuate this unjust social and economic order in Seattle. For them, the call to tax Amazon was a specific and timely demand of the Black Lives Matter protests.

"People correctly saw it's the ruling class that propagates and profits from racism and keeps it going," Swan said. "And this is fighting to make them pay taxes, in order to take wealth from them and put it in the hands of working-class people through union jobs, building affordable housing that's publicly owned, and prioritizing districts of historically marginalized people that have been driven out through gentrification. That's a process fueled by these major companies, and people just seemed to understand that intuitively," he said.

As June progressed, with the Tax Amazon movement closing in on the 30,000 signature threshold, it became clear that the initiative would qualify for the November ballot. Even with the COVID restrictions in place, the political establishment had failed to stop the socialist-led insurgency.

In *The Wall Street Journal*'s "Mindless in Seattle" editorial earlier that spring, the paper had warned its business readers that even if the Sawant-Morales legislation could be stymied, "One risk is that their fellow far-left councillors will pass a scaled-down version of the business tax and portray it as moderate." *The Journal*'s worry was prescient.

With hundreds of activists flooding city council offices with emails, phone calls, and public testimony, and with the Amazon tax demand echoing in the Black Lives Matter street protests, the political establishment fell back on their fourth and final line of defense: damage control. They introduced their own, more modest, Amazon tax bill.

The Democrats' substitute legislation—developed behind closed doors—adopted the exact same excise tax mechanism as Sawant's bill and proposed to tax the same pool of the largest businesses, those with payrolls above $7 million a year. But with a lower tax rate formula, the bill would bring in just $174 million a year—much less than the Sawant-Morales bill, yet a huge leap over the 2018 legislation. And the tax would expire after 10 years. The bill would fund some immediate COVID relief, along with new affordable housing construction beyond 2020. There was no money for Green New Deal projects.

The lead sponsor of the legislation was Councilmember Teresa Mosqueda, a former political director for the state labor federation who was first elected to City Council in 2016. In the 2018 Tax Amazon fight, she had opposed the tax repeal but had pointedly criticized Sawant and the rest of the movement for singling out Amazon. Now, in 2020, she gave her new legislation the insipid branding of "Jumpstart Seattle" and assiduously avoided the Tax Amazon tag, even though her bill—as with the Sawant-Morales bill—made Amazon far and away the single biggest payer of the tax.

Right after introducing her legislation, Mosqueda trumpeted the news that four of her Democratic colleagues had agreed to cosponsor the bill, assuring it of majority support on the nine-seat City Council. Labor leaders announced their support. Several large businesses—notably Expedia, which had just relocated its world headquarters to Seattle—sensed the movement's momentum and embraced the bill. Other businesses reluctantly came on board; better to accept Mosqueda's bill than to face Sawant and the prospect of a huge ballot fight. "Yes, harm mitigation was part of it," conceded one restaurant executive who had fought against the Amazon tax in 2018 but came around to support the 2020 measure.[140]

Lenin and other early socialists had observed that one key role of the state under capitalism is "moderating the collisions between the classes" so as to forestall deeper unrest. This was precisely the role of Mosqueda's tax legislation, just as the Democrats' $15 minimum wage bill had been six years earlier. In both instances, having failed to stop the movement, the Democratic political establishment brought forward their watered-down alternatives to forestall the tremendous class collision that would have ensued with ballot initiative fights.

The movement should welcome Mosqueda's legislation, Sawant said, "because it's confirmation that our movement for the Amazon tax and the George Floyd protest movement is having a huge impact and succeeding in putting pressure on the establishment." Yet, she noted, the fight was far from over. In 2014, Democrats had further weakened the minimum wage bill before finally adopting it. The task in 2020 was to prevent further erosion, and indeed to demand a stronger Amazon tax bill than Mosqueda's plan, which, Sawant said, "simply does not do nearly enough, quickly enough, to invest in communities and put real meaning to Black Lives Matter."[141]

---

140 Kroman, D. (2020, July 15). *What Seattle's new payroll tax says about the city's politics*. Crosscut.com. Retrieved March 28, 2023, from https://crosscut.com/news/2020/07/what-seattles-new-payroll-tax-says-about-citys-politics

141 [SeattleChannel.org]. (2020, June 18). Councilmember Sawant, faith leaders demand 1,000 affordable homes [Video]. Seattle Channell Council Press Conferences. https://www.seattlechannel.org/mayor-and-council/city-council/council-press-conferences/?videoid=x114887

No one recognized Sawant's point more acutely than Rev. Dr. Robert Jeffrey, Sr., pastor at New Hope Missionary Baptist Church in Seattle's Central District. Since arriving in Seattle in 1986, Rev. Jeffrey had been an outspoken community activist. He launched Black Dollar Days Task Force to promote Black businesses and support local community development. He called out corporations like Nordstroms for their racist hiring practices, often directly confronting executives.[142] He made enemies in the African American community by calling out Black leaders who gave political cover to predatory lenders like Washington Mutual when they accepted bank board positions while the institutions promoted gentrification. He was unafraid to call out politicians who tokenized the Black community when they showed up for the annual Martin Luther King Jr. Day marches but did little in substance the rest of the year. When Sawant was first elected, Jeffrey recognized a kinship, a fellow disturber of the peace. Over the years he worked closely with her council office as he advocated for more community investment and affordable housing. When the Tax Amazon fight developed, he played a prominent public role.

Rev. Jeffrey's church was a prime example of how past racist practices, left unreversed, magnify inequity over time. In 1969, City of Seattle officials presented Jeffrey's predecessor, Rev. C.E. Williams, with an offer he couldn't refuse: Sell your parking lot to the City. If you don't, they told him, the City would condemn the land and take it.

142 Strickland, D. (1992, February 9). *Blacks Give Nordstrom Dubious Award.* The Seattle Times. Retrieved March 30, 2023, from https://archive.seattletimes.com/archive/?date=19920209&slug=1474701

The African-American congregation acceded to the sale, getting $34,000 for a piece of land that in 2020 was worth $2 million, more than 8 times the inflation-adjusted property sale price.

The City's coercive seizure of land from New Hope was just one example of how the political establishment over the decades has been complicit in the impoverishment and destruction of the Central Area's African-American community. The city land appropriation, combined with developer-led gentrification in the Central District, drove Rev. Jeffrey's parishioners away from Seattle, torn from the social fabric of their historic neighborhood.

Rev. Jeffrey's demand to the City, which Sawant supported, was simple: Make reparations by returning the land it coercively seized 50 years ago. Jeffrey intended to use the land to build a 90-unit apartment building to house seniors, veterans, homeless people, and people with disabilities. The Amazon tax fight was an opportunity to fuse the demand for community reparations with the demand for money to build affordable housing.

Just after Mosqueda introduced her tax legislation, Rev. Jeffrey and Sawant convened a press conference outside his church, gathering many of the area's leading Black pastors and other faith leaders. They unveiled a clergy letter to Mayor Durkan and the City Council, calling for $500 million in progressive taxes—the level of funding of the Sawant-Morales Tax Amazon legislation—to build new homes in the Central District, more tiny house villages, and apprenticeship opportunities for young workers.

The clergy letter was a "challenge to the City Council as well as to Mayor Durkan. You must acknowledge the existence of the persistent and institutional racism that has decimated the Seattle

African-American population," said Rev. Willie Seals, pastor of The Christ Spirit Church.

"Simply put, if Black Lives Matter, then affordable housing for Black families in the Central District should matter," added Rev. Carey Anderson, pastor of Seattle's 134-year-old First African Methodist Episcopal Church. "It was Martin Luther King who said, 'Life's most important question is—what are you doing for others?' We are simply asking if we really believe in not the rhetoric, not the slogans, but the fact that Black Lives Matter, then do what's right, for what's right."

"Isn't it bad enough that the land was stolen from the Duwamish people?" asked Rev. Angela Ying of Bethany United Church of Christ. "And now it's stolen from New Hope Baptist Church right in their midst when they're trying to bring up their children in faith and make a difference in this society."

Like Rev. Jeffrey, Rev. Ying was another faith leader closely aligned with Sawant. The first Taiwanese-American ordained minister in the US, Ying had built a diverse congregation in Seattle's working class Beacon Hill neighborhood, and her church served as an incubator for various youth of color-led social justice groups. She had eagerly taken up the call of the Tax Amazon movement, traveling to Olympia earlier in the year along with the other activists to confront Macri and the other Democrats in the fight against preemption. Underscoring the connection between fighting gentrification and the Tax Amazon movement, Ying continued: "We know that economics and race stand hand in hand at intersectionality. So we stand to make sure that we can build thousands of new homes so that our Black and Brown brothers and sisters can return to their neighborhood where they belong, where they were to begin with."

Sawant applauded the clergy and then challenged Democrats to put substance behind their lip service to the street protests. "To the members of the political establishment who say Black Lives Matter, I urge them to put actions to the language that they use from our movement. I urge them to not co-opt the language, but to join with us, join with faith leaders, join with the Black and Brown community without reservation," she said.

The following week, when Mosqueda's bill came up for debate in the City Council's Budget Committee, Sawant introduced an amendment calling for boosting the tax rate, with the added funds dedicated to building new homes in the Central District. Sawant's amendment included a neighborhood preference policy for the new Central District apartments, to give tenancy priority to those who had lived in or who had past family ties to the neighborhood—a mechanism for beginning to undo racist gentrification. Her amendment would help Rev. Jeffrey and New Hope parishioners build the affordable housing that they had envisioned.

Over the course of the following two weeks, at Black Lives Matter rallies and in online meetings, the Tax Amazon movement mobilized hundreds of community members to write letters to City Councilmembers demanding the original tax rate of $500 million, dedicated funding for Central District homes and Green New Deal projects, and elimination of the 10-year "sunset," or expiration, of the tax. Rev. Ying organized an online letter signed by more than 220 area faith leaders backing the call of the Black clergy and Sawant for dedicated Central District housing investments.

Activists continued collecting signatures for an initiative in case the Democrats caved. But that seemed unlikely this time. In the 2014 fight for a $15 minimum wage, 15Now had been on the defensive in the final weeks as Democrats added weakening amendments. But this time the political momentum pointed in the other direction. Even the ironworkers union and other construction union leaders, who had eagerly done Amazon's dirty work in 2018, meekly announced support for Mosqueda's bill.

The political momentum on the streets was palpable—driven by a slew of crises local and global. Mayor Durkan was on the defensive because of the indiscriminate police violence she had unleashed on Black Lives Matter protesters. And no one—at least publicly—was willing to defend the company that, four months into COVID, had come to epitomize the worst of pandemic profiteering. The challenge would be harnessing this political energy to win more concessions from Mosqueda's bill.

The movement forced Democrats to bump the tax rates up another $40 million, to bring in $214 million a year, and to include $20 million a year in Green New Deal funding. The 10-year sunset clause was replaced with a 20-year sunset. That was still a shameful concession by the Democrats. What tax on working people ever sunsets? Yet it was a vast improvement over Mosqueda's original legislation. And, as a result of the movement pressure, led by the clergy, the Democrats agreed to set aside at least $18 million a year for new affordable housing in the Central District, a tangible and historic win for the Central District clergy and the Black Lives Matter movement.

On July 6, the City Council met to approve the tax measure—on Zoom, as the pandemic prevented in-person meetings. Tax

Amazon activists signed up to speak out in the public comment section—to point out the flaws in Mosqueda's legislation and fight for Sawant's amendments, like eliminating the sunset clause, but mostly to claim the movement win.

"When this Council passed a much weaker tax in 2018 before repealing it in a cowardly abdication to corporate power, this movement promised you we will be back for more," healthcare worker Sean Butterfield testified to the council. "Well, here we are: Bigger and stronger than we were two years ago, despite the organizing limitations of this pandemic, despite big business' withering attack on activists and community members fighting for this, and despite Amazon's unprecedented financial interference in last year's elections."

Matt Smith, the Amazon cargo worker and SA member, spoke: "I'm one of the 30,000 voters who have signed the petition to get an Amazon tax on the ballot. And we are prepared to fight all the way to November if the council fails to pass the strong Amazon tax today," he said. "It is absolutely because of the strength of this movement that we're even having this discussion today. Since March 1, Jeff Bezos has increased his wealth by $60 billion. Amazon stock price has skyrocketed, but Amazon workers like me have not seen that wealth and neither has our community."

When it was Sawant's turn to speak before the final vote, she, as with the public speakers, credited the grassroots movement. "Today's vote to pass an Amazon tax in Seattle is a historic victory for working people," she began. "This victory was hard fought and it was hard won by a movement that wouldn't give up and that faced down a seemingly endless series of obstacles, from the shameful attempts of corporate Democrats in the state Legislature to pass a ban on municipal big business taxes, to unfounded delays in the City Council to a pandemic and lockdown, which prevented signature-gathering, to relentless attacks in the corporate media in Seattle and nationally.

"We are winning because of the determination of workers and socialists to smash all obstacles and to find a path to victory," she said. After diplomatically giving nods of appreciation to Councilmembers Morales and Mosqueda, Sawant returned to address the broader audience. "For those watching from outside Seattle, don't let anyone tell you in your fight to tax big business in your city, that you are being divisive, because class struggle is what gets the goods," she said. "The private-for-profit housing market has utterly failed working people, not just here and now but everywhere and always, because capitalism is completely incapable of meeting the most basic needs of working people.

"Internationally the working class needs to take the top 500 corporations into democratic public ownership run by workers in the interest of human need and the environment, not billionaire greed," Sawant declared. "I have a message for Jeff Bezos and his class: If you attempt again to overturn the Amazon tax, working people will go all out in the thousands to defeat you. And we will not stop there because you see, we are fighting for far more than this tax, we are preparing the ground for a different kind of society."

This was more than a legislative speech. Sawant was coalescing 175 years of socialist struggle, gathering up the soaring declarations of the Communist Manifesto, the spirited energy of the Paris Commune barricades, the seering indictments hurled by Alexei Badayev from the Duma rostrum, and the analytical precision of Leon Trotsky's Transitional Program.

She continued: "And if you, Jeff Bezos, want to drive that process forward by lashing out against us in our modest demands, then so be it. Because we are coming for you and your rotten system. We are coming to dismantle this deeply oppressive, racist, sexist, violent, utterly bankrupt system of capitalism, this police state. We cannot and will not stop until we overthrow it and replace it with a world based instead on solidarity, genuine democracy, and equality—a socialist world."

Sawant's speech was both triumphant and a reminder to activists that the goal could not simply be incremental gains, life-changing as they might be, but societal transformation. Trotsky had called for Marxists to establish "the bridge between present demands and the socialist program of the revolution." Without transitional demands, he observed in 1938, movements stop challenging the underlying problem of capitalism and degenerate into minor players within the bourgeois systems, acting as a brake on revolutionary progress. Sawant recognized that if activists satisfied themselves with celebrating the Amazon tax they risked heading down the reformist path. It was essential to remind people in this moment of victory that the goal was much more.

The clerk called the roll, and each councilmember recorded their vote: 7 to 2 in favor. And just like that, the Amazon tax passed. It was a stunning development. The fight had come full circle. Just 25 months earlier, the movement had been badly beaten, a modest $47 million tax repealed, politically buried. Now we had just won a tax on Amazon 4 ½ times that size. We had won dedicated funding for the Black community. We had won money for Green New Deal projects. We had come back from bitter, ugly defeat, won reelection against all odds, built a democratic grassroots movement, stopped multiple attempts to block or ban the Amazon tax, and prevailed.

A Marxist-led movement of low-wage workers, students, Black Lives Matter activists, people living on the streets, socialists, disgruntled Democrats, retirees, union members, Black and Brown community members, clergy, and queer activists had put their collective shoulders to the wheel and had beaten the richest, most powerful symbol of capitalism in the world. No, we had not overthrown capitalism. But we had struck a blow for the working class in a power center of global capital, under an unapologetically socialist banner and against all odds.

And we had done it by hewing to the three pillars of political insurgency: a class struggle approach, bold demands, and movement democracy. Tax Amazon was a striking—and for the US, unique—archetype of Marxist struggle, drawing on the lessons of 175 years of socialist theory and practice.

And yet in the strange pandemic world of 2020, victory seemed surreal. This was not David slaying Goliath in the Valley of Elah as throngs of Israelites cheered on, ready to lift their hero up on their shoulders and lead a celebratory march, but a Zoom meeting flashed across thousands of computer screens in private homes. COVID assured us that there would be no victory parade, no high-fiving crowds, no round of toasts and speeches in a packed bar, no spontaneous street march. The council meeting adjourned; the Zoom room blinked closed. We turned off our screens, stepped out of makeshift COVID workspaces, stretched, sent texts, and made calls congratulating one another. We had made history.

7

Challenging the Guardians of the State

For a few convulsive weeks in the summer of 2020, America seemed poised to fundamentally transform the role of police. After Minneapolis police brutally murdered George Floyd on May 25, more than 20 million people around the country took to the streets. The Black Lives Matter (BLM) movement, constrained like other social movements during the initial weeks of pandemic lockdown, erupted in grief, anger, and determination. In Minneapolis, protests climaxed with the burning of a police precinct station, a bold action which one poll found a majority of Americans—some 54 percent—believed was justified.[143] Soon thereafter, Minneapolis politicians promised to dismantle their police

143 Impelli, M. (2020, June 3). 54 Percent of Americans Think Burning Down Minneapolis Police Precinct Was Justified After George Floyd's Death. Newsweek.com. Retrieved April 13, 2023, from https://www.newsweek.

department. Elsewhere, city leaders vowed fundamental change. From Seattle to Austin, Atlanta, Los Angeles, and New York, protesters demanded that cities slash their bloated police budgets and redistribute the money to social programs. The national movement coalesced around a bold demand: "Defund the Police!"

From the start, Sawant supported BLM's call to cut the Seattle Police budget in half. By early July, six of the eight other Seattle councilmembers joined her, with several profusely apologizing for their past failures to take seriously the epidemic of police violence in Black and Brown communities. A business-funded poll in the summer showed that most Seattleites supported defunding the police budget by 50 percent.[144] Just a month after Minneapolis police strangled the last breath out of George Floyd's body, Sawant and the Seattle BLM movement won a breakthrough law banning police chokeholds and the police use of pepper spray, tear gas, blast balls, rubber bullets, and other weapons of choice for "crowd control."

Soon, however, establishment leaders in Seattle and elsewhere regained their footing, exploiting divisions within the movement and playing a waiting game, anticipating—correctly—that over time the street marches would wane. In Seattle, Black Lives Matter protesters were sharply divided into three camps over goals and tactics. Some embraced Sawant's approach of

com/54-americans-think-burning-down-minneapolis-police-precinct-was-justified-after-george-floyds-1508452

144 Markovich, M. (2020, July 30). *Poll: More than half support defunding Seattle police but majority want chief to ID cuts*. KOMO TV. Retrieved April 13, 2023, from https://komonews.com/news/local/new-poll-says-more-than-50-percent-of-people-support-defunding-seattle-police-department

bringing forward grassroots demands that addressed the connection between police violence and the economic violence of the capitalist system. A second, reform-oriented group rejected Sawant's class struggle orientation and called for "Black capitalism" that raised identity politics over class considerations. They rebuffed any leadership that did not come out of the Black community and were eager to negotiate with the mayor and City Council Democrats. A third camp demanded an all-or-nothing approach toward defunding the police, rejecting a 50 percent budget cut as inadequate.

The local political establishment deftly exploited these divisions. They co-opted some leaders, isolated others, and marginalized street protests with more police violence. They appropriated the language of the protest movement while steering energy into symbolic performative activities. The mainstream media joined in the counterattack, calling police cuts rash and citing individual instances of crime to demand more police funding.

In August, less than two months after pledging to defund the police, the six City Council Democrats ignominiously backpedaled. Not a single councilmember seconded Sawant's fall budget proposal to redistribute half of the police's $409 million budget to Black and Brown community needs. A federal judge blocked Sawant's legislation banning the police use of chemical and other weapons. In 2021, the Democrats rescinded the weapons ban law, replacing it with a much weaker version shot through with loopholes. And in April 2021, the state Supreme Court, which had rejected a recall petition against Mayor Durkan for the indiscriminate police violence on her watch, authorized a corporate-instigated recall petition against Sawant. The recall charges against Sawant, ironically, included allegations that she had led illegal Black Lives Matter protests against the Durkan-ordered police violence.

The political turnaround was mirrored in other cities throughout the US. Minneapolis politicians walked back their promise to dismantle the police. In the lead-up to November, Democratic Party nominee Joe Biden derided BLM's defund demand and, once in office, cozied up to law enforcement.[145] In the fall of 2021, New York City voters elected a cop as their new mayor. He proceeded to cut social spending and hand millions more to the police department.

The national counterattack against the Justice for George Floyd movement served as an object lesson about what happens when a popular but unprepared movement runs headlong into state power. To be sure, in the latter half of 2020 BLM forced local governments to trim police budgets by about $875 million in aggregate, and they won $160 million in new community investments nationally. But that divestment represented only about 1 percent of annual US law enforcement spending.[146]

Within a year, police budgets in Seattle and elsewhere had resumed their upward trend. Meanwhile, police killings—disproportionately

---

145 Panetta, G. (2020, December 10). *Biden tells civil rights leaders that Republicans weaponized the 'defund the police' slogan to 'beat the hell' out of Democrats*. Business Insider. Retrieved April 26, 2023, from https://www.businessinsider.com/biden-told-civil-rights-leaders-avoid-defund-the-police-slogan-2020-12

146 Interrupting Criminalization (2021). *The demand is still #DefundThePolice*. Retrieved April 12, 2023, from https://www.interruptingcriminalization.com/defundpolice-update

of Black men—hit a new peak two years in a row[147] and mainstream media was awash with calls for "law and order" and sordid tales of drug-addicted homeless people. The drive to change policing, which had begun with such energy and broad appeal, was labeled dangerously naïve. The ferocious counterattack left many activists stunned and disillusioned. Too few of them recognized that in calling for defunding the police they were, in the eyes of political and business elites, declaring war on state power—a political war the movement was not ready to fight.[148]

That bitter conclusion was not what the Black Lives Matter movement anticipated in the days after Floyd's May 25 murder. Millions of people flooded into the streets in cities around the world. Collectively, the US protests constituted the largest mass mobilization in the country's history.

"We're tired of unlawful law enforcement," Rev. Dr. Leslie Braxton told a downtown Seattle crowd. "We're tired of a criminally unjust justice system. We're tired of police terrorism. We're tired

147 (2023, April 5). 1,080 people have been shot and killed by police in the past 12 months. The Washington Post. Retrieved April 5, 2023, from https://www.washingtonpost.com/graphics/investigations/police-shootings-database/

148 The recitation that follows focuses on how and why the street movement ran headlong into insurmountable barriers in the political arena, and the lessons that activists can glean from that experience. It does not attempt to capture the full range of anguish and frustration that boiled up from Black communities, the long history of anti-Black policing, the police abolition movement, and the full spectrum of experiences in the Justice for George Floyd street protests. Those stories, also vital, have been and remain best told by activists from within those movements and communities.

of blackness being a crime."[149] In the first 10 days of mass protests, it seemed everybody was joining in: 20,000 people, including many young children, marched through working class south Seattle. Healthcare workers led a downtown march of 10,000 people. Middle- and high-school students walked out of classes. Neighbors stood on street corners holding signs, ignoring Mayor Durkan's curfew orders. A huge silent weekend march wound through the city, estimated at 60,000. Led by young activists, thousands of protesters descended on City Hall and occupied the plaza outside the building until Mayor Durkan agreed to come out so they could directly deliver their three core demands: Defund the Seattle Police Department by 50 percent, use the money to fund community-based health and safety programs, and release all arrested protesters without charge.[150] These mass protests enveloped a wide range of people, from seasoned protesters to first-time marchers. But despite the enormous energy behind the slogan, "Black Lives Matter," it was unclear whether this movement—which had erupted so suddenly—would have the fortitude to follow through on its central demands. Taking the streets was one matter; actually wresting power from the political establishment was quite another.

The street movement gradually coalesced on Capitol Hill, adjacent to the Police Department's East Precinct building. This was

---

149 (2020, May 30). *Protests, then pandemonium: Seattle takes to the streets over death of George Floyd*. The Seattle Times. Retrieved April 5, 2023, from https://www.seattletimes.com/seattle-news/sadness-fury-violence-in-seattle-over-death-of-george-floyd-durkan-calls-for-curfew-national-guard/

150 [Facebook]. (2020, June 3). *No New Youth Jail* [Video]. Retrieved April 5, 2023, https://www.facebook.com/NoNewYouthJailSeattle/videos/533902837279250/

the heart of Sawant's district, the center of Seattle's LGBTQ community and a rapidly gentrifying area. Sawant participated actively in the street demonstrations, standing at the nighttime barricades with hundreds of other protesters and facing off against the brutal police reaction. Activists arranged barricades in the block around the East Precinct building and set up an outdoor community festival, with free food and music, dancing, speechifying, film screenings, and arts projects. They brought out couches and chairs for impromptu political salons. Some pitched tents to sleep in. Across the street, Cal Anderson Park became a scene of pick-up frisbee games and rallies. The area soon acquired the moniker "CHOP"—the Capitol Hill Occupied Protest.

Rather than stand down and let the gathering proceed, Seattle police, augmented by the Washington State Patrol, the National Guard, and other local police forces, chose to confront protesters, especially once the sun went down. They pushed demonstrators with their bikes, surrounded and cornered marchers, and attacked them with pepper spray and flash-bang grenades. Police injured hundreds, macing protesters and shooting them with blast balls while small groups of looters were left virtually unbothered by police. Unprovoked, an officer maced a nine-year-old Black boy standing and praying with his family and fellow church members. Another protester recorded the attack and posted the video online. Police tracked down the videographer and threw him in jail for two days.[151] Police shot a demonstrator

151 Golden, H. (2020, June 15). Outrage at video showing child who was maced by police at Seattle protest. The Guardian. Retrieved April 28, 2023, from https://www.theguardian.com/us-news/2020/jun/15/outrage-video-police-mace-child-seattle-protest

with a blast ball in the chest, stopping her heart; volunteer medics revived her.[152]

With the backing of Mayor Durkan, Seattle police unleashed torrents of pepper spray and tear gas—a chemical weapon banned in warfare by the Geneva Convention[153]— in residential neighborhoods. The assaults injured hundreds of street protesters, along with sidewalk bystanders and tenants sheltering in nearby apartment buildings who couldn't escape the clouds of chemical toxins.[154]

Taking a cue from the Hong Kong democracy movement, Seattle protesters brought umbrellas to defend against the chemical weapons; police ripped them away and shot streams of mace in their faces. "Don't kill them, but hit them hard," a state patrol officer was overheard instructing his troops.[155] Cops hunted down and assaulted community members whom they suspected were responsible for the protests. They kidnapped one woman out

---

152 Jones, L., & Raftery, I. (2020, June 10). This woman 'died three times' after Seattle Police hit her with a blast ball. KUOW. Retrieved April 28, 2023, from https://kuow.org/stories/this-26-year-old-died-three-times-after-police-hit-her-with-a-blast-ball

153 Sadeghi, M. (2020, June 6). *Fact check: It's true tear gas is a chemical weapon banned in war*. USA Today. Retrieved April 28, 2023, from https://www.usatoday.com/story/news/factcheck/2020/06/06/fact-check-its-true-tear-gas-chemical-weapon-banned-war/3156448001/

154 Graham, N. (2020, June 4). *Seattle Residents Got Tear Gassed in Their Own Apartments*. The Stranger. Retrieved April 28, 2023, from https://www.thestranger.com/slog/2020/06/04/43840246/seattle-residents-got-tear-gassed-in-their-own-apartments

155 Marx, K. (2020, June 2). Twitter. Retrieved April 7, 2023, from https://twitter.com/KrystalSMarx/status/1268009974170451968

of her car. They knocked protesters to the ground and punched and kicked them. They pepper-sprayed a mother and her child who were sitting in their parked car. Members of the public overwhelmed city investigators with more than 19,000 complaints of police misconduct during the course of Seattle's Justice for George Floyd protests.[156]

To instill fear and division in the movement, police faked radio reports of armed right-wing Proud Boys coming to confront the Black Lives Matter protesters.[157] Police Chief Carmen Best and deputies went on the airwaves to claim—falsely—that armed activists were extorting small businesses around CHOP.[158] In a dramatic, made-for-right-wing TV display, police abandoned the East Precinct building, bizarrely claiming that they had received threats that the building—a sturdy brick-and-concrete monolith—was about to be firebombed.[159]

---

156 Myerberg, A. (2021, April). *2020 Annual Report*. Seattle Office of Police Accountability. Retrieved April 20, 2023, from https://www.seattle.gov/Documents/Departments/OPA/Reports/2020-Annual-Report.pdf

157 (2022, January 5). *Seattle police faked Proud Boys threat during race protests, says watchdog*. The Guardian. Retrieved April 20, 2023, from https://www.theguardian.com/us-news/2022/jan/05/seattle-police-fake-radio-chatter-proud-boys-2020 and [You Tube]. (2022, January 5). *SPD Proud Boy Hoax Case* [Video]. Converge Media. https://www.youtube.com/watch?v=UEl1U7F2xHo

158 Baume, M. (2021, January 7). *SPD Finally Confirms: They Have No Reports of Extortion in the CHOP*. The Stranger. Retrieved April 20, 2023, from https://www.thestranger.com/slog/2021/01/07/54565189/spd-finally-confirms-they-have-no-reports-of-extortion-in-the-chop

159 (2020, November 18). *Who ordered the abandonment of the East Precinct?—UPDATE*. Capitol Hill Seattle Blog. Retrieved April 20, 2023, from https://

The movement responded energetically to the police violence. Pressed by scenes of thousands of protesters marching daily and nightly in the streets, dozens of political establishment and mainstream community leaders—many of whom themselves had directly witnessed or endured the police violence—called on the mayor to resign or be impeached. Activists started a petition to recall "Teargas Jenny," gaining thousands of signatures in short order. The grocery workers union, the largest private sector union in the state, called on Durkan to resign. Even local Democratic Party bodies, the mayor's traditional political base, demanded her resignation. "You can only pepper spray so many community members before even the non-radical members of your community are fed up," Devin Glaser, a local Democratic activist, observed.[160]

Sawant joined the call for Durkan's resignation. "It has been tragically ironic that this growing movement against police violence and brutality has been consistently met with more violence and brutality," she noted. "The responsibility for this vicious targeting of these overwhelmingly peaceful protests in Seattle lies with Mayor Jenny Durkan."

On June 8, following yet another night of police violence in which Sawant and hundreds of peaceful protesters were pummeled by police tear gas and pepper spray, the socialist announced she would introduce legislation to ban all police use of chemical

www.capitolhillseattle.com/2020/11/who-ordered-the-abandonment-of-the-east-precinct/

160 Graham, N. (2020, June 16). *More Seattle Democrats Call for the Mayor's Resignation*. The Stranger. Retrieved April 5, 2023, from https://www.thestranger.com/slog/2020/07/16/44102369/more-seattle-democrats-call-for-the-mayors-resignation

weapons and chokeholds, and to put the police under the control of an elected community board. In addition, Sawant's staff began drafting budget legislation to redirect police funds to community needs, using a list of priorities that Black community leaders had assembled: Restorative justice, recreation and other community programs, COVID relief, and affordable housing and small business development.

Sawant's legislation targeted the Seattle Police Department's bloated $409 million annual budget, which ate up 27 percent of the City's entire discretionary spending. It was more than what the City spent combined on eldercare, homeless and other human services, affordable housing, and neighborhoods, arts, and culture programming.[161] Fully 119 of the top 200 city salaries went to police officers, sergeants, and lieutenants who were paid an average of $268,000 in 2019. Chief Best and eight of her deputies each were paid more than all 50 US governors.[162]

Sawant linked the fight to rein in this shocking police spending with her demand to pass the Amazon tax, which was nearing its historic vote in the council. "Alongside these demands," she told hundreds of ralliers at Cal Anderson park, "we also have to fight to tax Amazon and other profiteering big businesses. Our city is not only reeling from the COVID crisis and joblessness, it was already reeling from the housing affordability crisis. We need a massive

---

161 (2020). *Summary charts and tables, City of Seattle - 2020 adopted budget*. City of Seattle. Retrieved April 11, 2023, from https://www.seattle.gov/Documents/Departments/FinanceDepartment/20adoptedbudget/Charts_and_Tables.pdf

162 (n.d.). Open the Books. Retrieved August 9, 2020, from https://www.openthebooks.com/members/employer-detail/?Id=3227&tab=1

expansion of social housing to begin to strike a blow against racist gentrification."

From the park, Sawant led 500 marchers through the streets of Capitol Hill, headed to City Hall downtown, where she planned a public speak-out inside the building's cavernous atrium. The decision to go inside City Hall was not made lightly. While the building technically was closed due to the pandemic, it was not empty; council members and staff had occasionally been working and holding meetings inside the building since the start of COVID, and as an elected official Sawant had every right to invite people into City Hall, whether for a meeting or a political rally. By bringing the marchers inside City Hall, we were taking the fight directly into the place of municipal political power. And, with night falling, a mass meeting inside City Hall hosted by an elected official was a haven from another wave of nighttime police violence. I went ahead of the rally with other council office staff to prop the doors open when everyone arrived.

Chanting, "Whose streets? Our streets!" the protesters marched downtown and once inside City Hall switched to chants for the mayor's impeachment, "Black Lives Matter!" and "Say his name: George Floyd!" The crowd filled the huge atrium on the main level, a wide-open stairway, and a surrounding second floor balcony, their voices reverberating off the walls. Organizers distributed masks.[163]

---

163 This and following quotations from: [Facebook]. (2020, June 8). Councilmember Kshama Sawant Facebook Page. https://fb.watch/jTZlu_3bWN/ and Turnbull, E. (2020, June 10). *Sawant and Protesters Take Over City Hall Tuesday Night, Demand Amazon Tax*. South Seattle Emerald. Retrieved April 13, 2023, from https://southseattleemerald.

"We want to have a general assembly," announced Emily McArthur, a Socialist Alternative organizer, from a microphone. "We want to have a conversation about what is next for our movement, because it's not just for the mayor to make decisions in this building. It's not just for the Democratic Party establishment to vote Yes on a racist police contract. It's for us to come here and decide how we want our city to be run."

Sawant urged the crowd to sign up for public comment at upcoming City Council meetings where her proposals to ban police chokeholds and chemical weapons, along with the Tax Amazon legislation and police defunding bill, would be coming up. "As inspiring as this moment is—and we need inspiration to be coursing through our veins because how else will we build this long and hard fight—we need to be sober," said told the crowd. "We are not going to win any of our demands unless we have a way to win them. And winning those demands needs clarity about who's on our side and who's not. And I think this is what this multiracial movement is beginning to show."

The speakers that followed were stoked. Many had never been inside City Hall, and if they had been, it certainly wasn't to join a popular assembly like this. The speakers were freewheeling, asking for volunteers for mutual aid and logistics support, telling tales of run-ins with cops, and leading raucous songs.

Their speeches also revealed the fault lines already showing up in the movement. "Please stop using Black Lives Matter for your political campaigns," said Moe'Neyah Dene Holland, a young

com/2020/06/10/sawant-and-protesters-take-over-city-hall-tuesday-night-demand-amazon-tax/

Black woman. "I'm really sorry, I want to tax Amazon, too. But this is not a movement for you to be politically active. . . . Please stop taking advantage of us." Many in the crowd applauded. In the preceding days, there had been rumblings among some activists that the Tax Amazon demand didn't belong in the protests because it didn't directly address police violence. Some asserted that it "didn't come out of the community." Never mind that Tax Amazon emerged from grassroots public assemblies involving hundreds of community members, committed to combat racist gentrification. Indeed, outside City Hall, clergy and other Black community members were publicly drawing the connection between the protests and Tax Amazon, rallying behind Sawant's call to dedicate a portion of the corporate tax receipts to affordable housing in the city's Central District.

A few minutes later, Tealshawn Turner, another young Black woman, took the mic. "Listen, I'm going to explain something to you guys real quick," she said. "We're all in here trying to figure out, what does Amazon have to do with Black Lives Matter? But let me tell you something: The Central District of Seattle was a predominantly Black neighborhood that was gentrified by Amazon." More applause. "People have the right to feel how they feel," she continued. "That's not my job to take that away from them, but I can educate people. . . . I don't see any Black people in the Central District anymore."

After more than an hour of speeches and chanting, the crowd chanted "We'll be back!" as they headed for the doors. A crew stayed behind to clean up. The occupation of City Hall had been a powerful demonstration of movement resolve, but it also had illustrated the internal challenges facing the movement.

Establishment media outlets were happy to amplify the fractures in the movement, especially when they impugned Sawant's leadership. "New accusations tonight that a Seattle city councilmember co-opted the BLM message for her own political purposes," proclaimed a TV reporter after the City Hall occupation. The reporter interviewed Harriett Walden, a longtime community leader and a member of the Community Police Commission (CPC), a city-appointed advisory board. Even though Walden hadn't been at City Hall, she held strong opinions about the occupation. "I didn't see any reference to Mr. Floyd last night. I saw reference to an agenda," Walden said. "We've been here 400 years. We don't need anybody to lead for us," she said, pointedly aiming at Sawant. "We need people to get out of the way so we can lead."[164]

Those fractures also were evident the previous evening, when Sawant joined the roiling energy at CHOP. Hundreds of people were gathered on the street outside the police precinct. A mic was passed around, and over the whine of the generator, Sawant engaged in an hour of give-and-take with activists. Many didn't know the socialist and didn't seem to differentiate her from establishment political figures. "What have you done for us?" asked one. "What are your demands?" Several demanded answers and promises from the politician; Sawant wanted to talk as an organizer about power. Others echoed Walden's dismissal of Sawant because she was not from the Black community; Sawant wanted

164 Markovich, M. (2020, July 30). *VIDEO: Sawant accused of putting city workers in danger during protest inside city hall*. You Tube. Retrieved April 13, 2023, from https://www.youtube.com/watch?v=Gz5nmMRHoq8

to challenge identity politics and reorient the conversation along class lines.[165]

"If we want to win anything that gives us substantial gains for our Black and Brown communities and for the working class as a whole," she said, "like defunding the police by 50 percent and investing in restorative justice—that is a substantial demand, right?—to be honest, to win we need to build an even more powerful movement than we have today," she said.

"I want to give you an example of why it will take a serious fight," she continued. "Two years ago, there was a police contract up for a vote. It was a bad contract, it was a racist contract, it was going to roll back the limited accountability measures that were hard fought for by community members. And the community spoke with one voice and pleaded, pleaded with Mayor Durkan and the Council, please vote 'no.' What do you think happened?" she asked.

"The city council at that time was majority people of color like me, and yet I was the only 'no' vote on that contract. We have to remember, what built the movement is not the people who are in power who look like you or me, but people who have shown through their actions that they are in solidarity with ordinary people and marginalized communities."

Several activists questioned the demand to defund the police by 50 percent. "We're not talking about 50 percent—we don't want them at all!" one argued.

---

165 This and following quotations from: [Facebook]. (2020, June 8). Omari Salisbury Facebook Page. Retrieved April 13, 2023, https://www.facebook.com/omarisal/videos/10220093426018456

Police abolition is not so straightforward, Sawant retorted. "Malcolm X said, 'you can't have capitalism without racism,'" Sawant said. "Capitalism has in its DNA oppression because capitalism's purpose is to have a divided society, where a sliver at the top can benefit hand over fist, generation after generation, at the expense of the rest of society. But in order to keep the rest of society from rebelling every day, it is necessary for the capitalist class to keep all of us at the bottom divided. And that is why you can never have zero police and elimination of racism and oppression on the basis of capitalism.

"You may agree or you may disagree with what I'm saying, but you're not going to get bullshit from me. I am not going to make false promises," she said. "I am not one of those politicians who will tell you that we can dismantle the police on the basis of capitalism. Any politician, whether in Minneapolis or in Seattle, who is telling you that the police force can be dismantled under capitalism is bullshitting you. The only way we can have a society free from oppression is if we fight against capitalism itself and fight for global socialism.

"And another item of no bullshit," she continued. "Winning 50 percent defund is going to be goddamn hard because overcoming the opposition of the establishment is going to be hard. You need a fighting movement to win it. Do you know why? Because it's not just the politicians. The politicians are cogs in the machine. They serve the multimillionaires and the billionaires, who are never going to agree to a society free of policing because they need the police to keep us repressed."

Sawant garnered applause, but it was not clear how much the socialist had swayed the crowd. Many of these late-night CHOP diehards had been drawn to the occupation by compelling slogans and the powerful vision of a section of the city liberated from state control. But now having taken control of the six-block zone, and having experienced the euphoria of that triumph, at least some of them were visibly impatient with Sawant saying how hard going up against state power was going to be. They wanted police abolition, nothing less. It felt similar to our debates with activists six years earlier who argued that anything less than $15/hour, immediately and without exception, was a sellout. Assessing the balance of forces in the fight and developing a battle plan around intermediate goals was far beyond the scope of this late-night political salon.

Close to midnight, Sawant was able to peel away from the street debate and head home. Journalist Omari Salisbury had been livestreaming the animated discussion for Converge Media, and he caught up with Sawant as she headed out of CHOP. "Kshama, a few things quickly, you tried to get your demands out. It's kind of—I wouldn't say volatile—but it's an up and down situation over here," he observed.

"Yeah," Sawant acknowledged. "First of all, just to give some context, if people have been watching this on the livestream, people shouldn't be fazed by a little bit of disagreement or a little bit of tension. This is part and parcel of building movements, and it's actually quite energizing that people are speaking their mind. We're never going to build a movement if we operate in an echo chamber, you know. If people already agree with you, that means that you're not building the movement wide enough. And in fact, most of my job as a socialist activist and organizer is talking to people who don't already agree with me, because I'm trying to win people over to what I believe is the most honest approach to winning a better society."

Away from the street debates, the movement was pressing hard on multiple fronts. On June 15, 116 people—about five times the usual number—signed up to give public comment at City Council meeting, with most of them blasting the police and mayor and demanding that the council adopt Sawant's bills outlawing police chokeholds and banning chemical and projectile weapons. The council passed both bills by 9 to 0 votes.

"Today, Seattle becomes the first US city to take these violent weapons out of the hands of police," Sawant said after the vote. "But let's be clear: Our victory today was not a result of enlightenment by the political establishment, but because of the thousands of ordinary people—led by young people, especially young people of color—who have marched in the streets . . . organized, spoken up at City Council meetings, and fought for systemic change.

"Our mass protest movement deserves all the credit for winning Seattle's historic ban on chemical weapons and chokeholds. If in the last few weeks you marched, rallied, organized, testified, or otherwise fought for Black Lives Matter and against police violence, then today's victory is your victory."

The street movement scored another victory two days later when, in a dramatic roll call vote, the Martin Luther King County Labor Council took the extraordinary step of expelling the Seattle Police Officers Guild (SPOG). The guild was fast becoming a reactionary force in the city. Earlier in 2020, officers had elected Mike Solan, a SWAT team member, as their new SPOG president. Solan defended police killings and was a frequent guest on right-wing media. In a dramatic campaign video for his guild election, Solan called on officers to "fight for your rights" and pledged to challenge "the anti-police activist agenda that is driving Seattle's politics." With video scenes of police pepper-spraying and assaulting protesters and with dramatic music playing in the background, Solan urged fellow officers to vote for him so he could "fundamentally change the activist narrative that negatively impacts our profession not only locally, but nationally."[166] Solan beat the incumbent president with 70 percent of the vote.[167] The first weeks of brutal police reaction in the wake of George Floyd's murder showed that Solan's colleagues were embracing his call to arms.

SPOG's truculence and the police violence provoked heated debate within the labor council. More conservative leaders, centered in the building trades unions, opposed expelling SPOG. But street protesters, many of whom were delegates to the labor council's monthly meetings, mobilized unions to kick SPOG out of the house of labor, by a 55 to 45 percent margin.

"Speaking as a Black woman and a mother of two young Black men, a labor leader, I know full well the obstacles that stand in the way of people who look like me," nurse and healthcare union

---

166 [You Tube]. (2019, November 6). *Mike Solan for SPOG president* [Video]. Wayback Machine. http://web.archive.org/web/20200307035619/https://www.youtube.com/watch?v=b6cJQ1XBH8M

167 Miletich, S., & Beekman, D. (2020, February 4). *Seattle police union elects hard-line candidate as president in landslide vote*. The Seattle Times. Retrieved April 25, 2023, from https://www.seattletimes.com/seattle-news/seattle-police-union-elects-hard-line-candidate-as-president-in-landslide-vote/

leader Jane Hopkins said at the meeting. When confronted earlier in the protests by labor council representatives, SPOG "didn't take our concerns seriously," she said, adding, "at this point, I just can't justify to our members, ones who are staffing the medical tents and getting gassed by SPD, having SPOG at the table."[168]

CHOP protest crowds shrank over time while other major rallies boomed through the city. Black-led organizations put together rallies and cultural events to celebrate Juneteenth. Community members, led by the families of people killed by police, organized a march through Mayor Durkan's tony neighborhood in late June. As a former US attorney who had been subject to personal threats, Durkan had received state approval to keep her address out of public records. Activists found the information anyway and led the march to her house. Sawant was a late invitee to the event, and she spoke among others from a makeshift stage with multi-million-dollar mansions in the background.

On July 1, Mayor Durkan ordered police to evict the remaining protesters from CHOP and return officers to the East Precinct. The scene at CHOP had devolved at night from a safe protest and organizing zone to a chaotic blend of parties and conflict. There were three shooting incidents in and around CHOP, driving most people away. Reasserting their dominance, police used pepper spray and rubber bullets—ignoring the new law banning these weapons—to complete the task. They arrested 44 people.

---

168 Takahama, E. (2020, June 17). *Seattle Police Officers Guild expelled from King County's largest labor council*. The Seattle Times. Retrieved April 13, 2023, from https://www.seattletimes.com/seattle-news/seattle-police-officers-guild-expelled-from-countys-largest-labor-council/

Back in City Hall, the council adopted the historic Amazon tax that Sawant and the movement had championed. The final measure included Sawant's amendment to dedicate at least $18 million a year to affordable housing in the Central District to combat racist gentrification. This was the third political win for the Black Lives Matter movement, following the police weapons ban and the chokehold ban.

With growing community pressure, by mid-July seven of the nine councilmembers—Sawant plus six Democrats—had publicly committed to the Black Lives Matter movement that they would support defunding the police by 50 percent. The Democrats seemed eager to outdo one another in their lofty pledges to the community.

"Now is the time to divest from the police department," declared Council President M. Lorena González. "Now is the time to zero out these budgets, and to reimagine, rebuild, build something from a community-led and community-driven perspective. . . . The status quo is no longer acceptable."[169]

"It is the institution of policing itself that must be dismantled," declared Councilmember Teresa Mosqueda. "Now is not the time for business as usual. . . . what we need is real change, radical change."[170]

---

169 [Decriminalize Seattle]. (2020, July 9). Facebook. Retrieved April 13, 2023, https://fb.watch/jUAveqqb8f/

170 Ibid.

"Don't let up on us, as your elected officials," tweeted Councilmember Dan Strauss, in committing to the defund pledge. "These are just words until actions are taken."[171]

"Shifting significant resources from SPD back to community is fundamental to achieving these goals," said Councilmember Tammy Morales. "That's how we'll build community wealth, health, and safety. We owe it to the Black and Indigenous community. We owe them about 500 years' worth of investment, actually."[172]

Movement activists took to social media to declare triumphantly that they now had a veto-proof majority of the City Council committed to defund the police. They pointed approvingly at a business-commissioned poll that showed a majority of Seattleites wanted to see the police budget cut in half. Some exulted that the defund victory was all but assured.

Not so quick, Sawant cautioned. A month earlier, during the first days of mass protest, Sawant had committed to advance the street movement's demand for a 50 percent police budget cut. Since then, she had warned activists repeatedly not to trust the Democrats. The quick retreat of Minneapolis city councilmembers from their June pledge to dismantle the police department could happen just as easily in Seattle.

Indeed, in the latter half of 2020, that is exactly what played out in Seattle: The political establishment's complete abandonment

171 (2020, July 9). Councilmember Dan Strauss Twitter Account. Retrieved April 13, 2023, from https://twitter.com/CMDanStrauss/status/1281303938608910337

172 [Decriminalize Seattle]. (2020, July 9). Facebook. Retrieved April 13, 2023, https://fb.watch/jUAveqqb8f/

of their public pledges to Black Lives Matter activists. Major warning signs came in August, when the Seattle City Council took up legislation addressing mid-year budget adjustments. The COVID shutdowns had wreaked havoc with City revenues. Mayor Durkan proposed further cuts to social programs. Sawant put forward amendments to cut $85 million from the police budget and redirect funds toward affordable housing, services in Black and Brown working-class communities, renter organizing and eviction defense, youth programming, and alternatives to repressive policing.

Only one of the eight Democrats supported her motion. Instead, they shaved $3.5 million from the remaining 2020 police budget—a cut of just 2 percent—and they punted the full defund issue, claiming they still supported the demand but could not implement it until the following year.

Among the trims that the council approved was a proposal from Sawant to reduce slightly the salaries of the top 13 police department executives, including the pay of Chief Best. Sawant had discovered that they were actually paid above the maximum limit of their city-assigned pay grade, in apparent violation of the City's own policies. Each were paid on average more than $230,000 a year, while Chief Best was paid $294,000, fully 45 percent above the national average for big-city police chiefs.[173] The Democrats agreed to make slight changes to executive pay for the remain-

173 Jeffrey, J. (2018, November 21). *Public Paychecks: America's police and fire chiefs have big jobs, and big salaries to boot. Here's the breakdown.* The Business Journals. Retrieved April 20, 2023, from https://www.bizjournals.com/bizjournals/news/2018/11/21/public-paychecks-americas-police-and-fire-chiefs.html and (2020, August 1). *Bloated SPD executive pay: It's worse than you think.* Councilmember Kshama Sawant. Retrieved April 20,

der of 2020, in Chief Best's case reducing her annual salary to $275,000. It was a pittance compared to the cuts endured by other City departments.

The day after City Council adopted the revised budget, Best, the city's first Black woman police chief, abruptly quit. She had been at the helm of a police department that had just assaulted and injured hundreds of peaceful protesters; was under years of federal oversight because of its track record of systemic racism and violence; whose officers, during Best's two-and-a-half-year stint as chief, had killed seven men, disproportionately Black and Brown; and now faced multiple lawsuits for police misconduct as a result of their violence during the Black Lives Matter protests. Even by the milquetoast metrics of the political establishment, Best's reign had been a disaster for meaningful police reform and for combatting the department's systemic racism; her track record ought to have merited dismissal.

But that's not why she resigned. Best said she was quitting in protest. The City Council's two percent budget reduction, including the executive salary tweaks, showed an "overarching lack of respect for the officers," Best complained, even though other city departments were facing even harsher austerity. "Targeting my command staff and their pay, it just felt very vindictive and very punitive, and I don't want them to be affected by that type of animus," she said, failing to explain how, if that was true, her departure would protect them from that animus.[174] She could not, she said,

2023, from https://sawant.seattle.gov/wp-content/uploads/2020/08/bloated-SPD-executive-pay.pdf

174 Ortiz, J. L., & Yancey-Bragg, N. (2020, August 11). *Seattle police chief blames City Council as she steps down after vote to cut $4 million in budget, 100*

bear to oversee department layoffs, even the minimal ones that the revised budget made likely. Best claimed the council's action would force her to fire newly hired officers of color because she was required to fire cops in order of seniority. This was patently untrue, as civil service rules allowed the chief to request exceptions to senior layoff order.

But the bald-faced assertion implying that the City Council was racist made for powerful media sound bites. "Seattle police chief quits after city council votes to strip funds," the BBC blared in an overwrought headline.[175] An area Chamber of Commerce statement read, "The Seattle City Council chose divisive rhetoric over responsible governance and it cost our city a respected leader." Even President Trump jumped into the fray, declaring that "Seattle has made a tragic mistake." Mayor Durkan told *The Stranger* that City Council "wanted to micromanage and play mini-police chief. Cut here and cut there, do this, do that. It showed a complete lack of respect and frankly a misunderstanding in how the department even operates."[176] Local right-wing talk radio host Jason Rantz picked up where Durkan left off. "Best is being driven out by councilmembers taking this city down a destructive path," he declared. "After the budget cuts, 100 officers will now lose their job, the

officers. USA Today. Retrieved April 20, 2023, from https://www.usatoday.com/story/news/nation/2020/08/11/seattle-police-chief-resign-following-nearly-4-million-budget-cuts/3342382001/

175 (2020, August 11). Seattle police chief quits after city council votes to strip funds. BBC. Retrieved April 20, 2023, from https://www.bbc.com/news/world-us-canada-53742006

176 Graham, N. (2020, August 11). Why Did SPD Chief Carmen Best Call It Quits? The Stranger. Retrieved April 20, 2023, from https://www.thestranger.com/slog/2020/08/11/44266867/why-did-spd-chief-carmen-best-call-it-quits

majority of them likely officers of color." Rantz posted a story on his station's website, featuring a picture of a pro-cop rally picket sign that read, "Carmen Best's life matters."[177]

Rantz's weaponization of identity politics was in line with the rest of the establishment's cynical counterattack to split the movement, and especially to split the Black community. "The vote yesterday was anti-Black," the CPC's Walden claimed. "I feel like it's a death," said Victoria Beach, chair of the police department's African American Community Advisory Council. "It's a huge loss, I think our community is in big trouble without her."[178]

Others tried valiantly to redirect to the systemic problem. "Best chose to be chief of an institution that has perpetuated racist policies and practices and perpetuated much harm on many communities," said Nikkita Oliver, a prominent young leader of the street protests. "Not to mention the violent policing of the recent protests. She could have chose to whistleblow but she protected the status quo," Oliver said.[179] "The task of rooting out anti-Black racism from the police department is too large for any one person," King County Equity Now, a coalition that emerged out of the BLM movement, said in a statement. "Black representation in lead-

177 Rantz, J. (2020, August 10). *Rantz: Carmen Best, Black female police chief, driven out by Seattle Council*. 770KTTH. Retrieved April 21, 2023, from https://mynorthwest.com/2084143/rantz-chief-carmen-best-resigns-seattle-council/

178 [King 5 TV]. (2020, August 11). *Community members react to abrupt resignation of Seattle Police Chief Carmen Best* [Video]. You Tube. Retrieved April 20, 2023, https://www.youtube.com/watch?v=zFSu0bLmyEo

179 (2020, August 11). Seattle and beyond react to Chief Best's retirement announcement. KIRO TV-My Northwest. Retrieved April 20, 2023, from https://mynorthwest.com/2085029/seattle-reactions-chief-best-retirement/

ership is critical and necessary, but only in-so-far as it works to upend the status quo and improve the health, safety, and equity of Black communities."[180]

But those community voices were drowned out by the right-wing caterwauling. By the end of the week, it would have been reasonable for casual observers to believe that, rather than abruptly quitting on her own volition, Best had been forcibly removed from office, a Joan of Arc martyred for challenging the rabid street mob. City Council Democrats were on the defensive, exclaiming they were surprised and sad to see her go. They lauded and whitewashed her troubled tenure. Some even expressed remorse at trimming her salary down to $275,000.

The council's failure to follow through on their defund promises, followed immediately by Best's resignation and the political establishment's bold offensive, drove a powerful wedge into the movement, accelerating the demobilization of Seattle's BLM movement.

Best exited the police department and promptly became a sought-after commentator on local and national TV stations, including Fox network, before landing a top executive position at Microsoft. But before leaving office, Best quietly took care to protect herself from future legal and political troubles. Beginning in June, the local Black Lives Matter chapter, many area businesses, and injured protesters each had sued the City for police abuse

---

180 Kroman, D., & Fowler, L. (2020, August 12). *Black Seattleites react to police chief's resignation with rage, hope*. Crosscut.com. Retrieved April 20, 2023, from https://crosscut.com/news/2020/08/black-seattleites-react-police-chiefs-resignation-rage-hope

and the City's handling of affairs around CHOP. As police chief responsible for directing her department, Best was a central figure in the lawsuits. Her recorded communications would be a central part of any court case. So she got rid of them. Best later admitted under oath that over the summer she had manually deleted text messages from her city phone. A forensic expert later determined more than 27,138 texts in all had been eliminated, wiping out vital evidence that plaintiffs could have used to demonstrate her role in directing the violence against the protesters.

Best wasn't the only city official to tamper with evidence. Mayor Durkan, her fire department chief, two of Best's top SPD executives, and two other top administration officials who had been deeply involved in the city's violent street response also destroyed evidence during the same period. Three of the executives said they had suddenly forgotten their numeric passcodes and had performed hard resets on their phones, wiping out all text messages. Two executives forgot their passcode numbers on consecutive days in October 2020, and the third forgot his two weeks later. For high-level public officials who surely had been briefed in their legal obligations, their mass text deletions—only discovered the following year by lawyers suing the city—were brazen violations of state public records law and court rules of evidence.[181] In many cases, they deleted messages after they had been explicitly directed by city lawyers not to.

181 Kamb, L. (2022, June 8). *Ex-Seattle police chief testifies that she deleted text messages in bulk*. Axois. Retrieved April 20, 2023, from https://www.axios.com/local/seattle/2022/06/08/ex-seattle-police-chief-deleted-text-messages

Durkan, a former federal prosecutor no doubt intimately knowledgeable about rules of evidence, offered various explanations for at least 5,937 missing messages from her city phone. She said she had dropped her phone in water, that she inadvertently changed the message deletion settings, and that an unnamed "someone" changed her deletion settings. A federal judge found that Durkan's "various reasons for deleting her text messages strain credibility." Durkan, Best, and the other officials had purged "thousands of CHOP-related text messages from their phones after they were under a clear legal obligation to preserve such information," the judge determined.[182]

Durkan's top aides tried to cover up the wide-ranging destruction of evidence. The mayor's general counsel, Michelle Chen, ordered city officials to conceal the fact that the texts were missing.[183] Two public records staff in the mayor's office refused to participate in the cover-up. They went to the media, were forced to resign, and sued the city.[184]

---

182 (2023, January 13). *Hunters Capital, LLC et al. V. City of Seattle*. United States District Court - Western District of Washington at Seattle. Retrieved April 20, 2023, from https://s3.documentcloud.org/documents/23579495/hunters-capitol-spoliation-order-1-13-23.pdf

183 Hiruko, A. (2021, May 10). *We asked for Mayor Jenny Durkan's text messages, and this is what we got*. KUOW. Retrieved April 27, 2023, from https://www.kuow.org/stories/we-asked-for-jenny-durkan-s-text-messages-and-this-is-what-they-gave-us

184 Trumm, D. (2021, September 4). *Durkan Text Scandal Whistleblowers Sue City for Retaliation*. The Urbanist. Retrieved April 28, 2023, from https://www.theurbanist.org/2021/09/04/durkan-text-scandal-whistleblowers-sue-city-for-retaliation/

The mind-boggling, shameless cover up proved costly, though not for Best, Durkan, and their confederates. The city—that is, Seattle taxpayers—had to fork over millions of dollars in forensic bills, legal settlements, and attorney fees in the ensuing years of litigation. Between lawsuits stemming from the police violence, the destroyed evidence, and the anti-whistleblower retaliation, the city paid out nearly $23 million settlements and legal fees in subsequent years.[185] The Seattle Ethics and Elections Commission found that Chen had violated state law; Chen protested, calling the investigation unfair and pointing fingers at other city attorneys. Durkan and Best skated free.

"There's been no accountability," one of the whistleblowers said when news of the retaliation settlement was announced. "These officials basically got away with it and the taxpayers are paying."[186]

Willful destruction of public records is a felony under state law, punishable by up to five years in prison. But as political elites, Durkan and Best had little to fear. Prosecutors were never going to go after Durkan and Best personally; after all, the mayor and police chief had performed a great service to the governing elites,

---

185 Carter, M. (2024, January 24). City of Seattle settles BLM protesters' lawsuit for $10 million. *The Seattle Times*. Retrieved January 25, 2024, https://www.seattletimes.com/seattle-news/law-justice/city-of-seattle-settles-blm-protesters-lawsuit-for-10-million/

186 Beekman, D. (2023, May 12). *Seattle to pay $2.3 million to employees who blew whistle on Durkan's deleted texts*. The Seattle Times. Retrieved May 12, 2023, from https://www.seattletimes.com/seattle-news/politics/seattle-to-pay-2-3-million-to-employees-who-blew-whistle-on-durkans-deleted-texts/

protecting the guardians of state power at the very moment when that authority was at greatest risk.

State power was advancing on other fronts as well, pushing back against the Black Lives Matter movement. Hand in hand with the Trump Justice Department, the Durkan administration secured a federal injunction to block Sawant's weapons ban legislation. With its longstanding history of using excessive force, especially in Black and Brown communities, Seattle was under Justice Department oversight—a "consent decree." US District Court Judge James L. Robart determined that denying police blast balls, pepper spray, tear gas, flash-bang grenades, and similar "less lethal" weapons would leave them only with their guns, which would therefore "create a risk that SPD officers will resort to excessive force," and, in so doing, violate the consent decree. It was pure pretzel logic: To mitigate the police's use of excessive force, the police must be given back the very weapons they had used to inflict excessive force on thousands of people in the preceding weeks.

Back in the real world, protesters were continuing to experience plenty of brutal, excessive force from police. In late July, police assaulted a peaceful group, the "Wall of Moms," who had locked arms in an attempt to separate police from demonstrators. It was a complete violation of a separate federal injunction barring police from attacking nonviolent protesters. Moms and others were knocked to the ground, bleeding, burned, and unable to see or breathe.[187] Black Lives Matter appealed to federal court for a con-

187 (2020, July 27). Motion for Order to Show Cause Why City of Seattle Should Not Be Held In Contempt for Violating the Preliminary Injunction. United

tempt of citation against the city, but to no avail. Later that summer, cops assaulted demonstrators outside the police guild's office, and then used pepper spray and blast balls to break up a memorial vigil for Summer Taylor, a BLM protester killed by a car in July.

The unremitting police violence was a powerful component of the state's broad counterattack. It deterred street participation and marginalized the remaining protesters. Tens of thousands of people from all walks of life, including people who didn't normally hoist picket signs and march in the streets, had eagerly joined Black Lives Matter demonstrations in the early, heady days of the uprising. But as TV and social media broadcast horrific images of demonstrators pushed to the ground by police, being choked and blinded by pepper spray, or limping away with deep abrasions and painful burns, protest numbers dropped precipitously. Why protest if there was such risk of getting hurt? Among the remaining protesters were a few individuals who were poorly disciplined or who likely were outright provocateurs. They turned peaceful demonstrations into chaotic scenes of clashes with police, further undermining the credibility of and support for Black Lives Matter. A single firecracker or water bottle tossed from the crowd would trigger overwhelming, indiscriminate salvos of toxic chemicals and blast balls from the police. No court order was going to stop this reaction. The police were determined to control the streets, with even more vigor than before their Minneapolis colleagues had choked the life out of George Floyd.

States District Court - Western District of Washington at Seattle. Retrieved April 22, 2023, from https://s3.documentcloud.org/documents/7008096/Motion-for-Contempt.pdf

The state's counteroffensive also took direct aim at Sawant. At the end of June, Mayor Durkan called on City Council Democrats to launch a formal investigation of the socialist. "Disagreements on policy contribute to a robust public debate," the mayor wrote. "However, policy disagreements do not justify a Councilmember who potentially uses their position in violation of law or who recklessly undermines the safety of others, all for political theatre." Durkan urged the full council to consider punishing and expelling Sawant "for disorderly or otherwise contemptuous behavior."

Durkan issued several charges in her demand, including that Sawant, in her official capacity as a councilmember, had illegally brought hundreds of Black Lives Matter demonstrators into City Hall for the June 9 rally and that she had led the June 28 march to Durkan's neighborhood and home "with reckless disregard of the safety of my family and children," knowing that the mayor's address was private under a state confidentiality program. Durkan also charged Sawant with illegally using council funds to promote a Tax Amazon ballot initiative earlier in the year.

In fact, there was nothing illegal about the June 9 political demonstration that Sawant led inside City Hall. The socialist had been a late invitee to the demonstration in the mayor's neighborhood, and of course did not know where the mayor lived. And the charge against her support of the Tax Amazon campaign was clear political retribution for her leadership in securing passage just weeks earlier of the big business tax.

Sawant's public retort was sharp. "Durkan's attack on my office is an attack on the grassroots campaigns we've participated in and helped lead alongside many others, and the progressive victories we have all won together. While her words are directed at me and my elected office, I don't take it personally," she said. Noting that more than 47,000 Seattle residents had already signed petitions calling for Durkan to resign or be impeached, she added that, "In reality, this is an attack on working people's movements, and everything we are fighting for, by a corporate politician desperately looking to distract from her failures of leadership and politically bankrupt administration."[188]

The City Council Democrats declined to take up Durkan's call to investigate Sawant. But the mayor's letter was only an opening volley in a battle that would come to dominate the city's politics for the next year and a half. Three weeks after Durkan's demand letter, anti-Sawant forces announced they were launching a recall campaign against her. The recall petition used Durkan's charges almost word-for-word. Sawant and Socialist Alternative now would have to fight the recall while at the same time waging legislative battles." Months of court hearings would precede any recall vote. City Hall went into the fall budget season with both Sawant and Durkan facing the prospect of recall campaigns, Sawant for her peaceful participation in Black Lives Matter protests, the mayor for her brutal repression of those protests.

In tandem with the stick—the unremitting police violence and the political attack on Sawant—Durkan and City Council Democrats also began to unveil carrots to the BLM movement. They invited in select community members to discuss housing, education,

188 (2020, June 30). *Mayor Durkan's attack on my office is an attack on working people's movements, and everything we are fighting for*. Councilmember Kshama Sawant. Retrieved April 23, 2023, from https://sawant.seattle.gov/mayor-durkans-attack-on-my-office-is-an-attack-on-working-peoples-movements-and-everything-we-are-fighting-for/

apprenticeship, and other public programs that might be funded with a repurposed police budget. Officials dangled the promise of new funding for research and services, part of which, they said, could be controlled by community nonprofit organizations, as the King County Equity Now group had demanded. Some of the activists involved in these conversations began to say quietly in protest circles that maybe a 50 percent defund demand wasn't immediately feasible, and perhaps it was better to negotiate a smaller amount of funding now. They became less interested in mobilizing for street actions, and more invested in negotiating with the mayor and City Council Democrats. Many of these activists clung publicly to the language of "police abolition," even as they privately tempered their demands with city officials.

Durkan's deft co-optation of the BLM participants put the political establishment back in the driver's seat for the city's fall budget process. In Seattle, the mayor proposes a budget in late September for the upcoming calendar year, and the council has two months to debate and amend it before adopting a final budget in late November. Durkan's proposed 2021 budget trimmed the police budget from $409 million to $360 million. Most of the reduction was achieved not by actual cuts but by shifting around funds—moving the 911 call center, emergency management, and parking meter enforcement staff out of the police department. Meanwhile, Durkan made huge cuts to libraries, parks, bus service, and road and building repairs.[189]

---

189 Goldstein-Street, J. (2020, September 29). 'A start' — Durkan 2021 budget proposal cuts police funding by 12%, adds record homelessness spending, and makes brutal decisions for the next year under COVID-19. Capitol Hill Seattle Blog. Retrieved April 25, 2023, from https://www.capitolhillseattle.com/2020/09/a-start-durkan-2021-budget-proposal-cuts-police-funding-by-12-adds-record-homelessness-spending/

City Council Democrats further shaved the police budget by about 8 percent compared to the previous year's, bringing the total amount transferred from the cops to community programs to $31 million. Hundreds of community members testified in council budget meetings calling for a 50 percent defund, but Council Democrats had no intention of honoring their enthusiastic summertime pledges. Not a single councilmember seconded Sawant's amendments to cut the police budget in half. They also unanimously opposed her proposal to create an elected community oversight board with power to hold the police accountable. Only one Democrat supported Sawant's amendment to freeze police hirings; her proposal to ban police from sweeping homeless encampments also failed, 2 to 7. Democrats had felt the powerful political reaction in the wake of Best's resignation, and they had seen how the protest movement had faded under the twin blows of internal division and sustained police repression. Forced to choose between the community and the police, the Democrats chose the police.

"In the middle of a pandemic and a spike in COVID infections, in the context of the worst recession for working people since the Great Depression, Democratic Councilmembers will be carrying out brutal austerity,"[190] Sawant said. The movement had for the first time in memory trimmed the bloated police budget.

190 (2020, November 24). Councilmember Sawant denounces Democrats' austerity budget while hailing victories by People's Budget and Solidarity Budget for affordable housing and shelters, renters rights and eviction defense, Green New Deal, and $31 million shift from bloated police budget to community-led programs. Seattle City Council Blog. Retrieved April 25, 2023, from https://council.seattle.gov/2020/11/24/councilmember-sawant-denounces-democrats-austerity-budget-while-hailing-victo-

They had limited some of the worst of Durkan's social service cuts and prevailed in winning new housing and cultural funding in the Central District.[191] But, she added, "taken as a whole, the budget that Democratic Party Councilmembers have approved today is a budget that deeply fails working people and marginalized communities, including working-class and poor communities of color."

The police budget cuts turned out to be but a temporary pause in expanding police power. Seattle police suffered no budget-related layoffs as a result of the budget trim, and within two years police budgets resumed their upward trend.

The defund demand, of course, was not just about dollars; it was a call to change the nature of policing and in particular to stop racist policing. That did not happen. Police abuse and killings picked up their sordid pace after 2020. In the two years following the uprising, Seattle police killed five men, including a man in mental distress.[192] That was about the same rate of Seattle police killings as before the Justice for George Floyd uprising.

ries-by-peoples-budget-and-solidarity-budget-for-affordable-housing-and-shelters-renters-rights-and-evic-2/

191 Russillo, J. (2020, November 24). *After Council Vote, Solidarity Budget Celebrates Victories but Battle Against SPD's "Hugely Bloated Budget" Continues*. South Seattle Emerald. Retrieved April 25, 2023, from https://southseattleemerald.com/2020/11/24/after-council-vote-solidarity-budget-celebrates-victories-but-battle-against-spds-hugely-bloated-budget-continues/

192 Kroman, D. (2021, March 3). *Family and friends wonder why Seattle police killed Derek Hayden*. Crosscut.com. Retrieved April 26, 2023, from https://crosscut.com/news/2021/03/family-and-friends-wonder-why-seattle-police-killed-derek-hayden

Seattle police officers operated with virtual impunity in the wake of 2020's turbulence. An officer involved in the June 2020 fake Proud Boy radio reports was rehired by the department.[193] The new police chief fully exonerated the officers who had ordered tear gas and blast balls against Black Lives Matter protesters, overruling a watchdog agency that recommended discipline.[194] The city paid $3.5 million to settle a wrongful death lawsuit by the family of a pregnant Black woman whom Seattle police had killed in 2017; the officers skated free.[195] Police guild members pressed a defamation lawsuit against Sawant for speaking out against another police killing.[196] Communities of color continued to feel the sting of racist policing: In 2021, a year after the political establishment loudly proclaimed their determination to end racist policing, 27 percent of all complaints against Seattle police

---

193 Beekman, D. (2022, January 12). *Seattle police officer involved in 2020 Proud Boys hoax has been rehired*. The Seattle Times. Retrieved April 25, 2023, from https://www.seattletimes.com/seattle-news/politics/an-officer-involved-in-seattle-polices-2020-proud-boys-hoax-was-rehired-last-month/

194 Takahama, E. (2021, May 12). *Seattle police chief overturns watchdog's discipline recommendation in 'pink umbrella' protest clash*. The Seattle Times. Retrieved April 26, 2023, from https://www.seattletimes.com/seattle-news/politics/seattle-police-chief-overturns-watchdogs-discipline-recommendation-in-pink-umbrella-protest-clash/

195 (2021, November 30). *Seattle to pay $3.5M to settle police wrongful-death suit*. AP News. Retrieved April 26, 2023, from https://apnews.com/article/police-lawsuits-seattle-1d1f3156fa868fc420980cfe6d637daf

196 (2021, November 10). *Reversal: 'Murdered by the police' defamation lawsuit against Sawant can go forward*. Capitol Hill Seattle Blog. Retrieved April 25, 2023, from https://www.capitolhillseattle.com/2021/11/reversal-murdered-by-the-police-defamation-lawsuit-against-sawant-can-go-forward/#jp-carousel-2067268012

came from Black residents, who constituted only 7 percent of the population.[197]

The Seattle Police Department's infamy spread beyond the city. Six Seattle police officers participated in the January 6, 2021 violent insurrection at the US Capitol building, the single-largest contingent of any police department. Guild chief Solan, who earlier had called some Seattle protesters "domestic terrorists,"[198] falsely asserted that Black Lives Matter protesters were partially responsible for the Jan. 6 right-wing attack.[199] Solan defiantly brushed aside politicians who called for him to resign for his incendiary remarks, declaring "I will never bend to cancel culture as I lead this union with conviction."[200]

---

197 (2022, April). *Office of Police Accountability 2021 Annual Report*. City of Seattle. Retrieved April 26, 2023, from https://www.seattle.gov/documents/Departments/OPA/Reports/2021-Annual-Report.pdf

198 Smith, R. (2020, July 21). *SPOG President Repeatedly Says It "Might" Be Time for Trump to Send Feds to Seattle*. The Stranger. Retrieved April 25, 2023, from https://www.thestranger.com/slog/2020/07/21/44132674/spog-president-repeatedly-says-it-might-be-time-for-trump-to-send-feds-to-seattle

199 Kamb, L. (2021, January 9). *President of Seattle police union lambasted for comments claiming Black Lives Matter among those to blame for U.S. Capitol siege*. The Seattle Times. Retrieved April 25, 2023, from https://www.seattletimes.com/seattle-news/president-of-seattle-police-union-lambasted-for-comments-blaming-black-lives-matter-liberal-activists-for-u-s-capitol-siege/

200 Gutman, D. (2021, January 12). *Seattle police union president won't resign after Capitol attack remarks, blames 'cancel culture'*. The Seattle Times. Retrieved April 26, 2023, from https://www.seattletimes.com/seattle-news/politics/seattle-police-union-president-wont-resign-after-capitol-attack-remarks-blames-cancel-culture/

He defended the January 6th Seattle officers, even sponsoring a lawsuit to stop public disclosure of their names.[201]

The rollercoaster events of 2020 offered a remarkable display of the state recovering from the movement's initial blows to reassert its power and to reestablish the preeminent role of police in violently curbing political dissent. The counterattack deployed the full range of state apparatus—the legislative and executive branches, the court system, and of course the police themselves. The reaction was amplified by the media and abetted by divisions and weaknesses in the movement: Street activists, many clustered around CHOP, who demanded an all-or-nothing approach to police abolition, and then the more mainstream community activists, who failed to recognize state power as the enemy, placed identity politics over class analysis, and willingly jettisoned Defund the Police goals for much more modest reform.

Both of these groups, in varied ways, rejected Sawant's three pillars of political insurgency.

The former group, street activists, many of whom were newly radicalized community members, failed to grasp that protest and occupation alone would not be enough. You need strategy, too, encompassing not just street movement but political struggle. Sawant's second pillar of Marxist insurgent politics is movement-building around immediate material struggles that are

201 Kamb, L., & Carter, M. (2021, July 8). *Two Seattle officers trespassed on U.S. Capitol grounds during riot and should be fired, investigation finds*. The Seattle Times. Retrieved April 25, 2023, from https://www.seattletimes.com/seattle-news/two-seattle-officers-trespassed-on-u-s-capitol-grounds-during-riot-and-should-be-fired-investigation-finds/

explicitly connected to the call for broader societal change. The street activists were correct to call for transformational demands, such as police abolition, as a way to inspire and mobilize the movement. But they failed to connect these demands to an effective strategy, such as the city budget fight, where demands could be made specific and concrete, and where city councilmembers would be forced to take sides. Many street activists also rejected Sawant's first pillar of insurgent politics, which is recognizing the primacy of class struggle, even in a fight in which race was a central feature. They mistrusted Sawant because she was not Black. Like many of the mainstream community activists, they elevated identity politics over class analysis and failed to develop an understanding of the power dynamics at play.

One can appreciate why activists rejected Sawant's efforts to bring street energy into a political battle in City Hall. After all, for many of them, radical politicians were people like Bernie Sanders and Alexandria Ocasio-Cortez—leaders who campaigned on bold demands, like Medicare for All and a Green New Deal, but once in office, pivoted to dead-end insider politics. Activists' deep skepticism of politicians blinded them to what Sawant was offering: Not a legislative battle fought on the terms of the political establishment, but an insurgent class struggle waged by bringing the street movement's disruptive energy, militancy, and creativity into City Hall.

The community leaders who took a more conciliatory approach toward the political establishment could point toward the $31 million in budget transfers from police to social programs. That was an accomplishment, and a credit to the mass movement. Yet it paled in comparison to the original demand to defund the police by 50 percent. Once engaged in negotiations with the political establishment—often out of public sight—these BLM community members jettisoned the sharp rhetoric and movement demands of the first weeks of the Justice for George Floyd protests. When City Council Democrats abandoned their summertime pledges to cut the police budget in half, the BLM leaders were unprepared to hold them accountable. They had failed to appreciate that class interests were central to the defund fight, and that the Democrats, while mouthing the slogans of the BLM movement, were working overtime to co-opt and block any real police defund movement.

Emerson Johnson, the restaurant worker and SA organizer, also faulted the movement for not hewing to the third pillar of Sawant's theory of political insurgency, movement democracy. "Without democratic structures and a way for people to get organized in a movement like this, it's extremely easy for demands to be taken up and then never followed through on," he observed. "Politicians can make all the promises in the world, but if there's no movement to fight back, then they're going to strip those concessions as quickly as they can because that's fundamentally what any reform is, is a concession, and the work of the working class is to maintain those concessions and build on them."

In contrast to the BLM community members, Durkan and the other major state actors understood very clearly that class interests were at play. Their two-fold strategy—repress and marginalize the street protests, divide and co-opt the broader popular movement—effectively exploited movement weaknesses. The result left Sawant's forces, and indeed all those who advocated for defunding the police, isolated from the other BLM forces and completely outmatched.

In the aftermath of the 2020 uprising, the movement's balance sheet provided a sobering lesson about the lengths to which the capitalist system will go to maintain control. As Sawant had told the late-night crowd at CHOP back in June, taking money and power away from the police was going to be "goddamn hard" because the police were defending the real power in capitalist society. The big corporations and the billionaires "are never going to agree to a society free of policing because they need the police to keep us repressed," she had reminded them. In challenging the guardians of the state, the street movement was in fact contesting much more than a city department budget. It was declaring war on state power itself. Notwithstanding the passion and convictions of the millions who organized and bravely marched for Black Lives Matter in Seattle and worldwide in 2020, the street movement was not prepared for this herculean task.

8

'You Give Them Hell'

At the start of 2021, with the recall election all but certain to happen, the forces uniting against Sawant had every reason to believe that this would be the year they would finally boot the Marxist from City Hall.

Having stymied Black Lives Matter's core demands and throttled street protests, the establishment had political momentum. Progressives, cowed by the right-wing backlash, were on the defensive and fighting amongst themselves. Democratic politicians, who had aligned with Sawant just months earlier demanding justice for George Floyd, abandoned her. Construction union leaders were avidly pooling resources into the Recall Sawant campaign, alongside major real estate developers, big landlords, Amazon and other tech executives, and finance CEOs. These were daunting obstacles for any politician, let alone a Marxist in America. Indeed, throughout 2021, Sawant and those closest to her expected this would be their last year in office.

The first task of the anti-Sawant coalition was to stage-manage the 2021 electoral calendar, a responsibility that fell to the nine-member state Supreme Court. To green-light a recall campaign, the state court must determine whether the petition charges are specific and serious enough for an elected official to be removed. The state court does not determine the veracity of the charges themselves—rather, it simply determines whether the charges, if true, meet the legal standard. Once the state court approves a recall petition, the campaign has six months to collect the signatures necessary to qualify the issue for the ballot—not a hard task to accomplish, especially with paid signature-gatherers. The recall election, a simple yes-or-no vote, must be conducted between 45 and 90 days after the signatures are verified.

Sawant wasn't the only elected official facing the prospect of a recall. Anti-Durkan campaigners had hoped for a fall 2020 ruling that would allow them to get a recall vote in the first half of 2021. Their recall petition charged that Durkan endangered the community and violated her oath of office by allowing police to use chemical weapons on hundreds of peaceful protesters and bystanders during a respiratory pandemic. To anyone on the streets of Seattle in the summer of 2020, brutalized repeatedly by the police, it was obvious that the mayor had run roughshod over the legal and constitutional rights she had sworn to uphold. Yet in October 2020, the state high court issued its decision: no recall vote for Durkan. The massive attacks on peaceful protesters had been "alarming," the justices acknowledged, but they were "insufficient to support a recall election." By a unanimous 9 to 0 vote, they ruled that the anti-Durkan recall could not advance.[202]

For the anti-Sawant forces, the demise of the Durkan recall campaign helpfully removed one complication from the electoral calendar, as a vote to recall the mayor would have re-energized the street movement and given a boost to Sawant. Durkan herself removed a second potential problem shortly after the court ruling by announcing she would not run again in 2021. Her decision meant that she wouldn't have to face public accountability over police violence, nor would she and her allies have to spend the year explaining her administration's audacious coverup of their complicity in police brutality.

The same nine court justices took much more time to rule on the Sawant recall petition, ensuring that any recall campaign would gain distance from the peak of the Black Lives Matter uprising and scenes of police violence. At first, court officials said a decision would come in January. But January came and went without a ruling. So did February, then March.

Were internal divisions among the justices to account for the delay? Absolutely not. On April 1, 2021, the court ruled unanimously that the recall against Sawant could move forward. Even though Sawant had broken no law by opening up City Hall to the June 9, 2020, Black Lives Matter protest, or by attending the June 28 rally in Durkan's neighborhood, the court ruled that voters

202 (2020, December 10). *In the Matter of the Recall of Jenny Durkan, City of Seattle Mayor*. Justia.com. Retrieved April 27, 2023, from https://cases.justia.com/washington/supreme-court/2020-98897-8.pdf?ts=1607616356

should be allowed to decide whether her actions at those rallies constituted malfeasance.

The court also greenlit a third charge: that Sawant had illegally funded the Tax Amazon ballot initiative using city resources. This charge was unalloyed political retribution for her leadership in winning the breakthrough tax. At the beginning of 2020, Sawant's council office had spent $1,759 printing posters and issuing solicitations for the Tax Amazon action conferences, advertising that the movement would, among other agenda items, consider an initiative at these events. The initiative was purely a discussion point at the time; no paperwork was filed until several weeks later. But in a novel interpretation of the law, the judges ruled that even the discussion of a potential future initiative could not be done with city resources; that would be electioneering, they asserted. In approving this third charge, the court agreed with the Seattle Ethics and Elections Commission, which earlier had ruled the expenditure illegal and fined Sawant.[203]

Two City Council Democrats had been found guilty of similar ethics violations in previous years—one for promoting a different initiative—and had not faced recalls. And just two years earlier, all eight Democrats had faced no repercussions when they violated city ethics code by conducting illegal secret discussions to repeal the first Amazon tax. The Supreme Court's decisions in both the Durkan and Sawant recall petitions revealed the Court to be not a place where blind justice was dispensed, but an

203 (2021, April 1). In the Matter of the Recall of KSHAMA SAWANT, City of Seattle Councilmember, Appellant. Casemine.com. Retrieved April 27, 2023, from https://www.casemine.com/judgement/us/606bcec34653d00386523452

integral component of state power, insulating Durkan from the recall while applying double standards to facilitate an electoral assault on the socialist.

Sawant was defiant. "I plead guilty to fighting unapologetically to tax Amazon and big business. I plead guilty to spending much of the year 2020, in the midst of a pandemic, fighting alongside hundreds of other activists to make Jeff Bezos fund affordable housing," she said.

"As long as I sit on the City Council," she continued, "I pledge to continue to fight in solidarity with working people and marginalized communities. I pledge I will continue to be accountable to working people and to never join the establishment's club. I pledge I will uphold my oath of office as I understand it. And most importantly, I pledge to never waver in my fight for social justice and a different kind of society."[204]

Privately, Kshama Solidarity Campaign staffers knew they faced a huge uphill battle even more daunting than the 2019 reelection campaign. "We were very clear from the beginning that even if we're going to lose this seat, the example that we need to set on our way out is extremely important," recalled Kailyn Nicholson, an organizer for Socialist Alternative. "No matter how strong and intense the attacks are, no matter how much the balance of forces is stacked against you, you never just roll over and give up. You fight as hard as you possibly can and you expose

204 Sawant, K. (2021, May 12). Kshama Sawant: Why I Settled the Ethics Complaint On My Support for Tax Amazon. Socialist Alternative. Retrieved April 28, 2023, from https://www.socialistalternative.org/2021/05/12/kshama-sawant-why-i-settled-the-ethics-complaint-on-my-support-for-tax-amazon/

what's happening and how much all of these different forces, the lengths that they will go to try to kick out a genuine fighter. You give them hell."

Nicholson and her comrades also believed that defeat, while likely, was not inevitable. "We probably were more optimistic than most people because we understand the strength of our ideas and our methods and we've seen before how we've been able to beat the odds," she said. "So we had to convince people that if we do go all out, we have a shot. We need to do everything we can to make that window as big as possible and just be laser-focused on it."

On the other side of the emerging battlefield, Henry Bridger II, the manager of the Recall Sawant campaign, must have been delighted with the Supreme Court decision. For him, the ruling was great, but the timing was even better. By waiting until April 1 to issue their court decision, the judges gave Bridger's team some good options to collect signatures. Primary ballot electorates tend to be more conservative than in the November general election, when the multiplicity of candidates and ballot issues tends to draw higher turnout and a more progressive-leaning electorate. As such, Bridger could collect the necessary signatures from District 3 voters in a couple of months and qualify for the August primary ballot. Or, more enticingly, he could use the full 180-day signature-gathering period and submit the signatures in September or October. That would be too late for the November ballot and would trigger a special election at the very end of the year—right between the Thanksgiving and Christmas holidays—when a much lower turnout, skewing conservative, would be expected. Either way, Bridger wanted to avoid getting on the November general election ballot. And thanks to the timing of the Supreme Court decision, he had options: Go fast, or go slow. Publicly, he said the campaign wanted to get on the November ballot, but that was never his intention. Bridger chose to go slow and aim for December.

Bridger also had to raise campaign funds, but this was a rather straightforward task. He turned to people like George Petrie, who needed no persuasion to give money and fundraise. As the CEO of Goodman Real Estate—the $5.2 billion national landlord firm, with 45 buildings in the area and headquartered in Seattle—he surely understood how Sawant represented a challenge to his business. Petrie invested heavily in politics. In 2021, he was Trump's top Washington state donor. But he supported the two-party duopoly, over the years giving generously to both Republicans and Democrats. The recall was a time for the CEO and his associates to go all-in to protect their profits. Petrie donated the $1,000 legal maximum to the recall campaign. So did his company's chairman and founder, John Goodman, along with the company's president, Kelli Norris, and his wife, former banker Alyssa Petrie. Billionaire commercial real estate developer Martin Selig, also a major Trump donor, anted up the maximum to the recall. Frank Shrontz, who as Boeing CEO waged war on the Machinists union at Boeing and oversaw some of the biggest layoffs in company history, maxxed out. So did hotel owner and union foe Richard Hedreen and a host of venture capitalists, developers, corporate lawyers, and real estate, investment bank, and high-tech C-suite executives. All told, over the course of 2021 some 130 Trump donors and more than 850 millionaires donated to the recall effort, building a war chest for Bridger that eventually topped $1 million, an unprecedented figure for a Seattle City Council race.[205]

For these leading capitalists, 2021 was shaping up as the year when they could finally rid themselves of the socialist nuisance. On the other side of the class divide, the growing economic crisis facing working class households put the recall squarely in the spotlight of Seattle politics: As much as the billionaires wanted Sawant out of office, tenants needed her in. As 2021 got underway, close to 100,000 Seattle-area renters reported being unable to make payments.[206] The initial infusion of federal emergency aid had kept working people afloat. But that money was dissipating. And the blanket citywide moratorium on evictions, which Sawant had won alongside renters, unions, and housing groups, was about to expire.

Arianna Laureano was one of those workers on the precipice. An itinerant young trans woman with chronic health needs, abandoned by her family since she was a young teenager, she had moved to Seattle in 2016 after learning that Washington state offered an affordable healthcare plan for workers with disabilities. She went back to school to become a baker, worked a bunch of

---

205 Walicek, T. (2021, December 5). *Recall Campaign Against Socialist Kshama Sawant Is Backed by Billionaires*. Truthout. Retrieved May 23, 2023, from https://truthout.org/articles/recall-campaign-against-socialist-kshama-sawant-is-backed-by-billionaires/

206 (2021, March 1). Housing Insecurity (Missed Payment and Low Confidence). US Census Bureau - Household Pulse Survey. Retrieved May 4, 2023, from https://www.census.gov/data-tools/demo/hhp/#/?s_metro=42660&areaSelector=msa&periodSelector=25&measures=HINSEC

low-wage jobs, and by early 2020 had landed full-time work at a union grocery store. Between the paycheck and her meager Social Security Disability check, she could manage. "I was trying to do things on the side to make up money for bills and for toilet paper and basic needs," she later recalled. "And I had always had this idea that my existence was like this because I was disabled. That if I could just figure out a way to deal with health care and to make enough money, to find a job that would take me, that all of that suffering would just disappear."

Then the pandemic struck. "I was suddenly spending a small fortune on masks and gloves, and getting to and from work every day," she said. Then the grocery reduced her hours. Her roommate was stuck at home, waiting for unemployment checks to come through. "She basically was someone who was supporting me before when I was on disability, and now she had nothing, and I was basically the main income for the household," Laureano said.

"COVID flipped my entire life on its head in a way, and it directly hammered in that nobody's lives matter, nobody's in our society, unless you're rich. The only people that the politicians care about are the business owners and the rich, because they bailed all of them out and they didn't bail us out," she said. "My whole life slowly fell apart over seven months to the point where I was back to being hungry, rationing meds and stuff while working. So now I'm working my body to the bone—and my body is not as capable as other people's bodies—and still having this grueling life where rent's taking up 60 percent, 70 percent of my income. . . . So, basically, that kind of broke me. I realized that there was no height I could reach where I would be treated with human dignity in our society. And when I realized this, I was just angry. I was really, really angry."

One day her roommate came home from a workshop organized by the tenants' rights group, Be:Seattle. Until then, "I was a computer chair warrior sitting around complaining about how nobody cared about disabled people in our country," Laureano recalled. Her roommate talked about how the director of Be:Seattle, Kate Rubin, was recruiting people to testify about a tenants' rights bill coming up.

"Ari, you're constantly complaining about this stuff. Ranting about how human life doesn't matter. Talk to Kate. She has something for you to do," Laureano's roommate said.

Laureano dove in. She joined the burgeoning Cancel Rent and Mortgages movement, testified in support of state relief measures, got connected to Sawant's council office, and in early 2021 became one of a growing army of volunteer tenant organizers, handing out Sawant's leaflets in her apartment building and neighborhood and mobilizing friends to attend online City Council and state legislative meetings. She found a wellspring of energy among her fellow renters.

"I could just talk about what I was doing and people were like, 'How do I get involved in that?'," Laureano recalled. "It was very easy to get people to open up because we were all going through very obvious suffering. I was a disabled person who just got my life together. My roommate had a good job for years and her life was destroyed. My neighbor was a single mother, an artist who was making $4,000 a month before COVID, and went to nothing because she's an artist. . . . The impact was universal. If you didn't lose your job, you still lost wages."

The national scene for the working class mirrored the desperate straits of Laureano and her neighbors. In the first six months of the pandemic, 57 million Americans filed for unemployment, with Black unemployment 50 percent higher than white unemployment, the largest racial jobless gap in five years.[207] By the start of 2021, nearly 12 million US renters owed an average of $5,850 in late rent and utility bills.[208] Fully 28 percent of all renters—more than half of whom were Black renters[209]—started the new year with rent debt. There was little prospect of seeing a turnaround in the near term, even as COVID vaccination programs started to roll out.

On the other side of the class ledger, corporate behemoths like Amazon and Starbucks and the rest of the billionaire class were doing quite well, often even better financially than they'd been doing pre-pandemic. Amazon headed the pandemic profiteering

---

207 Kelly, J. (2020, August 20). Jobless Claims: 57.4 Million Americans Have Sought Unemployment Benefits Since Mid-March—Over 1 Million People Filed Last Week. Forbes.com. Retrieved May 3, 2023, from https://www.forbes.com/sites/jackkelly/2020/08/20/jobless-claims-574-million-americans-have-sought-unemployment-benefits-since-mid-marchover-1-million-people-filed-last-week/?sh=159aa7da6d59 and Marte, J. (2020, July 2). Gap in U.S. Black and white unemployment rates is widest in five years. Reuters.com. Retrieved May 3, 2023, from https://www.reuters.com/article/us-usa-economy-unemployment-race-idUSKBN2431X7

208 Long, H. (2020, December 7). Millions of Americans are heading into the holidays unemployed and over $5,000 behind on rent. The Washington Post. Retrieved May 2, 2023, from https://www.washingtonpost.com/business/2020/12/07/unemployed-debt-rent-utilities/

209 Warnock, R. (2021, January 14). Rent Debt & Racial Inequality in 2021. ApartmentList.com. Retrieved May 2, 2023, from https://www.apartmentlist.com/research/rent-debt-2021

parade, logging a record $23 billion in 2020 profits, nearly double the previous year's astounding figure.[210] By January 2021, while unemployed baristas and Laureano's neighbors were going deeper into debt and wondering if they would ever gain economic stability, Starbucks stock was trading at record highs.[211] "I could not be more pleased with our U.S. sales recovery," the Starbucks CEO boasted to investors.[212]

Corporate landlords cashed in, too. One of the biggest residential landlords in the country, Equity Apartments, with 79,000 units nationally including 9,400 in the Seattle area, registered $700 million in profits in the first nine months of 2020. Essex Property Trust, another huge company with 12,000 apartments in the Seattle area, recorded $473 million in profits during the same period. And in the first eight months of 2021, as vaccines rolled out and jobs began to return, the average Seattle rents soared 25 percent, more than recovering from the brief 2020 rent dip.[213] The rest of

---

210 (2021, February 2). Amazon.Com announces financial results and CEO transition. Amazon.com. Retrieved May 3, 2023, from https://s2.q4cdn.com/299287126/files/doc_financials/2020/q4/Amazon-Q4-2020-Earnings-Release.pdf

211 (2023, May 3). Watchlist. MSN.com. Retrieved May 3, 2023, from https://www.msn.com/en-us/money/watchlist?tab=Related&id=a22k9c&ocid=ansMSNMoney11&duration=5Y&relatedQuoteId=a22k9c&relatedSource=MIAI&src=b_secdans

212 Kalogeropoulos, D. (2021, January 20). Starbucks Earnings: What to Watch. The Motley Fool. Retrieved May 4, 2023, from https://www.fool.com/investing/2021/01/20/starbucks-earnings-what-to-watch/

213 Peha, J. (2021, September 27). Sawant Congratulates Renter Organizing for Winning Bills Requiring Landlords to Provide 6 Months' Notice for Any Rent Increases, Plus Relocation Assistance. City of Seattle. Retrieved May 4, 2023, from https://council.seattle.gov/2021/09/27/

the nation's landlords followed suit, hoping to make up for their 2020 losses. This spiked rents "well above where they would be if growth had remained on its pre-pandemic trend," according to industry analyst ApartmentList.com.[214] Landlords showed a cruel indifference to human suffering, pressing evictions even as communities reeled from the epidemic. Corporate landlords were the biggest evictors, and the top evictor in the area was none other than George Petrie's firm, Goodman Real Estate.

The chasm between the lived experiences of Laureano and other working class renters on one side, and the George Petries and Martin Seligs of the world on the other, could not have been wider. Sawant was determined that since the recall battle had to be waged, it would be on this terrain of class struggle.

The newly reinvigorated renters' rights movement fired its opening salvo in early January. "A tsunami of evictions will hit Seattle in the coming year without bold action by the Seattle City Council," Sawant declared in a January 2021 op ed co-signed by 17 other union and community activists, including Laureano. "Tens of thousands of evictions, disproportionately in communities of color, will likely overwhelm the courts, shelters, and streets, as people lose their homes." What followed over the next nine months was an extraordinary series of breakthroughs led by Sawant and an energetic tenants' rights movement—even more extraordinary

sawant-congratulates-renter-organizing-for-winning-bills-requiring-landlords-to-provide-6-months-notice-for-any-rent-increases-plus-relocation-assistance/

214 Long, H. (2021, August 4). Twitter post. Twitter.com. Retrieved July 28, 2024, from https://x.com/byHeatherLong/status/1422927794867167236

because the movement achieved these victories at the same time it was defending the council seat against the recall.

In late January, dozens of tenants, including Laureano, testified at Sawant's Renters Rights Committee about the need for a moratorium extension. Prodded by community petitions that Sawant's City Council office organized, the mayor did so—albeit in stages—for another 14 months. Meanwhile, Sawant also put forward a right-to-counsel bill, which would create a right to an attorney for all tenants facing eviction—a protection that had already been won by tenant movements in New York City, San Francisco, and Newark, New Jersey. In March, the bill passed after Sawant and tenant activists successfully warded off Democrats' last-minute efforts to water it down.

Just two and a half months later, the movement recorded three more victories. In early June, with the help of the educators' union, they won a ban on school-year evictions of students, their families, and school workers—the strongest ordinance of its kind nationwide, which, combined with the previous year's ban on wintertime evictions, further constrained landlords from uprooting people's lives post-COVID. At the same June meeting, City Council passed a new "just cause" law requiring landlords to offer tenants a new lease unless the landlord had a valid reason under city law. And the council also adopted a bill banning evictions for non-payment of rent that had become due during the COVID civil emergency. This additional measure would protect tenants struggling with debt after the civil emergency officially was lifted.

Even as—outside the council office—she and activists were consumed with fundraising and building campaign infrastructure to fight the recall, Sawant and the movement pressed their advantage as spring turned into summer. "Our movement won not by our council office agreeing to concessions and making inside deals, but rather by turning outward and organizing working people and fighting boldly for our needs," Sawant noted. "Renters came out by the hundreds to demand that the other city councilmembers vote for our bills."[215]

Sawant intended to force Democrats to choose sides between tenants and big landlords. "None of our campaigns have ever been just election campaigns. They've also been offensive campaigns around concrete demands," SA's Kailyn Nicholson recounted later. "And, yeah, we said from the beginning, if we want any chance of winning, it's going to have to not just be a defensive campaign, it's going to have to also be an offensive campaign."

Flanked by tenants, small business owners, and union members, Sawant staged a press conference in the Central District to announce she would introduce a City Council bill to trigger rent control as soon as state restrictions on rent limits were lifted. That bill would not come up for a vote before the following year. But Sawant also announced she would introduce two complementary renters' rights bills, which she intended to bring before the council in advance of the recall. One would oblige landlords to provide six months' advance notice for any rent increase. The other would require landlords to pay tenants the equivalent of three months of rent in relocation assistance if a rent increase of 10 percent or

215 Peha, J. (2021, June 7). Sawant Congratulates Seattle Renters for Monday's Victories, Urges Fight for Rent Control and to Cancel COVID Debt. City of Seattle. Retrieved May 4, 2023, from https://council.seattle.gov/2021/06/07/sawant-congratulates-seattle-renters-for-mondays-victories-urges-fight-for-rent-control-and-to-cancel-covid-debt/

more forced the tenant to move. The six-month notice and relocation assistance bills would operate in tandem to place a powerful brake on future rent increases.

Over the summer, as people ventured out more, activists collected thousands of petition signatures demanding that City Council act on Sawant's new measures. More than 200 union members and tenants held an outdoor rally nine days before the City Council was to vote on Sawant's six-month notice and relocation assistance bills. Community members wrote hundreds of letters to councilmembers and signed up for public comment at the online council meetings.

It was hard for the Democrats to put up substantial roadblocks to Sawant's legislation. Unlike the Tax Amazon fight, where Democrats fought tenaciously to forestall and then water down the bill, in 2021, given the social crisis induced by COVID, they were on the back of their heels when it came to renters' rights. Landlord lobbyists also found it hard to fight back. Predictably, they put forward self-described "mom-and-pop landlords" to testify against the bills. In the past, this tactic had served them well. But on September 27, Democrats approved the six-month-notice bill with only one dissent. The tenant relocation assistance bill passed unanimously. "De facto rent control," groused the statewide landlord association.[216]

216 Waller, B. (2021, November 12). *Two Steps Forward, One Step Back: Latest Data Shows Seattle Lost 6785 Rental Properties since 2018*. Washington Multi-Family Housing Association. Retrieved July 31, 2023, from https://www.wmfha.org/news/two-steps-forward-one-step-back-latest-data-shows-seattle-lost-785-rental-properties-since-2018

The movement celebrated. In just half a year, activists had run the table on the landlord lobby, winning—if not rent control itself—legislation that overall would suppress future rent increases and empower tenants with new legal rights. "Today's victories will benefit tens of thousands of renters in Seattle, who are facing skyrocketing rent increases from profit-hungry corporate landlords and the venture capitalists and big banks who are fueling a speculative bubble," Sawant said, adding that "we won because renters organized alongside my council office, unions, socialists, communities of color, the LGBTQ community, and others to demand their rights."

If the anti-Sawant forces thought going into 2021 that their recall election would force the socialist-led movement onto the defensive, they were wrong. The new laws represented the biggest advance of renters' rights in the city in modern times. They changed lives; in the months following the bills' passage, Laureano was among thousands of tenants now protected from major rent increases and eviction threats. When, a few months after the spate of new legislation, Laureano's landlord announced that she was raising the rent by 14 percent, the new activist balked. "I said, 'Hey, if you raise it by more than 10 percent, I'm going to have to leave,'" she recalled telling the landlord. Under the new law, "'You will have to give me three months rent back, and that's like $4,500.' And she said, 'Oh, oh, okay.'" They negotiated a much lower increase.

Laureano had learned an important lesson. Previously, she'd been turned off by politicians who said tenants should be satisfied with incremental change. What Laureano learned from Sawant's tenants' rights battles was that "something revolutionary makes a huge, huge difference in people's lives and it brings people into a movement."

"I think it's an amazing thing," she said. "I never would have gotten involved in any of this if I didn't have someone saying, 'Hey, maybe we could reach for a star.'"

These wins also set the terms of debate for the recall election. Laureano, Nicholson, and the newly invigorated tenants movement had no chance to exhale. Three days after Sawant and the activists declared victory on the six-month notice and tenant relocation bills, the recall campaign turned in its signatures to election authorities, triggering the countdown for the epic recall vote. The submission represented the culmination of the political establishment's engineering of a low-turnout December ballot: First, with the Supreme Court's delaying ruling, and then with campaign manager Henry Bridger's slow-walking signature-gathering. But in maneuvering for this electoral advantage, Bridger hadn't reckoned that the socialists would respond with their own daring political gambit, one that would cost the recall forces dearly.

After the April 1 Supreme Court green light to proceed with the recall, nobody doubted that the recall campaign would collect the requisite signatures. They needed 10,700 valid signatures from Sawant's District 3 to qualify; with 13,000 signatures, they would have plenty of padding to account for some invalid names. With a paid canvass operating in the district's wealthier neighborhoods, the recall campaign would be quite capable of reaching the goal. By early July, the campaign announced it had collected 9,000 signatures. Yet the recallers seemed to be in no hurry to collect the remainder by August 3, the deadline to make the November general election ballot. After all, the Supreme Court had given them until October.

In early July, in the immediate wake of the school year eviction ban victory, the seven-member Kshama Solidarity Campaign strategy team puzzled over the recall campaign's lethargic pace. Before July, "they had previously released a number that was very close already to 9,000," said Nicholson, the Socialist Alternative organizer. "They would have had to basically have stopped collecting signatures for a span of weeks in order to be at this number now. Why? What's going on here? And that's when we realized, oh, they're intentionally trying to miss the general election deadline because a special election will be more favorable for them because the turnout is lower."

Nicholson and her comrades knew they already faced an uphill battle with a recall vote in November. A later special election, which typically has significant drop-off among working-class voters, would be even more difficult to win. "So first we thought, 'Okay, we need to call out the fact that they're doing this, we need to try to make them pay as big a price as possible for doing this undemocratic thing,'" Nicholson recalled.

She recalled Calvin Priest, the SA political director, intervened with a provocative suggestion. "Calvin's like, 'Well, what if we collect signatures *for* them?' And there was definitely a moment where everyone's kind of like, 'Is that even possible? Wait, that would be crazy. People would be confused by that.' But we also pretty quickly realized that if our main goal is to try to do whatever we can to get on the general election ballot, which would dramatically increase the size of that window of opportunity for us to actually win, then this does make sense. And even if we fail at that, if our goal is to make them pay the biggest possible political price for taking this really undemocratic strategy, then collecting signatures for them will make that statement in a much bigger way than just calling them out."

Nicholson and the others presented the idea to the campaign staff. "People were a little bit skeptical at first, but by the end of the discussion, they were really excited and were like, 'Oh man, this is a really badass thing to do,'" she said.

Standing before the media on July 9, Sawant signed her own recall petition with a flourish. "Our message to the recall is 'put up or shut up,'" she said. "You say you want to turn in your signatures and get on the ballot in November, then do it. The solidarity campaign will collect the rest. Let's have a vote in November." Noting that turnouts in winter elections were historically 25 to 50 percent lower than November ballots, Sawant said the recall campaign's delay tactic amounted to undemocratic voter suppression.[217] "They don't want a normal November election because that's when most people vote," Sawant said. "They don't want working people, people of color, young people, or renters to vote. They feel, correctly so, that the only way they can win is an election dominated by the wealthiest, whitest possible electorate. In short,

---

217 Graham, N. (2021, July 9). *Sawant's Campaign Will Help Gather Signatures to Put Her Own Recall on the November Ballot.* The Stranger. Retrieved May 9, 2023, from https://www.thestranger.com/slog/2021/07/09/58911378/sawants-campaign-will-help-gather-signatures-to-put-her-own-recall-on-the-november-ballot

if you are an ordinary person, a working person, or a renter in District 3, then they are afraid of you."[218]

Every two days, the Kshama Solidarity Campaign delivered to the recall campaign, via legal courier, new batches of recall petitions that their volunteers had collected. More volunteers came out for this novel canvass, getting voters to sign two petitions: First, a pledge to support the Kshama Solidarity Campaign, and then, a copy of the recall petition. Many of these new signers also donated to the solidarity campaign. The campaign focused signature-gathering in renter-heavy neighborhoods, where the spate of legislative victories was fresh on voters' minds. "The first thing we ask people is, 'Will you stand with Kshama against right-wing voter suppression?'" Nicholson explained. "We are not looking to collect signatures from or do anything to mobilize people who plan to vote for the recall. We just want to talk to and mobilize our supporters."

When the Kshama Solidarity Campaign hit the streets with recall petitions, "people loved it," Nicholson recalled. Many had heard of Sawant's press conference; others needed a little more of an explanation. "We would say, 'These are the demographics of people who are less likely to vote in a special election,' and that's not surprising to anyone." By helping the recall qualify for November, "there will be no room for them to pretend that, 'Oh, we just weren't able to get the signatures,'" Nicholson said. "There will be no space at all, and they will be completely exposed as taking

218 Kreig, H. (2021, August 11). *Chess game underway between Sawant supporters and recall campaigners*. Real Change News. Retrieved May 9, 2023, from https://www.realchangenews.org/news/2021/08/11/chess-game-underway-between-sawant-supporters-and-recall-campaigners

a conscious decision to try to disenfranchise all of these people. People just thought it was brilliant."

On August 2, the Kshama Solidarity Campaign delivered the last of its batch of 3,000 recall petition signatures, posing for pictures outside the recall campaign's law office. With Bridger announcing he had nearly 11,600 signatures collected by the recall campaign, the socialists' contribution assured that even with a 25 percent cushion for invalid signatures, Bridger would have more than enough to file for a November election.

To no one's surprise, he did not do that. The recall campaign instead waited until the end of September to file, securing a December 7 ballot date from elections officials. It would be the first local December ballot in anyone's memory, an election held between holidays in the darkest, rainiest part of the year in Seattle, the hardest time to do grassroots organizing. The Recall Sawant campaign got the date they wanted. But because of the creative organizing of Nicholson and her comrades, it was at the price of being widely branded as the political movement that was trying to suppress voter turnout. It was a label that dogged Bridger for the rest of the campaign and cost him crucial support.

9

Against All Odds

Among the many hurdles that Socialist Alternative organizers anticipated in the 2021 recall campaign, a fractious split within a key constituency was not one of them. Yet in September, that's exactly what happened. An open war broke out within the area labor movement, pitting Sawant, rank-and-file Carpenters union members, and several area progressive unions against an entrenched bureaucracy in the building trades unions and the central labor council. It was not a civil war that the recall campaign proponents planned, but doubtless they were gleeful to see union officials publicly attacking Sawant and the socialists. The division could only benefit them.

Over the summer, the area's 11,000 union carpenters had rejected three successive contract proposals negotiated between their union leadership and the Associated General Contractors, the main alliance of construction companies. Each proposal failed to match carpenter pay increases with the area's galloping cost of living, let alone keep up with the industry's huge profits. Carpenters, along with most other construction trades workers, could no longer afford to live in the city. Early morning start times precluded taking public transit, and besides, many had to bring their own tools to the job every day. So they were essentially forced to pay $100 or more every week to park near the major downtown construction projects, with only meager parking subsidies offered to a fraction of workers. For some carpenters, the parking tab came to thousands of dollars a year.

Art Esparza was a rank-and-file carpenter who had opposed the union's previous contract in 2018. He was inspired to hear about the historic West Virginia educators' strike of the same year, when 20,000 teachers and other school workers struck the state, occupied the state Capitol, and won raises. Esparza began his own dissident carpenters Facebook group. His initial efforts to organize a strike fell short, but in 2021 he revived the Facebook group and began networking at job sites after workers turned down the second contract offer. He was encouraged when 200 carpenters showed up at a rally he called. They were ready to fight for better terms, and named themselves the Peter J. McGuire Group after the union's 19th century founder. The fledgling caucus coalesced around three core demands: A $15 increase in the base journey-level wage over three years, paid parking, and strengthened contract protections against sexual harassment on the job. The budding rank-and-file caucus mobilized to achieve a decisive rejection of the third agreement just before Labor Day, and they won resolutions at several area Carpenters union meetings calling for strike action.

Carpenters were angry that their union leadership had brought three inadequate proposals to them. Most of the rank-and-file carpenters' ire was aimed at Evelyn Shapiro, the principal officer of the regional Carpenters union. Shapiro was anomalous among carpenters: Rising quickly through the ranks from apprentice to journey-level carpenter, she became the first woman in the US to head a regional Carpenters union. She was an outspoken supporter of the Black Lives Matter movement and, as a fluent Spanish speaker, worked to bring more Latinx workers into the union. The previous year, she had been reelected to head the six-state Pacific Northwest Regional Council of Carpenters. Leaders in other unions hailed Shapiro as the new face of labor, evidence that past days of exclusion and corruption were no more.

In the summer of 2021, however, union members increasingly saw that Shapiro was undermining their prospects of fighting for better standards. She urged members to accept contract proposals that failed to keep up with the local cost of living, publicly downplayed the power of striking, and did little to mobilize members for a better contract. Worse, to some carpenters, she encouraged members to accept a four-year contract with the industry, which would put the agreement's expiration date out of alignment with those of electricians, plumbers, operating engineers, and the other trade unions. Workers understood that they would have more power taking on the industry together. That required having contracts that expired at the same time. Union members pointed to Shapiro's lavish $253,000 a year salary as evidence that she had grown out of touch with the interests and needs of the rank and file.

After Labor Day, Shapiro brought a slightly tweaked fourth proposal back to the members and assigned staff to call around urging a "Yes" vote. The members again rejected it, and this time demanded that the union strike.

"Seattle has been booming since 2010," union member John McCallum said. "Every time the contract comes up, the same crap is spewed: 'We did the best we could. We'll get you better next time.' . . . It's coming to a head and we need to stand up for ourselves."[219]

Forced to act, Shapiro announced the Carpenters union would strike beginning September 16. The evening before, carpenters gathered at their union hall to prepare for the action. Shapiro and her staff shocked the membership by announcing that out of hundreds of construction sites in the region, the strikers would picket only four—and that out of 11,000 union carpenters in the region, only 2,000 would be on strike. The rest would continue working as usual. She said that was because most job sites were covered by Project Labor Agreements (PLAs), which, she argued, required that carpenter work continue uninterrupted.

PLAs are a détente arrangement first developed fifty years earlier between the construction industry and building trades unions. In exchange for contractors promising union-covered jobs that pay the prevailing area wage, unions promise not to strike or otherwise disrupt work for the duration of the project. PLAs give

219 Groover, H. (2021, September 16). *Seattle-area carpenters on strike, slowing construction projects across the region.* The Seattle Times. Retrieved May 16, 2023, from https://www.seattletimes.com/business/real-estate/seattle-area-carpenters-on-strike-slowing-construction-projects-across-the-region/

developers assurance of "labor peace," and the confidence that large projects can get finished on schedule.

Construction union leaders are fond of PLAs because they guarantee union work and increase union membership. But the price is surrendering workers' most powerful tool, the right to strike. By 2021, most construction union leaders—typically carrying the title of "business manager"—were comfortable with that arrangement, even if their members weren't. Instead of building power through collective action, they had become glorified labor brokers for an industry willing to share a sliver of profits in exchange for a compliant, reliable workforce. This business union model, as it has become known, was why area carpenters hadn't struck over the previous 18 years.

Shapiro's invocation of PLAs did not completely explain why she wanted to severely limit picketing. On the eve of the strike, she had privately committed to the business managers from the other construction unions that "Roving or alternating picketing on multiple sites throughout the day will not be performed" and that "Pickets will not be concentrated on a single site for a long duration or for consecutive days throughout the workweek," according to a leaked email obtained weeks later by *Labor Notes*.[220] Limiting pickets in that way would mean other trades workers could stay on the job. It also would render the strike essentially toothless, devoid of any actual economic pressure on the bosses.

---

220 Leon, L. F. (2021, October 19). *After Strike, Washington Carpenters Approve New Contract by Slim Margin*. Labor Notes. Retrieved May 21, 2023, from https://labornotes.org/2021/10/after-strike-washington-carpenters-approve-new-contract-slim-margin

Shapiro surely understood the broader risk to her and the other construction union business managers if carpenters picketed a wide range of worksites, which, given that their contract had expired, they were well within their rights to do. If they did so, workers from other trades were likely to walk out in solidarity, PLA or no PLA, shutting down area construction. Beyond that, if the Carpenters—the largest single union in the construction trades—could win paid parking, then the industry would face tremendous pressure to extend the benefit to other workers. Indeed, this was the very purpose of a strike—to force a better contract by inflicting economic pain on the contractors.

Shapiro and her fellow business managers had pledged in PLAs and in their contracts to provide the industry with an uninterrupted supply of labor. In a wider strike, they would be trapped between the demands of their members to walk out in solidarity and the contractors' insistence that they bring the strike to heel. This was a problem entirely of their own making, a direct consequence of their attachment to the business union model. Jammed into a no-win situation, Shapiro must have feared the other business managers would turn on her if she failed to control her own members.

To Esparza and his union siblings, it was clear that in practice, Shapiro was no different from the leaders who preceded her. Tensions were high as workers gathered at the union hall on the eve of the strike. Fights nearly broke out as rank-and-file carpenters confronted Shapiro's staff. The members demanded that the union leaders expand the strike significantly. Striking only a fraction of the industry was a dead loser of a strategy; anyone could see that. Esparza and others pointed out that Shapiro had excluded other projects not covered by PLAs from picketing. At the very least, they insisted, the union should sanction picketing at Microsoft's suburban Seattle headquarters, at the time the largest private sector construction site on the west coast. Facing an outright rebellion, Shapiro relented, agreeing to add Microsoft to the picket list.

The strains only heightened the next day, when Shapiro's staff instructed picketing carpenters to choose from a small selection of chants, and advised them of the few activities that would be permitted. Worse, some of the sites were what carpenters called "holes in the ground"—construction sites that had been excavated but were not yet in full operation. Picketing them was a purely symbolic act.

One of the many incensed picketers was Nina Wurz, a self-described "33-year-old queer journeyman carpenter out of Local 30, but my number one title is mom." In the summer Wurz had plunged headlong into the task of helping build up the Peter J. McGuire group. Wurz had just graduated from apprentice to journey-level status and was working on a public transit construction project, one of the many that Shapiro had exempted from the strike. When the strike started, she quit the job and joined the union-sanctioned pickets. "I wanted to get an idea of what the official pickets were like," Wurz recalled. "And it was pretty depressing." Attempting to liven up the picketing, Wurz picked up a megaphone and led the picketers in her own chant. Union staff came up to her and confiscated the megaphone. This was not just leadership incompetence, Wurz and her union siblings concluded. This was outright sabotage.

Sawant and Socialist Alternative members had been in touch with Esparza, Wurz, and other members of the Peter J. McGuire

Group since that summer. Logan Swan, the union ironworker and SA organizer, had long since overcome the jobsite tensions that are common between carpenters and ironworkers because of the two unions' frequent jurisdictional disputes. Years earlier, he had spoken out in support of carpenters when their pension was being threatened. Rank-and-file carpenters remembered this act of solidarity, and as the union members rejected successive contract offers, they reached out to Swan. When they went on strike, Swan and Sawant joined the Peter J. McGuire Group on the picket line, along with other SA members, electricians, ironworkers, and other building trades workers.

Sawant issued a public statement supporting the rank-and-file call for a better deal and pledged to support the strike and whatever democratic decision the carpenters made. An extraordinary political alliance was emerging: Building trades workers, many of whom openly supported Trump and other right-wing causes, reaching out to unabashed Marxists to strike the industry for better pay and benefits. At one picket line, a bulky carpenter towering a foot over Sawant asked to shake her hand. "We probably don't agree on anything else," he said, "but you are the only person standing with us."

Swan observed, "That must have scared the pants off everyone in power to see the right-wing workers and socialists reaching rapprochement around naked class struggle. Like it's their worst fears come to life."

Swan wasn't just referring to the construction bosses. Shapiro and the other building trade union leaders were working aggressively to break strike enthusiasm, and they saw Sawant's participation as their biggest threat.

As a staff organizer in Sawant's council office, I fielded a string of messages and calls from local and even national union leaders, including text messages from the head of the regional grocery workers union, the largest private sector union in the state and a heavyweight in the labor movement. The private messages warned Sawant to stay away from the rank-and-file members. Shapiro had been subjected to sexist attacks within the Carpenters union, the grocery union leader noted, and any association by Sawant with Shapiro's internal political opponents was intolerable. More ominously, I was warned that if Sawant didn't cease aligning with the members, then unions would stop opposing the recall she faced.

Publicly, in the first days of the strike the leaders of several other unions and Democrats rallied to defend Shapiro. They blamed union members who were on strike, and they red-baited Sawant and other strike supporters. Nicole Grant, the head of the Martin Luther King County Labor Council, the federation of area unions, told a reporter that she'd "never seen anything quite this serious in the course of my career, where a small faction of Marxist extremists, with the backing of an elected official, have been able to not just wreak this much havoc inside of a union but been this undermining."[221]

There's no question that Shapiro faced a barrage of sexist attacks and threats from some union members in online messages, at union meetings, and on picket lines. It was a function of deeply ingrained chauvinism and misogyny welling up against the

221 Barnett, E. C. (2021, September 16). *Misogynistic Attacks, Accusations of "Interference" By Sawant, as Carpenters' Union Strikes*. Publicola. Retrieved May 19, 2023, from https://publicola.com/2021/09/16/misogynistic-attacks-accusations-of-interference-by-sawant-as-carpenters-union-strikes/

widespread exasperation with Shapiro's leadership. And it was extremely destructive to the workers' cause. The Peter J. McGuire Group leaders were keenly aware of the power of sexism to divide and harm the movement, and they regularly reminded members at rallies and in social media postings that sexist, racist, or homophobic attacks would only help the bosses and weren't allowed within the caucus. They noted that one of the caucus' core bargaining demands was stronger worksite protection against sexual harassment. Sawant, too, spoke up against the sexist attacks on Shapiro, but emphasized that the horrific bile directed at Shapiro did not excuse her failure to support the members and their demands once they democratically had chosen the strike path.

On the fifth day of the strike, Sawant and the Peter J. McGuire Group members called an early morning press conference in downtown Seattle's Pioneer Square to announce several legislative measures that would up the ante against the bosses. First, Sawant said, she would bring forward an ordinance requiring all contractors to provide fully paid parking to their workers in Seattle. If the bosses wouldn't negotiate paid parking in union contracts, then the movement would impose a legislative solution, she said, noting that her ordinance would cover all construction workers, not just carpenters. Second, Sawant said she would introduce a bill restoring workers' right to strike by banning no-strike clauses from city construction projects. And third, she would bring a bill to strengthen enforcement and penalties for wage theft, a common problem in the construction industry. She invited Shapiro and other labor leaders to join her in pushing for the bills. Sawant announced that strikers and community members would begin gathering signatures on petitions demanding that the City Council act promptly on these measures. The measures would open a new battleground in the strike, increasing pressure on the Democrats, who had stayed on the sidelines except to defend Shapiro, and on the industry bosses, who had refused to negotiate on parking and other issues.

Just before the press conference kicked off, carpenters began streaming into Pioneer Square to announce a dramatic picket line development. Earlier that morning the Peter J. McGuire activists and other construction workers had taken matters into their own hands, setting up roving wildcat pickets—strike lines not sanctioned by the union leadership. Already carpenters had shut down one construction site by picketing and successfully persuading workers from other crafts to down their tools and join them.

"We would just show up with homemade signs and a megaphone," Swan recalled. "We would chant things like, 'Down your tools, join the line.'" One very tall and imposing carpenter, Monty Wills, grabbed a megaphone. "He would start a whole tirade about how the carpenters were on strike, you need to stand with the carpenters. If we all shut everything down, then, that's how we're going to win," he said.

On the other side of the battle line, Shapiro's business agents raced to get ahead of the wildcatters, rushing onto job sites to tell workers to ignore the pickets. "They're getting told by their union reps that we're with BLM, and we're Antifa, and we're communists, and it's not a sanctioned picket, and not to respect the picket line. And just to ignore us. They're getting told by their foreman and their general foreman that it's work as usual. And these are just protesters," Swan said. "But we would see workers who are doing the work on the ground floor, and we would engage into the fence and make appeals for them to down their tools. And we'd see workers, peering out through the windows, heads coming over the parapet, as they're looking at us, and we'd yell at them, and appeal to them to come down. And we just went job site to job site." Slowly but steadily, one construction site after another went quiet as the workers stopped construction and joined the carpenters on the street.

At one point, a wildcat picketer passed by a job site on the way to his car. "All the workers are kind of just milling around by the fence and the gates," Swan said. "And they're like, 'Hey, are you with the picketers?' And he's like, 'Yeah,' and they say, 'When are you going to come here?' They were just waiting for us to show up so that they could leave." Other wildcat picketers were getting texts from friends, urging the pickets to come to their sites so they could join in.

For two days, the roving pickets of carpenters and other construction workers, Socialist Alternative members, and other community supporters went site to site, getting hundreds to stop work.

"Our group would at least double in size from when we started to when we finished, because workers would come down off of the job and be like, 'Well, I already paid for parking for the day and this is exciting.' And they would grab a picket sign and come with us to go shut down the next job," Swan said. "The energy was great."

On the second day of roving pickets, a crew of strikers took a break in the afternoon on Seattle's First Hill, just east of downtown, assessing their progress and the verbal battles they'd had with the union business agents. "We were standing up on the hill being like, 'What are we going to do?' Should we call it and cut our losses and maybe we can try and connect with those guys who are shutting down Microsoft? Because there was a whole other group that was doing unsanctioned pickets there," Swan recalled.

As they sat deliberating, an elevator operator from a nearby job site approached. "Hey," he said, "are you the guys going around shutting down job sites?" His coworkers were eager to pack up their tools and join the action.

It had already been a long, exhausting day. "We didn't feel like we had the momentum to go and keep shutting down jobs," Swan told me later. "But it basically came to us and it was like, if you show up, they're going to walk. So we said, fuck it. And we headed down there and picketed them and shut it down."

Compared to the union-sanctioned pickets, Wurz found the wildcat actions elating. They were building solidarity across the construction trades and escalating pressure on the bosses. After the second day, "We were like, let's shut down Climate Pledge Arena tomorrow," she recalled. The Amazon-branded arena was a huge construction project near Seattle's iconic Space Needle. It was the crown jewel of area PLA agreements. Picketing it would put the strikers in direct confrontation with the union business managers.

The pickets began at 5:00 a.m., starting in Pioneer Square downtown, and again snowballed from site to site. By midmorning the carpenters and socialists were outside Climate Pledge Arena. They heckled Chris McClain, the business manager for the Ironworkers and president of the local construction unions council, as he crossed the picket line along with other business managers to lobby workers already inside to stay.

Shapiro was determined to stop the wildcat actions at any cost. On Thursday night, September 23—after the second day of wildcat job shutdowns—the Carpenters union leader announced a halt to all picketing the next day. One *Seattle Times* headline blared, "Carpenters union pauses picketing in Seattle after wildcat strikes, dispute with Kshama Sawant." Shapiro blamed Sawant for exposing the union to lawsuits from employers. She accused the socialist of "interfering in the NW Carpenter Union's democracy just to grab the limelight for her own political agenda."[222] It was a bizarre choice of words, considering that Sawant had sided with the democratic decision of Shapiro's members to go on strike. Picketing would resume on Monday, Shapiro said, at more sites but under tighter union staff control.

Shapiro's pivot made zero sense to rank-and-file carpenters. "We can't stop picketing because once we stop picketing, all these trades are going to see that we're weak and start crossing," Joe Sosa said. "Our intention is to keep the momentum going."

Sosa was glad to have Sawant on his side. "I don't really believe in her politics," he said. Sosa had joined with union ironworkers in 2018 in shouting down Sawant at a Tax Amazon rally, but now things were different, he said. "I'm not a socialist. I'm not on board with defunding the police, the head tax or anything like that. But I'm with her in support of the unions."[223]

---

222 Groover, H. (2021, September 23). *Carpenters union pauses picketing in Seattle after wildcat strikes, dispute with Kshama Sawant*. The Seattle Times. Retrieved May 19, 2023, from https://www.seattletimes.com/business/carpenters-union-to-pause-picketing-in-seattle-after-wildcat-strikes-dispute-with-kshama-sawant/

223 Ibid.

More than 200 people, about half of them carpenters, turned out the following day for a weekend rally and march to the Associated General Contractors headquarters. The action was organized by the Peter J. McGuire Group and Sawant's office. Mingling among the carpenters and their families were other construction trades workers, schoolteachers, university workers, doctors, bookstore workers, and state employees.

"Look through our history. Union victories and strikes were made when the leaders represented the rank and file," Wurz told the crowd. "They were made by breaking the rules set by the forces in power who want us to be weak. They were made by bridging solidarity across other worker movements."

Wurz described the pointlessness of following the union leadership's orders: "Picketing empty job sites, brothers and sisters shouting themselves hoarse while no one's listening. Morale is a precious resource on a strike. And they're running near empty.

"We need to do better than this and we need to do better by them," she said. "Strikes succeed when we threaten the boss's profit margins, not by becoming a nuisance. And when you threaten the profit margins, they will strike back and they always have, but we cannot fear that.

"I spoke with workers who left their jobs during our protest, and they had nothing but solidarity for us. . . . We've seen solidarity from outside the trades as well. We've seen teachers and students and nurses and doctors, and workers from all across the spectrum show up and express their solidarity with us," she said, scanning the crowd. "We carpenters see you here showing up for us, and I promise you that we will show up for you!"

The crowd roared in approval. Members from other unions spoke up, alternately pledging support for the carpenters and parrying union leaders' charges against Sawant and the rank and file who were supporting the strike.

The striking carpenters "deserve nothing but respect and solidarity from our labor community," said Book Workers Union member Jacob Shear. "Unions should be a radical and disruptive force, not shields or cushions for management," he declared.

"We are here to show solidarity and our gratefulness to the carpenters union for taking the lead in showing the bosses that we are ready to fight back," said Heather Barnett, a doctor and member of the local physicians' union.

"The bosses would love unions to fight each other. . . because they just want to make an extra buck off of your labor," Barnett said. "We're not meddling – we're standing here in solidarity," she said.[224] Following the speeches, the crowd marched down the block to the contractors' headquarters, chanting "15 over 3!" – the wage demand for $15 in wage increases spread over three years.

Carpenters welcomed the broader support. "I've been picketing for a week and a half – my feet are tired, my voice is tired," Carpenters union member David Wang told a reporter. "I'm glad

224 [Facebook]. (2021, September 25). *Livestream* [Video]. Councilmember Kshama Sawant. Retrieved May 19, 2023, https://www.facebook.com/watch/live/?ref=watch_permalink&v=3048868858731579

to see non-carpenter, community supporters add their feet and their voices to our struggle."[225]

The rally, coming after a week of energetic pickets and job shutdowns, was a high-water mark for the rank-and-file insurgency. The wildcat pickets and rallies forced the union leadership to make concessions on strike tactics. The following week, Shapiro and the union business managers expanded authorized picketing to 18 sites. But there were not enough Peter J. McGuire activists to keep the pressure up on further expanding the strike. Getting non-carpenters to walk off the job site for more than a day or two was increasingly difficult, especially in the absence of a unified, industry-wide escalation plan. Members were fighting against both their employers and the union business managers, who day by day became more aggressive about enforcing the no-strike clauses.

Shapiro resumed bargaining with the contractors and in a few days emerged with a fifth proposal. There was little change in workplace anti-harassment protection. Workers would receive raises of $10.02 an hour over the next three years. This was far from the "$15 over 3" demand, but it was better than the original offer—$8.64 over four years. For some workers, parking subsidies were improved, but they still only covered a portion of the cost. Still, the length of the contract—three years—was a victory;

225 Krieg, H. (2021, September 30). *A Fractured Carpenters Union Sits Together at the Bargaining Table for the First Time*. The Stranger. Retrieved May 21, 2023, from https://www.thestranger.com/slog/2021/09/30/61593735/a-fractured-carpenters-union-sits-together-at-the-bargaining-table-for-the-first-time

it ensured that in the next round Carpenters could bargain alongside other construction unions.

In October, members ratified the offer, 54 to 46 percent, and returned to work. Some, like Wurz, became politicized through the fight, got more active in the union, and joined Sawant and the socialists in community struggles. Just days after the contract was ratified, construction workers and allies signed into an online City Council meeting where Sawant was introducing the employer-paid parking ordinance. In the previous week, several hundred construction workers had signed petitions to City Council calling for adoption of the bill.

Their excitement to elevate the parking fight ran headlong into a rock-hard political firewall. All eight Democrats united in refusing to provide even a courtesy second to Sawant's ordinance, blocking the bill from getting discussed by the council. It was a particularly brazen display of the political establishment's loyalty to big business, likely spurred on by the Democrats' judgment that Sawant would be gone within a few weeks. With the socialist about to be recalled, there was little holding the Democrats back from openly revealing their true class allegiances.

Monty Anderson, executive director of the construction union council, thanked the Democrats for blocking the bill that would have provided employer-paid parking to thousands of the union members he claimed to represent. "We collectively bargain. We don't need Councilwoman Sawant in the middle of our bargaining process," he told the City Council during the meeting's public comment period. "The contracts that we're talking about are very unique and nuanced between our employers and ourselves and we don't need grandstanding."

Rank-and-file construction workers had a completely different perspective. "I'm mother to a sick child, and I currently pay $31 a day for parking," carpenter Mandy Richardson told the City Council. "It's just like a second mortgage payment."

Marissa Bertaud, an apprentice union electrician, told the politicians, "When I moved here I was making bottom salary for apprentices, paying $20 parking, which is cheap." Parking costs "completely wiped me out weekly. It cost me grocery money. It cost me rent money. . . . We as workers are coming to you right now and telling you what we need, and you're not paying attention. I'm disgusted."

"You folks who oppose this are out of touch with the boots on the ground rank-and-file workers, who lose upwards of $500 a month on parking," Wurz told the Democrats. Workers, she said, "are intensely disappointed with supposed leaders who can't put aside party politics to support workers. The least you could do is make sure we're not taxed to go to work."[226]

Apprentice union electrician Taylor Werner told the Democrats that "this legislation that Councilmember Sawant put forward would have been game-changing." As a single mom starting out in the trade, Werner said she was paid a starting wage of $15 an hour. "There were days when I paid three times that much to park."

---

226 [Seattle Channel]. (2021, October 18). *City Council 10/18/2021* [Video]. Seattlechannel.org. Retrieved May 21, 2023, https://www.seattlechannel.org/FullCouncil?videoid=x132248

The Democrats' smackdown of Sawant's paid parking ordinance was a relief to the union business managers. They had headed off a nasty carpenter uprising and now, thanks to the Democrats, did not have to get put in the awkward position of explaining to their members why paid parking legislation was a bad idea. But any celebration was cut short by stranger-than-fiction drama that exploded in the immediate aftermath, undercutting the establishment's narrative that union leaders and Democrats were nobly defending a progressive Carpenters union leader against wildcatters and Marxists.

Just one week after the Democrats blocked Sawant's parking bill, Shapiro was leading a meeting of her regional Carpenters union executive board when national Carpenters union leaders burst unannounced into the room. They declared that the northwest council was being placed under immediate trusteeship. Shapiro was charged with directing her staff to commit election fraud on several contract ratification votes, including one of the summer 2021 votes. She was fired from her job, expelled from the union, and sued for allegedly directing vote-rigging to engineer "yes" votes on contracts. The lawsuit described in detail how Shapiro allegedly directed her staff to "fix the fucking vote" by submitting contract ratification ballots on behalf of members who hadn't yet voted. One Shapiro staff person was accused of submitting nearly 1,000 false "yes" votes. The fraud was discovered when dozens of those members subsequently tried to vote, only to find that they couldn't. The national union also charged Shapiro with concealing huge pension fund losses from the members and mismanaging the union's finances.[227]

---

227 (2021, December 17). *Letter to all members of the local unions affiliated with the Northwest Regional Council of Carpenters*. Laborpains.

Shapiro denied the vote fraud and financial mismanagement charges. In turn, she declared she was being railroaded by the national union president, Doug McCarron, because she refused his demand that she crush a newly-formed staff union at her regional Carpenters council. She counter-accused McCarron of vote-rigging and said that the national president had ordered her to sign union contracts without membership votes. Adding yet another bizarre twist to matters, Shapiro asked a federal court for immunity from prosecution, claiming that while in union leadership she was working undercover for the Seattle Police Department to root out contractor fraud.[228]

There was no shortage of finger-pointing as Carpenters union staff scrambled to rescue their reputations, dodge lawsuits, and avoid prison time. The national union canceled internal leadership

org. Retrieved May 22, 2023, from https://laborpains.org/wp-content/uploads/2022/01/UNION-HEARING.pdf and (2022, March 2). *United States District Court Western District of Washington - UNITED BROTHERHOOD OF CARPENTERS AND JOINERS OF AMERICA, an unincorporated association, and PACIFIC NORTHWEST REGIONAL COUNCIL OF CARPENTERS, an unincorporated association, Plaintiff, v. EVELYN SHAPIRO, an individual, Defendant. Case 2:22-cv-00245*. CourtListener.com. Retrieved May 22, 2023, from https://storage.courtlistener.com/recap/gov.uscourts.wawd.307829/gov.uscourts.wawd.307829.1.0.pdf

228 (2022, May 5). *Declaration of Evelyn Shapiro. United States District Court Western District of Washington - UNITED BROTHERHOOD OF CARPENTERS AND JOINERS OF AMERICA, an unincorporated association, and PACIFIC NORTHWEST REGIONAL COUNCIL OF CARPENTERS, an unincorporated association, Plaintiff, v. EVELYN SHAPIRO, an individual, Defendant. Case 2:22-cv-00245*. CourListener.com. Retrieved May 22, 2023, from https://storage.courtlistener.com/recap/gov.uscourts.wawd.307829/gov.uscourts.wawd.307829.19.0.pdf

elections and unilaterally restructured the regional council. Members were stunned, angry, and confused.

Neither the lurid allegations nor the ensuing chaos got Esparza, Wurz, and the other Peter J. McGuire Group activists closer to building the kind of union they sought. The national union leadership had intervened to remove a political liability, not defend democracy. But the unseemly and sordid accusations lobbed back and forth between Shapiro's faction and the national union only proved what the rank-and-file members and Sawant had been saying all along: The union had been hijacked by people who utterly betrayed the interests of the members. The area labor council leaders, other construction union business managers, and City Council Democrats, who just weeks earlier had loudly rallied to Shapiro's defense and assailed Sawant, suddenly had nothing to say about the precipitous downfall of their erstwhile hero.

There was no time following the strike for Sawant and the campaign to draw up a balance sheet of the experience. Carpenters were consumed with the internal turmoil of their union, and the socialists dove headlong into the recall fight, which was just a few weeks to conclusion when the strike ended. But there were important lessons. The Peter J. McGuire Group members had not realized most of their bargaining demands. And yet they, along with Sawant and the socialists, could claim a remarkable achievement: Facing the combined headwinds of implacable employers, hostile union business managers, and a united political class, they had waged a militant three-week strike that put bold working-class demands in the spotlight. They had attracted other trades workers into the fight and demonstrated the tremendous power of construction workers when they move beyond single-craft actions to striking as a united class. And they had done it by building a remarkable alliance between the most conservative elements of the union movement and Marxist socialists—united through bold bargaining demands. Sawant had shown workers, jaded after being repeatedly abandoned by the entire political establishment, how a principled pro-worker officeholder acts. Swan and the other members of Socialist Alternative had gained the trust of conservative building trades workers, not by hiding or downplaying their Marxist politics but by mobilizing pickets and rallies focused on the material demands of the workers.

In an age when mainstream political pundits wring their hands about their inability to connect with Trump voters, when Democrats demean, blame, infantilize, and write off workers who jump on right-wing bandwagons as "deplorables," or simply throw their hands up, claiming workers are too conservative, Sawant and the socialists had demonstrated a way forward: Not by marginalizing or ignoring people with vastly different political orientations, nor by insincerely papering over differences, but by reaching out on the principled basis of class struggle.

The strike's roller-coaster drama delivered a huge dividend to recall advocates: a more polarized Seattle labor movement. As the pickets were coming down, Ironworkers union business manager McClain filed papers to set up a new pro-recall PAC called A Better Seattle, collecting money from executives, developers, corporate landlords, millionaires, and others who had already given the $1,000 legal maximum to the Recall Sawant campaign and wanted to do more.[229]

Some 20 unions had endorsed the Kshama Solidarity Campaign earlier in the year, but in the wake of the carpenters strike the officers of many of these unions backed away from Sawant, not rescinding their endorsements but also giving few resources to fight the recall. Rank-and-file union members and the leaders of the more progressive unions—those who had rallied and picketed with the carpenters, including state employees, university workers, doctors, educators, healthcare workers, and hospitality workers—remained the core of Sawant's labor support. Many union members were more energized than ever. The strike had demonstrated that, without Sawant in office, it would be much harder to build a fighting labor movement.

A sweeping victory for right-wing candidates in the November municipal elections was more bad news for Sawant. The business-backed mayoral candidate cruised to victory. A conservative business owner beat community organizer and BLM leader Nikkita Oliver for the open council seat. The City Attorney race went to an attorney with almost no courtroom experience, who joined the Republican Party during the Trump administration and who was buoyed by high-profile Democratic establishment

229 Seattle Ethics and Elections Commission (2021, October 27). *Report history*. SEEC - Committee Registration Statement. Retrieved July 14, 2023, from https://web6.seattle.gov/ethics/filings/popfiling.aspx?prguid=06F49785-1EA3-4F16-A4A1-516AF242C355 and (2023, July 14). *Contributions to A Better Seattle 2021 Election Cycle*. Seattle Ethics and Elections Commission. Retrieved July 14, 2023, from https://web6.seattle.gov/ethics/elections/poplist_v2.aspx?cid=826&listtype=contributors

endorsements and right-wing talk radio hosts. The local results mirrored the national political scene, where right-wing law-and-order candidates swept hotly contested local and state races.

Just as the dust began to settle from the November election and as households turned attention to the Thanksgiving holiday, ballots arrived in the mailboxes of the 77,000 voters in Seattle's District 3.

Recall proponents wanted to make a final fundraising push to pay for huge television buys in the final weeks, but to do so they needed a legal work-around. State law limited individual campaign donations to $1,000, and a similar $1,000 cap also applied to McClain's A Better Seattle PAC. Many of the recall funders had already maxxed out to both the Recall Sawant campaign and the PAC. So McClain's PAC petitioned the state's Public Disclosure Commission to be exempted from all contribution limits. The petition was explicitly contrary to state law, but the PAC lawyers argued that A Better Seattle technically was an independent political committee deserving unlimited fundraising rights under the US Supreme Court's *Citizens United* ruling. Just before Thanksgiving, with ballots already out, the public disclosure commission members—appointed by a Democratic governor—unanimously voted to override state law and lift the PAC contribution limits.[230] With restraints off, the recall backers collected another $200,000 for the final push.

---

230 (2021, November 24). *Minutes - Special meeting, November 24, 2021.* State of Washington - Public Disclosure Commission. Retrieved May 23, 2023, from https://www.pdc.wa.gov/sites/default/files/2022-03/Minutes%252011.24.21.FINAL_.pdf

The Kshama Solidarity Campaign managed to raise just over $1 million, closely matching the combined Recall Sawant and PAC backers. They achieved this historic level with an aggressive grassroots fundraising push—everything from collecting coins and single bills at apartment doors to staging online fundraisers. Some 11,626 people gave money to defend Sawant, more than twice the number of donors to the recall campaign and the pro-recall PAC.[231]

The fundraising supported a huge canvassing effort, with campaign staff augmented by more than 1,500 volunteers who logged time over the course of 2021. In the last two months, hundreds of volunteers along with staff fluent in eight different languages knocked on tens of thousands of doors every week, getting people involved in renters' rights struggles, soliciting contributions, and educating voters about the right-wing and corporate forces behind the recall campaign. Many of these volunteers were newly activated renters, drawn into the fight as a result of the multiple tenants' rights wins earlier in 2021 and determined to preserve their beachhead in City Hall.

Even while balloting was underway, Sawant continued to demonstrate her brand of insurgent politics, organizing with tenants at the Rainier Court Apartments who were fighting against rent increases and for their landlord to fix housing code violations. Sawant called out the Democrats for their hypocrisy in ignoring the tenants' plight at the senior housing complex. "What does

---

231 (n.d.). *Recall - City Council District 3.* Seattle Ethics and Elections Commission. Retrieved May 23, 2023, from https://web6.seattle.gov/ethics/elections/campaigns.aspx?cycle=2021&type=contest&IDNum=195&leftmenu=collapsed

it mean to say Black Lives Matter when hundreds of Black and Brown working-class renters, low-income seniors in this case, can be forced to live in nightmarish conditions, then subjected to unjust rent increases en masse which will lead to continued displacement of our Black and Brown neighbors?" she asked. Sawant and her council office staff, along with the Tenants Union, organized a march on the landlord to deliver their demands, and then staged a press conference and public rally. The Rainier Court landlord rescinded the increases for the 600 tenants, and pledged to accelerate apartment repairs.

On the election front, campaigners did not shy away from framing the fight in class terms. They pointed to the Rainier Court Apartments fight, and also contrasted working-class demands for rent control and the tenant protections Sawant and the movement had won in the previous months with the big-moneyed developers and CEOs who were backing the recall. Campaign literature named names, pointing out that recall champions like CEOs George Petrie and Martin Selig were big Trump donors. The campaign also had no hesitation calling the recall racist, noting that two of the three recall charges against Sawant involved her participation in Black Lives Matter demonstrations.

"We had a very sharp fighting edge, where it was you either vote no and support Kshama Sawant or you stand with these Trump supporters and these billionaires and these capitalists that are funding this campaign," recalled Cat Ngo, a tech worker and a new member of Socialist Alternative. "We took that sharp edge because we knew it was necessary to polarize people to make a choice." That was jarring to some voters, especially Democrats and self-described moderates, but showing the class conflict underlying the recall made it clear what the ballot choice was about. "There were people who said, "Why are you calling me a Trump supporter?' And with those people we have to be like, 'Okay but you're voting with these millionaires, these union busters, these people who run these terrible companies,'" Ngo said. One conversation at a time, the campaign successfully defined their adversary and undermined the recall campaign's narrative about ordinary District 3 voters outraged by the socialist.

Campaign staff knew that overall voter turnout would be decisive. If overall turnout was low, then the higher-propensity voters in the richer, whiter neighborhoods—a minority of District 3 voters—would carry the recall to victory. If renters and homeowners in low- and moderate-income neighborhoods failed to turn out in similar numbers, Sawant was finished. In 2021, the campaign registered 1,775 new voters, mostly students and workers from immigrant communities.

Kailyn Nicholson, the SA organizer, described how canvassers would remind voters that the recall had scheduled the December election "because they're counting on people not voting. The only way we're going to win is if we have a bigger grassroots 'get out the vote' campaign than has ever been seen in Seattle's history. We need you to be a part of that." Once a voter agreed to oppose the recall, canvassers would have them fill out a pledge card describing their plan to vote and identifying three people they would encourage to vote against the recall. Campaign staffers then followed up with pledge signers a few days later to see how their outreach efforts had gone. Some 919 voters signed pledge cards, each one an organizer in their own social circle.

Natalie Bailey dove headlong into the canvassing work. A trans woman who had moved to Seattle years earlier from Salt Lake City, she had struggled to get by and was not politically active until she attended a Tax Amazon rally in 2020. Inspired by Sawant's rally speech, she became a regular petitioner for the Tax Amazon campaign.

For Bailey, pressed to pay the bills every month and eager to see rent control, Sawant offered political clarity and a fighting path forward. The political work was physically challenging for her. Bailey suffered from a congenital spinal condition that forced her to walk slowly. Every shift, whether standing at a campaign table or traipsing up and down stairs to knock on doors, was painful. She pushed through it. When the 2021 tenants' rights bills came before City Council, Bailey was an avid participant, signing up to testify. When the recall burst onto the scene, she signed up for tabling and door-knocking shifts.

At one door, a woman challenged Bailey about the charges levied against Sawant. "Did she learn her lesson yet?" the woman asked Bailey. "And I was like, 'What exactly, what lesson?' And she said 'Oh, well they found her guilty of all this stuff,'" Bailey recalled. She explained that Sawant hadn't been found guilty by the Supreme Court; it was up to the voters to decide if she should be recalled or not. Bailey shared a flyer about the issue.

"She was like, 'Oh, well, I didn't know that. That's not how people are talking about that. I really thought that she had done something wrong. I wanted her to learn her lesson because I wanted her to stay in office. But I didn't want her to be a criminal or whatever,'" the woman told Bailey.

The woman took the flyer, promised that she would show it to a bunch of her friends, signed a pledge card, and listed three people she would reach out to. "Thank you for actually telling me the truth about what's happening with this recall," Bailey recalled the woman telling her. And then the woman, who minutes ago had not been in Sawant's camp, donated $25 to the campaign.

For other voters, the challenge wasn't misinformation; it was a complete lack of information. This was especially common in immigrant communities, where it was easy for non-English speakers to be totally unaware of the recall. Ngo, the new SA member, was a native of Saigon and fluent in Vietnamese. He showed up one cold, rainy fall morning at a food bank line in Yesler Terrace, a public housing community that was home to many elderly people from his home country.

Handing out translated campaign literature, Ngo told the residents that the political and business establishment were angling to kick Sawant out of office. Nearly everyone he talked to was supportive of fighting the recall. Many knew Sawant, as she had been a regular guest at the meetings of the Vietnamese Senior Association and the annual New Year's Lion Dance festivities. Over the years, Sawant's council office had worked with the elders to win city funding for senior cultural programming and bus passes. And, living on fixed incomes, they were worried about the rising cost of groceries and rent. Sawant was the singular political figure who had defended them over the years. As Ngo talked to them in the food bank line, they declared that of course they would oppose the recall.

From the food bank tabling Ngo began door-knocking on weekends along with campaign staff fluent in Mandarin, Cantonese, Korean, Somali, Swahili, and other languages. They focused on public housing complexes and large apartment buildings, reaching hundreds of voters who previously had scant, if any, knowledge of the recall.

When voting began, Ngo began door-knocking along with campaign organizer Chris Gray, who carried a portable printer in a bag as they went door to door. They asked people if they had voted yet. Almost no one had. Many didn't even know where their ballots were. Ngo offered to help them vote on the spot. "I would do all the talking and Chris would do the logistics of feeding the paper into the printer, print the paper out, get them to vote on the spot, and then telling them, 'Hey, please submit this when you get a chance.'" They got about 50 people to vote in this manner.

The ballot printing was entirely legal. Balloting was all by mail, and the King County Elections Department had a website portal for registered voters to download and reprint ballots that had been spoiled or misplaced. They had even made an accompanying tutorial video. After seeing the success that Ngo and the other multilingual organizers were having, Nicholson said the campaign strategy team realized that "if it's legal to do that, couldn't we try to do it on a mass scale by instead of just going to people's doors?"

At sites throughout working-class neighborhoods, the campaign began to set up ballot printing stations with Wifi-connected portable printers. Consulting closely with King County Elections officials, Sawant campaigners made sure that the ballot stations were separated from any of the campaign tables, and that only trained organizers staffed the ballot printing stations to ensure there was no electioneering. They quickly found that the tables were enormously popular with voters, especially low-income voters who didn't have access to personal printers.

"It made it qualitatively easier for people to vote," Nicholson said. "If we are out there every day in the same place reliably, and we have posters on every telephone pole with the addresses of where we'll be and when, and right there we have the ballot for you, all you have to do is stop at the table, fill it out, put it in the envelope, sign it. It takes less than a minute to do the whole process." This was a game-changer for voters who had lost their ballots or who thought voting was over for the year. "We pretty quickly realized that this was a bigger thing than we even initially thought. This could be decisive," she said.

Recall advocates hated the tactic. In the final days of voting, recall supporters would drive past ballot-printing stations and shout obscenities at or heckle the staff. *The Seattle Times*—which earlier in the year had editorialized against the rise of voter suppression in other states—complained about Sawant's grassroots ballot stations and demanded that the state legislature outlaw the practice. But it was entirely legal, as long as people staffing the ballot-printing stations did not electioneer. In the final days leading up to the special election, the campaign staffed 14 ballot-printing stations in student- and renter-heavy neighborhoods. All told, more than 600 people voted using the printing stations.

Bailey was one of the campaigners assigned to ballot stations. Training was thorough before anyone went out: Verify voter eligibility through the county elections website; no electioneering, no campaign literature allowed, no touching the ballot; point the voter to a nearby ballot drop box or mailbox where the vote could be deposited; and be aware that the recall advocates were watching carefully and one misstep would hurt the entire campaign. It was not a simple operation. Staffers had to make sure they had enough paper, backup batteries, phones to set up local Wifi hotspots, canopies, pens, hand sanitizer, and that the equipment worked before they headed out into the December rain to their tabling spot.

Voters learned about the ballot-printing stations from campaign tables or from one of hundreds of posters stapled to telephone poles. "A couple people I talked to had lost their ballots," Bailey recalled. "Some people just hadn't done it yet, and this was a very convenient option for them to actually vote so they didn't forget. And I think that that was really helpful. Some people expressed that this should just be a thing that you can do. You just have a place to go, and it just gets done and you can vote right away in that way."

The recall staff and the PAC ran a more traditional election campaign, piling on in the final weeks with a torrent of mailers and internet, TV, and radio ads, supplemented by editorials in *The Seattle Times* calling for Sawant to be recalled. Turnout was high in the rich neighborhoods abutting Lake Washington, and those votes overwhelmingly favored the recall. But the recall's massive air war and turnout could not match the herculean grassroots campaign squeezing out every potential "no" vote.

On election night the recall was leading, 17,048 to 15,055, but about 9,000 votes were left to count. That was better than Sawant had hoped for on the first night of vote-counting. The campaign was confident that late votes would swing heavily for the movement, just as they had in 2019. That was a correct assessment. Within two days, the "no" vote was in the lead, and when the final votes were tallied 10 days after the election, Sawant had beaten the recall by 310 votes, 20,656 to 20,346. It was exceedingly close.

But it was a socialist victory—again—over the combined power of the business and political establishment and their allies.

The ballot stations, the language-specific door-knocking, and the massive grassroots canvasses in low- and moderate-income neighborhoods had lifted voter turnout significantly. Turnout in big working-class apartment buildings—the ones that Ngo, Gray and their colleagues had knocked repeatedly—doubled compared to the 2021 primary election. In one building it was nearly 10 times the primary turnout, Sawant's campaign determined. Overall, turnout in this first-ever December election was 53 percent—about 20 percentage points higher than previous special elections,[232] or an additional 15,000 votes.

"The wealthy took their best shot at us, and we beat them. Again," Sawant declared after the final tally to about 100 supporters gathered outside Rev. Jeffrey's New Hope Missionary Baptist Church. "We did not back down in our socialist City Council office. Instead we went on the offensive, and we won some of the most crucial victories for renters' rights this year. We did not back down in fighting for workers. . . . We did not back down one inch in our socialist election campaign to defeat the racist, right-wing big-business-backed recall."[233]

---

232 (2020, November). *King County Elections Historical Turnout Information*. King County Elections. Retrieved May 24, 2023, from https://kingcounty.gov/~/media/depts/elections/about-us/data-and-statistics/historical-turnout-data.ashx?la=en and (2021, December 16). *Election Results*. King County Elections. Retrieved May 24, 2023, from https://aqua.kingcounty.gov/elections/2021/dec-recall/results.pdf

233 [Facebook]. (2021, December 10). *Kshama Solidarity Campaign* [Video]. Kshama Solidarity Campaign. Retrieved May 24, 2023, from https://www.facebook.com/watch/live/?ref=watch_permalink&v=953199935278539

Sawant called out progressive Democrats, the vast majority of whom stood on the sidelines while the corporate and political establishment flailed away at the socialist. "Why is it when progressive people get elected, even well-meaning ones, they don't do anything much? Or they utterly sell out. There is no big mystery—fundamentally it's because this system puts enormous pressure on elected representatives to operate within the status quo. And it is only by basing yourself on movements that you can fight back," she said.

Sawant's extraordinary grassroots movement had gone up against the full forces of state power that had ganged up to expel her—the millionaires and billionaires, the courts, the politicians, the media, state government, and their allies in positions of community power. And they had prevailed in another epic round of class struggle. For the hundreds of SA members and allies who had door-knocked, tabled, and called in the final weeks, "there was this huge overwhelming feeling of pride," Nicholson said.

"Every day you're talking to all of these people, turning them out to vote, getting them to get their friends and family out to vote," she said. "Just knowing how many people it took to play an active role in making this happen, realizing just what a monumental lift it was and it worked. Yeah, just this huge feeling of pride in the working people of the district who had accomplished this against all of those odds being stacked against us."

When the vote-counting began, "All of a sudden it's like, this is proof that we were strong enough to overcome all of those things. It's an extremely empowering feeling. And then it was also like, 'Okay, on with the work,'" Nicholson said.

For Sawant and Socialist Alternative, the biggest lesson of the extraordinary victory resonated well beyond District 3 and the city. "If a small revolutionary socialist organization can beat the wealthiest corporations in the world here in Seattle, again and again," Sawant said, "you can be sure that the organized power of the wider working class can change society."

10

Revolutionary Politics: The Way Forward

Socialist rise – then disappointment

Sawant's improbable victory against the recall was a shock to the ruling elites. In the right-wing backlash to the George Floyd uprising, the local and national political tides were running fully in their favor. They had assembled the full forces of state power—the courts, big business, the political establishment of both major parties, the elections bureaucracy, and the media—to pry the socialist out of City Hall. They had raised record funds, even manipulating fundraising limits at the end of the campaign to pour extra money into the recall coffers. They had arranged the election at the most inauspicious time for Sawant's supporters. They even had the unexpected gift of a civil war inside Sawant's labor movement base in the runup to the vote.

And yet, despite all those factors, they had failed to defeat the socialist. Again. For the fourth time in eight years, an unrelenting, Marxist-led grassroots movement had beaten the elites.

After the recall, Sawant and the movement continued fighting from their socialist beachhead inside City Hall, in early 2023 winning the first-in-the-nation ban on caste discrimination. The new law outlawed the practice—originated in South Asian countries but also common in diasporic communities—of dividing and excluding people based on the social grouping they were born into. In the Seattle area, with more than 100,000 people of South Asian ancestry, this was a major breakthrough, and it garnered global attention. Media from India, England, and around the world reported extensively on the socialist-led win. Community activists in other regions of the US and Canada mounted similar campaigns.[234]

In January 2023, just weeks before the caste discrimination ban victory, Sawant announced she would not run for reelection in November. She said she would leave office at the end of the year on her own terms, concluding a remarkable decade of Marxist office-holding, unprecedented in US political history. Sawant's socialist movement had not merely survived. It has set the terms of political debate in Seattle and won breakthrough legislative and community battles by practicing disciplined class-struggle organizing.

234 (2023, March 2). *Media Coverage — Ban on Caste Discrimination.* Councilmember Kshama Sawant. Retrieved June 10, 2023, from https://sawant.seattle.gov/news-coverage-of-ban-on-caste-discrimination-victory/

Following her departure from City Hall, Sawant said, she and Socialist Alternative would take the fight from Seattle to a national battleground. They would launch Workers Strike Back, a new organization encompassing both socialists and non-socialists and aiming to advance independent political fights nationally. Workers Strike Back would seek to do on a national level what the 15Now and Tax Amazon movements, led by SA, had successfully done in Seattle.

"We have no illusions that a mass movement can be built overnight, but we urgently need to get started," she said. "While I'm sure the corporate establishment in Seattle will be very happy with the news that I am not running again, they shouldn't rush to mix their martinis just yet, because we are not done here. My Council office will continue fighting relentlessly for working people right up until the final days of my term. . . . And when this term is over, we will continue to be disturbers of the political peace in Seattle, as well as nationally, whether inside or outside City Hall."[235]

Indeed, Sawant led a flurry of successful fights in the socialist office's final chapter. She led a push to win city abortion funding after the Supreme Court ended the constitutional right to abortion in *Dobbs v. Jackson Women's Health Organization*. She mobilized hundreds of community members to force City Council to adopt a ceasefire resolution in the wake of Israel's 2023 genocidal attack on Gaza. And working with public middle- and high-school

---

235 Sawant, K. (2023, January 19). *Why I'm Not Running Again for City Council*. The Stranger. Retrieved June 10, 2023, from https://www.thestranger.com/guest-editorial/2023/01/19/78821484/why-im-not-running-again-for-city-council

students, she secured $20 million in new funding for youth mental health services—paid for by a small increase in the Amazon tax.

In early December 2023, Sawant gathered with 150 supporters to celebrate their achievements and commit to spreading their fight beyond Seattle through Workers Strike Back. Speakers traced the arc of Seattle's decadal political revolution. "When I moved to Seattle, one of my first memories was being handed a flier outside my grocery store for a meeting launching the Tax Amazon campaign," Joan Wright, an office workers' union member, told the crowd. "I was intrigued, but to be honest I was skeptical. I'd never heard of Socialist Alternative, and I thought defeating Amazon couldn't be done. But our movement showed me what it looks like to win. . . . Our victories here in Seattle provide a roadmap of what is possible."[236]

Wright was certainly correct that the revolutionary Marxist movement provided a hopeful beacon. But it also was a tough act to follow. Strained by the sheer energy required to maintain the City Hall post over the years, Socialist Alternative made no plans to run another comrade in Sawant's stead. And once there was no longer a socialist political office to defend, tension and internal differences within SA welled to the surface and led to a split the year after she left office. Some argued for focusing energy on Workers Strike Back as the vehicle for building campaigns on a national level, such as Medicare for All. Others wanted to concentrate more explicitly on building SA as a revolutionary political organization. Sawant led a portion of the SA's local and national membership

236 Wright, J. (2023, December 14). Unpublished, in author's possession [Speech at council office celebration].

into Workers Strike Back, and into a new Marxist political group, Revolutionary Workers; other members stayed with SA, also on the front lines of labor and political battles. I watched the unraveling of SA from the sidelines, a close ally but never an official member, in touch with comrades on both sides of the fight but not in any position to alter the divorce's trajectory. Lost in the sharp internal debates, it seemed to me, was a universal appreciation of this tiny organization's remarkable achievements in Seattle. It was painful, and also unsurprising—yet another factional split on the left, a sorry tradition as old as socialist movements.

The SA split underscored the huge challenges that contemporary socialists face in trying to scale up victories, but it shouldn't detract from the extraordinary lessons and experiences during Sawant's decade-long tenure in Seattle City Hall. The period following Sawant's departure from City Hall demonstrated the lasting effect of Seattle's socialist insurgency, in Seattle and also beyond. The City's income from the Amazon tax ballooned from an anticipated level of $214 million in 2021 to actual revenue of $360 million in 2024—a function of the high-income payrolls of Amazon and other tech firms.[237] The Amazon tax, insistently called "Jumpstart" by lawmakers who remained politically allergic to naming the tax's dominant revenue source, funded new housing construction and Green New Deal projects throughout the city. The tax's outsized success in raising funds also meant that it became an annual target for raiding by Democrats seeking money for their own pet

237 City of Seattle (2025, March 1). *Office of Economic & Revenue Forecasts - 2024 Q4/Year-end Revenue Report*. Seattle.gov. Retrieved April 30, 2025, from https://www.seattle.gov/documents/Departments/OERF/Reports/2024/2024%20Q4%20Year-end%20Revenue%20Report.pdf

programs or to backfill budget shortfalls. In early 2025, Seattle voters added onto the Amazon tax, approving an additional levy on employee compensation above $1 million a year to fund a new social housing program. Democrats, the Chamber of Commerce, and big business vociferously opposed the voter initiative but it passed by an overwhelming margin.[238]

Then in April 2025, Washington lawmakers reversed the half-century state ban on rent control. Their enacted measure was weak—it capped annual rent increases at 10 percent and allowed landlords to raise rents even higher when tenants vacated—but merely adopting this law was a concession to the movement that Sawant had inaugurated.[239] The local renters' rights laws that the socialist movement had won in Seattle continued to benefit tenants throughout the city; several were copied by surrounding municipalities. Unsurprisingly, property developers and managers bellyached about the "the crippling rental regulation ordinances." None other than George Petrie, the corporate landlord and top Trump supporter, filed a lawsuit claiming that the tenant protections constituted an illegal deprivation of his right to make a profit. A county judge dismissed the case.[240]

---

238 National Low Income Housing Coalition (2025, February 18). *Seattle Voters Approve Ballot Initiative to Fund Social Housing Developer*. NLIHC. Retrieved April 30, 2025, from https://nlihc.org/resource/seattle-voters-approve-ballot-initiative-fund-social-housing-developer

239 Bellisle, M. (2025, April 29). *Washington lawmakers pass rent-control bill, approve unemployment for striking workers*. Associated Press. Retrieved April 30, 2025, from https://apnews.com/article/rent-control-washington-state-285d94e38e9e10092ec020f8f0da12ab

240 Hjalseth, C. (2025, March 1). *King County Judge Dismisses GRE Downtowner's Lawsuit Against the City of Seattle*. RHAWA. Retrieved April

Sawant's decade in City Hall coincided with a national reemergence of socialism in US political discourse. Bernie Sanders energized millions of new voters with his 2016 presidential run, campaigning within the Democratic Party primary but calling himself a democratic socialist. In November 2018, some 40 candidates backed by the Democratic Socialists of America (DSA) won local, state, and federal races. Most notable among them were Alexandria Ocasio-Cortez of New York and Rashida Tlaib of Michigan—both of whom became high-profile members of the Squad, the nickname given to the new progressive cohort in Congress, which continued to grow in the following two years.

Many supporters had high expectations that these emerging radicals would use their new platforms to bring a combative approach to office-holding and to organize nationally around key movement demands. Shortly after being elected, Ocasio-Cortez, or AOC, joined 200 Sunrise Movement protesters who occupied Congresswoman Nancy Pelosi's office, demanding that the incoming House Speaker commit to passing Green New Deal legislation. AOC's participation in the civil disobedience action signaled that she and the rest of the Squad were ready to bring the street movement into the halls of power. For a moment, it appeared that the Seattle movement's combative socialist politics might be taken up in Congress.

Alas, that hopeful moment soon faded. Just a year later—and only months after six million people around the world walked out of workplaces and schools to demand action on climate justice—AOC

30, 2025, from https://www.rhawa.org/blog/king-county-judge-dismisses-gre-downtowners-lawsuit-against-the-city-of-seattle had pivoted away from the politics of disruption. She criticized other progressives as being too "conflict-based" and affectionately referred to Pelosi as "mama bear" even while the Squad's signature Green New Deal bill languished in the Speaker's legislative dungeon.[241] Members of the Squad held the balance of power in the House but refused to employ it to force votes on Medicare for All, the Green New Deal, a raise in the $7.25 federal minimum wage, or other progressive legislation. And in the fall of 2022, with railroad workers threatening to strike over the right to paid sick leave, AOC and other self-described progressives joined the Biden administration in outlawing the railroad strike and imposing contracts that had been democratically rejected by the union members.

This spectacular betrayal of the working class came amidst historic political setbacks on many fronts: In *Dobbs,* the Supreme Court eliminated the constitutional right to abortion, sending women's rights back by decades; meanwhile, the Biden administration extended Trump's brutal first term treatment of immigrants at the border, right-wing attacks escalated on LGBTQ communities, and the White House and Congress terminated COVID-era protections including eviction protections, student debt relief, and food aid.

241 Thompson, A., & Otterbein, H. (2020, March 30). The 'new' AOC divides the left. Politico. Retrieved June 10, 2023, from https://www.politico.com/states/new-york/city-hall/story/2020/03/30/the-new-aoc-divides-the-left-1269548 and Herndon, A. W. (2020, March 18). Progressive Ideas Remain Popular. Progressive Presidential Candidates Are Losing. Why? The New York Times. Retrieved June 11, 2023, from https://www.nytimes.com/2020/03/18/us/politics/bernie-sanders-progressives-elizabeth-warren.html

The US working class was reeling from multiple body blows, yet the Squad and the other newly elected leftists failed to use their offices as movement counterweights. Within 24 hours of President Biden announcing he was running for reelection, Bernie Sanders rushed to endorse him, notwithstanding Biden's extraordinarily unfavorable polling numbers. AOC followed shortly after. And when Biden ceded his candidacy to Kamala Harris in the fall election, Sanders and AOC folded snugly into Harris' political camp, even as her disastrous campaign tacked ever more rightward. The nominally socialist officeholders had traded the mantles of outside movement leaders for marginal roles inside the Democratic Party structure. They were repeating the same errors of Europe's socialist reformers of a century earlier: the mistaken belief that legislative activity could substitute for disruptive outside movements, and the failure to recognize that bourgeois forms of government were relentlessly hostile to the socialist idea.

Defenders of AOC, Sanders, and other nominally socialist electeds typically point to the legislative accomplishments of the Biden administration, like Build Back Better, the Inflation Reduction Act, and the CHIPS Act, as proof positive that their insider strategy garnered results. But those were paltry offerings compared to the signature issues the reformers campaigned around but quickly cast aside—Medicare for All, Green New Deal, taxing the rich, raising the minimum wage, strengthening workplace and civil rights. Reformers lamented the multiple difficulties of advancing a radical political agenda in office: the crush of legislative demands that compete with movement-building, the rules and procedures that marginalize insurgents, and the political duopoly's implacable opposition to radical change. Yet the obstacles that these officeholders cited were no different from those confronting Sawant and Socialist Alternative. By the end of Sawant's time in office, the movement she led could claim the $15 minimum wage, the Amazon tax, transformative renters' rights, and a first-in-the-nation caste discrimination ban among the highlights of a decade of legislative accomplishments that changed the political terrain, raised living standards and protections for hundreds of thousands of area workers, and energized a new generation of activists.

The three pillars

How did Sawant succeed where reformist socialists failed?

First, she practiced class analysis. Sawant recognized that state institutions—legislative bodies, courts, and their bureaucratic adjutants—are hostile to working-class interests. They are organized to reinforce the existing relationships of power in society by "protecting the economy." As such, these institutions restrict policy choices to those acceptable to capitalism. To overcome that, Sawant and the socialists knew they had to break rules and disrupt state power. They built campaigns bearing in mind the first pillar of Marxist insurgent politics—a class struggle approach—which utilized disruption and rule-breaking in small and big ways: From interrupting City Council meetings with chants and signs, to leading the walkout at the Seattle Housing Authority (SHA) meeting, to using voter initiative threats to force council action on the $15 minimum wage and the Amazon tax.

Of course, merely having class analysis and a set of disruptive tactics does not guarantee success. The amount of movement pressure necessary to extract a concession will vary greatly from one battleground to the next. In fighting to stop SHA's mass eviction program, or in the second round of Tax Amazon, Sawant's movements were sufficiently creative, agile, and resilient to force concessions. In the case of fighting for rent control in Seattle, political establishment resistance was greater and the movement strength was insufficient. The same equation holds true in all arenas of struggle. Contemporary disruptive movements to defund the police or to force university divestment from the Israeli war machine have largely fallen short, not for lack of creativity and tenacity, but because opposition forces are much more deeply entrenched; the threshold for extracting a concession is much higher. What we win in the final analysis is not what's right or just or fair, but what the balance of forces dictates we have the power to wrest from the establishment.

Progressive activists view struggle and state institutions differently. They gloss over class analysis, placing faith in elected officials' rhetoric and on the personal relationships they develop with those officials. They believe that other politicians can be won over with persuasion and relationship-building, failing to properly analyze the class interests that those officials represent. Or they build campaigns that make aggressive demands but keep tactics within the boundaries established by state power, as AOC did in the months following her sit-in in Pelosi's office. Many may run as outside political organizers, but once in office, they shed organizing for legislating. This is a recipe for failure.

In contrast, it did not matter to Sawant, in the fight to defund the racist police, to levy a greater tax on Amazon, or to increase the minimum wage, that most City Council Democrats were self-identified progressives, that most were women of color, or that six out of eight had publicly vowed to halve the police budget. What mattered was recognizing that when legislation came to a vote, the Democrats would reliably defend the class interests that kept them in office. The only way to prevail over that class dynamic was a movement consistently strong and disruptive enough to force a concession from the establishment.

Choosing class allegiance—whether to align with state institutions and state power or with the working class—happens very early on in the formation of any political movement, whether issue-based or electoral. Some 175 years ago Marx observed, "The executive of the modern state is but a committee for managing the common affairs of the whole bourgeoisie." That remains true today. No matter how much they declare left-wing bona fides, political movements will default to joining the political establishment "committee"—destined to reinforce, not oppose, state power—unless they consciously distinguish themselves from the get-go. Sawant did this in several ways. She boldly advertised her socialist affiliation in campaign literature and speeches and refused alliances with the Democratic Party. She rejected the six-figure City Council paycheck, accepting only an average worker's salary. She refused to engage in backroom deal-making, instead building outside forums of workers and other community members to bolster and steer her work inside City Hall. She treated the council office as a beachhead for the movement, opening up the office to activists and speaking from the City Council rostrum not to persuade the other councilmembers but to energize and organize community members, to amplify movement demands, and to expose the hypocrisy of the Democrats.

Contemporary reform-minded socialists have tried to straddle the line between outside agitator and inside player. This quickly becomes an impossible position. Even while running on third party lines, they seek dual endorsements with the Democratic Party; quietly accept the full financial benefits of political office; and focus on inside-the-legislature cajoling and relationship-building instead of outside movement building. Crucially, they see themselves and their office as distinct from the movement, not a political arm of the movement and not directly accountable to rank-and-file community members. They set re-election as their paramount goal, foregoing the purpose of a revolutionary holding office in the first place.

One needn't be a full-throated defender of the ruling class or accept direct funding from the Chamber of Commerce and big business to fit snugly into the folds of the political establishment. Simply shedding the politics and tactics of class struggle once in office renders a formerly radical leader part of the establishment and strips them of any effective movement leadership role. Reformists, Rosa Luxemberg observed more than a century ago, "do not really choose a more tranquil, calmer and slower road to the same goal, but a different goal. Instead of taking a stand for the establishment of a new society they take a stand for surface modifications of the old society."[242] Today progressives serve as useful foils for the political establishment, advancing "surface modifications" and thereby providing tangible proof to the Democratic Party's left-leaning supporters that the party accepts dissenting perspectives within its ranks. Rather than undermine

---

242 Luxemburg, R. (1999, January 1). Reform or Revolution, Chapter VIII: Conquest of Political Power. Marxists.org. Retrieved April 18, 2025, from https://www.marxists.org/archive/luxemburg/1900/reform-revolution/ch08.htm

the system, reformism with no greater objective in mind actually *strengthens* capitalism—lending legitimacy to bourgeois hegemony and maintaining the core of the exploitative system while relieving pressure to overthrow it.

This brings us to the second pillar of Marxist insurgent politics: movement-building around immediate material struggles that connect to a broader call for socialism. This was the central argument in Trotsky's 1938 Transitional Program, calling for fights to build "the bridge between present demands and the socialist program of the revolution." In the battle for a $15 minimum wage, Sawant called for democratic, public ownership of major corporations, pointing to their insatiable exploitation of workers. In the fight for the Amazon tax, she called for bringing housing under public control because of the failure of the private housing market to supply quality homes. She called for a democratically-elected renter oversight board because neither bureaucracy nor private business could be trusted to properly manage social housing.

Economic destitution, racism, and homelessness are features, not bugs, of capitalism. It would not be sufficient, Sawant underscored, to attenuate human misery by winning the material issue at hand without pointing to the root cause of the problem. In advancing the movement's immediate demands, Sawant's tenure in City Hall exposed the systemic inability of big business and capitalism to meet people's needs. It was a political master class in Transitional Program strategy.

Today's reform-minded socialists and progressives, on the other hand, advocate for material demands without extending a call for broader societal change, or perhaps with only perfunctory reference to the need for socialism. In doing so they detach the immediate demand from the source of the problem. A common example is demanding more affordable housing but failing to lay blame on those who control the privatized housing market. In this manner reformers move from one campaign to another, taking aim at the maladies of capitalism without parsing why these problems persist. But you can't properly treat a cancer without first having a correct diagnosis. A policy demand without root-cause analysis will not solve the problem it aims to address. It will train activists to become reform advocates instead of promoters of revolutionary change. The results are campaigns that begin with lofty slogans and ideals—"Housing for All!"—but degenerate into appeals for liberal reforms that only attenuate injustice but fail to inspire and mobilize working people, let alone build politically independent, democratically-accountable movements.

Instead of socialized universal healthcare, we end up with an exasperatingly complex health insurance system that denies needed healthcare and further enshrines profiteering; instead of universal housing, we end up with dehumanizing vouchers, privatized systems, and growing masses of people struggling to survive in sidewalk tents and unsafe shelters. Instead of true workers' organizing rights we end up with weak and ineffective labor laws. Instead of a real fight against institutionalized racism and the carceral state we end up with performative identity politics, symbolism and empty gestures from politicians, along with window-dressing "police accountability" commissions that do nothing to alter the status quo of police killings and mass incarceration of Black and Brown people.

The reformist failure to demand broader change springs in part from a lack of confidence in working people. Today's reform-minded socialists and progressives—just like their reformist progenitors of more than a century ago—worry that they could lose votes or alienate parts of the movement if they raise bold demands. They would rather appeal to narrow thinking than broader perspectives, arguing that people "aren't ready" for socialist-oriented demands. Or they start off with a bold program but make compromises because they believe people are unprepared to fight for a radical program. They count votes and give up rather than develop a fighting program to win. They think that by making compromises they can tame the opposition. But in the absence of a powerful movement, compromises only reveal a movement's weakness and embolden opponents to escalate demands for yet more concessions.

The Sawant experience demonstrates what happens when movement leaders trust workers to think big and act boldly. Working people alienated by mainstream politics get engaged because they see a movement that speaks to their material needs, explains the underlying systemic problem, and provides a course of action for newly energized community members.

In the first, failed round of the Amazon tax fight, the Democrats framed the fight around the need to build more housing and fund social service programs. They were afraid to call out Amazon by name, thinking that to do so would alienate community members. They repeatedly ratcheted down their demand, ultimately settling on a tax rate that would bring in only $48 million a year, arguing that any higher figure would be politically untenable. When the predictable corporate blowback arrived, they lacked confidence to mobilize supporters and fight back. They surrendered. Conspiring behind closed doors, they cooked up a plan to repeal their own measure.

In the second round, led by Sawant and Socialist Alternative, the movement shined the spotlight on the corporate behemoth and emphasized that affordable housing needed to be placed under public control because of the inescapable failure of the private housing market. They added the demand for Green New Deal jobs. By making bold demands, the Tax Amazon movement pushed through political boundaries and won a tax rate 4 ½ times the size of the original measure.

Certainly, movements must be skillful in how bold demands are developed and articulated, and they must account for the actual, not imagined, balance of forces in different fields of contest. Slogans and campaign tactics that work in Seattle, which demonstrate that working people, especially young people, are eager and ready to join movements that articulate bold, explicitly socialist demands, must be adapted for communities like Tulsa and Phoenix. Activists must be tuned in to the political consciousness of the local communities they are organizing within.

The final pillar of Marxist insurgent politics, movement democracy, seeks to address this reality. What do I mean by democracy, and in particular, movement democracy?

On an individual level, democracy means having a voice in determining the economic, social, and ecological conditions in which you live. On a collective level, it means having agency—that is, power—to use that voice to effectively challenge oppressive systems, advocate for material changes, and construct a new social order. "Democracy" as it's talked about today in mainstream US society is narrowly defined, typically cast in reductionist examples like quadrennial elections or the roll calls that conclude legislative battles. Democracy in this construct is something that you're only marginally involved in. Elections offer limited choices. Racist voter suppression laws ban millions from participating. Arcane and bewildering rules govern legislative debates. Unelected courts roll back popular gains. Government bodies meet during times that preclude most people from taking part. It's no wonder that increasing numbers of Americans see "democracy" not as an expression of their own social agency but rather as something alienating, outside their control, manipulated by the political establishment to meet the desired ends of the elites. It is something that is done *to* them. That narrow, contorted manifestation is not true democracy.

Democracy can't be divorced from the question of collective power. For today's political establishment, democratic practices like elections are mechanisms for legitimizing their own hold on society, serving to tame radical currents and channel popular energy into activities that reinforce the state and the hegemony of the political duopoly. But if you have electoral rights yet no real ability to challenge the status quo and effect social change, then you don't have true democracy. This façade of democracy is dominant under capitalism, serving to reinforce and reproduce the status quo: The hegemony of the ruling class over the rest of us.

In contrast, movement democracy involves ongoing, collective engagement and action by community members to fight for the things they need, without institutional gatekeeping. Movement democracy means scheduling meetings accessible to ordinary community members, actively soliciting ideas from workers and tenants, creating organizing spaces and resources for activists, formulating concrete demands, mobilizing people around those demands, and ensuring that campaign leaders are accountable to the community.

The $15 minimum wage movement's decision to push forward with a ballot initiative if the City Council failed to act—a decision approved democratically in a 15Now assembly attended by hundreds of people—was decisive in prodding the political establishment to approve the $15 legislation. Sawant made clear to the mayor and the rest of the political establishment that while she would participate in the mayor's minimum wage advisory committee, she would not be beholden to any confidentiality agreement within the group. As the "shop steward for the working class" on the committee, she would coordinate with and take direction from 15Now activists. Later, as chair of the City Council's Renters Rights Committee, Sawant often scheduled evening meetings in working class neighborhood community centers or in local churches so that more people could participate. By converting the council office into an organizing center, Sawant also ensured community activists had a place to meet and access resources like lists of allies, research materials, and printing and rally supplies. The movement's Tax Amazon action conferences were attended by hundreds of people each with one vote, no matter their day job, union affiliation, or expertise. The democratic process instilled participants with strong ownership over the campaign. It underscored to the political establishment that Sawant was speaking not just as an individual elected official, but for a broad, committed constituency.

This practice of working class movement democracy is essential to revolutionary political struggle because only by building a mass base of support can workers wield the power they need to advance demands, win, and then enforce those victories.

Rank-and-file members of many unions will recognize similar characteristics in how their union—if it is a healthy organization—democratically develops bargaining demands, builds internal support for them, assembles a campaign strategy, and makes decisions about how and when to settle or strike.

While the political establishment occasionally invites constituents to "town halls" and "listening sessions," set up to mobilize public opinion around a program with predetermined boundaries, this is performative democracy. Take "participatory budgeting" programs, for example, in which local governments set aside a tiny fraction of their overall budget and convene community members to decide how to spend those funds. The discussion proceeds within limits set in advance. This is the outward appearance of democracy, but contained within narrow parameters that preclude any potential for disruptive challenges to the political status quo.

Meanwhile, the huge expense of running electoral campaigns practically restricts candidacies to those who are willing to serve the state's interests. The vast majority of contested partisan elections are between defenders of the capitalist status quo, albeit with distinguishable variations in how they articulate that defense. Additionally, the electoral arena is a prime place for ruling elites to steer people away from seeing the world in class terms. Elections are fertile grounds for promoting personality conflicts, identity politics, and myriad petty controversies, real or imagined, that distract from class conflict. The sharper the controversy, the greater the opportunity to steer voters away from class struggle. At the end of the election, the media and political establishment declare that "the people have decided," which is true only in the narrow sense that "the people" have decided among the extraordinarily limited choices given to them by this money-driven process. It's no wonder that every election cycle tens of millions of American voters don't bother casting ballots. There is no one running who genuinely speaks to their needs.

This is not true democracy. It's a modern version of century-old parliamentarism, which the 1920 Communist International Congress declaimed as "a 'democratic' form of the rule of the bourgeoisie, which at a certain stage of development requires the fiction of popular representation which outwardly appears to be an organization of a 'popular will' that stands outside the classes, but in essence is a machine for oppression and subjugation in the hands of ruling capital."

True movement democracy also requires leadership accountability to rank-and-file activists. Whether deliberately or unconsciously, most progressives and even reform-minded socialists have abandoned working class movement democracy practices. They become immersed in the day-to-day schedule inside the political establishment's fortress and drift from organizing to legislating. In doing so, they have joined the "committee for managing the common affairs of the whole bourgeoisie."

When Sawant first took office, many figures in the political establishment thought it was odd that she spoke typically in the first-person plural. She introduced bills as "our legislation" or "our movement's demands" and referred frequently to "our council office." For Sawant and the socialists, the council position was not a personal office, even though her name appeared on the ballot and her name was on the office door frame. The office was an integral part of the working-class movement, the insurgency's beachhead inside enemy territory; she just happened to occupy it. Sawant was accountable to the movement, acting always as a representative of the organization that had led the insurgent election, Socialist Alternative, and more broadly, the working-class members who had elected her and who came together to make decisions on how to do battle.

Reformist delusion and weakness on the US left

Activists might reasonably ask why Sawant's Marxist insurgent politics haven't been more widely adopted on the US political left. Certainly one factor is that challenging capitalism in the 21st century is an enormously intimidating task. Consider the systemic obstacles: The ruling class has a consolidated hold on power, much more so than in earlier days of capitalism's development. Especially after the US Supreme Court's *Citizens United v. FEC* decision opened the corporate cash spigots, the electoral arena is an extraordinarily challenging field of contest for political insurgencies. Bourgeois forms of governance are more mature, their architects having learned over the last century to hone the instruments of limited democracy while tightening the grip that elites hold on the actual levers of power. They have become more skilled than their predecessors at co-opting sections of the working class and dividing and sabotaging emerging movements.

The aura of political invincibility also reinforces today's capitalist hegemony. The 1990-1991 dissolution of the Soviet Union and the Eastern Bloc removed a political counterweight and emboldened elites to insist that "there is no alternative" to capitalism, as the late British Prime Minister Margaret Thatcher once declared. Under today's ascendant neoliberal ideology—and its latest iteration, Trump's neofascism, the brazen fusing of big capital and government into a single hegemonic force—the ruling class has freed restraints on capital, slashed social spending, broken unions, and adeptly disciplined the working class through the manipulation of markets, public debt, trade policy, and interest rates. Racism, sexism, xenophobia, and homophobia remain potent tools to divide workers. The mainstream media, increasingly corporate-controlled and cowed by the new Trump era, is a reliable channel for reinforcing ruling class will and capitalist ideology.

Those obstacles make it understandable why resistance to capitalism can seem futile; why so many political activists on the left give up on revolutionary politics, even as they acknowledge the mounting economic, social, and climate crises. Indeed, reformism exerts a powerful gravitational pull precisely because of the severity of the global crises: By immersing themselves in campaigns that seek only incremental policy change, or by supporting DSA-endorsed Democrats, activists feel that they are at least doing *something*. This understandable impulse explains the meteoric rise of left reformist politics in the 2010s, when DSA peaked at nearly 100,000 members. But the reformist path reaches a distinct dead end, as we saw in the early 2020s, when nominally socialist standard-bearers like Sanders and AOC surrendered their banner demands and folded meekly into Biden's Democratic camp. The enemies of the working class cannot alone be to blame for our predicament. Factors within activists' control have contributed to the historic weakness of the US left and have held back revolutionary movements. New activists and emerging movements must acknowledge and confront these obstacles directly, and not simply duck out of the fight because the revolutionary socialist project seems too daunting.

We must ask ourselves: Where does the reformist approach to political change end up? The climate crisis provides a useful framework. The Republican Party offers a reckless program that ignores basic science and will speed the destruction of our planet. The Democratic Party blocks Green New Deal initiatives and continues to cater to fossil fuel industry executives and major shareholders. Any remedies that party leaders propose are trivial compared to the crisis. Its leaders have joined with political establishments worldwide to adopt unenforceable and distant climate goals that scientists agree will only delay but not stop the planet from reaching an irreversible climate tipping point. The two branches of America's political duopoly offer somewhat different timelines but they both end up in exactly the same place: An uninhabitable planet.

In unguarded moments, the political establishment confesses this truth. In her tweet on Earth Day 2024, Hillary Clinton wrote . . . "What's at stake for our climate in this November's election? Absolutely everything." She displayed a chart from the website Carbon Brief that found Trump's climate policies would add 4 to 5 billion tons of greenhouse gases a year to the atmosphere. But the same chart showed that Biden administration policies would add 3 to 4 billion tons of greenhouse gasses a year, and that both men's policies disastrously fail the goal of reaching zero net tons of emission by 2050.[243]

---

243 Clinton, H. (2024, April 22). *What's at stake for our climate in this November's elections?* Twitter.com. Retrieved July 29, 2024, from https://x.com/HillaryClinton/status/1782400479743324603; citing report at: Carbon Brief (2024, March 6). *Analysis: Trump election win could add 4bn tonnes to US emissions by 2030*. CarbonBrief.org. Retrieved July 29, 2024, from https://www.carbonbrief.org/analysis-trump-election-win-could-add-4bn-tonnes-to-us-emissions-by-2030/

Picture two cars running parallel to one another, rapidly approaching a cliff. In one car, the driver has their foot on the accelerator and speeds impulsively forward. In the other, the operator drives at a more moderate speed, but is headed toward the same cliff. Reformers would have us run after the second car and grab onto the bumper in a vain effort to commandeer it. What the working-class needs is a new car steering in a different direction.

Unfortunately, many of today's DSA reformers and left-wing Democratic Party activists are repeating the same mistakes that European socialist reform advocates made more than a century ago in the runup to World War I. Those forerunners insisted that they could successfully resist the imperial war drive while navigating within the political establishment. The reformers' decision to work within the political confines of a system marching relentlessly toward global conflict had tragic consequences. Today, we face circumstances at least as grave. By downplaying the central role of class conflict, today's reformers are repeating the historic mistake.

Moreover, attempting to convince fellow working-class members that our best shot lies within the Democratic Party breeds discouragement and cynicism as transformational ideas get crushed time and again by party leaders, or worse, as Democratic leaders meekly protest while Trump attacks marginalized communities and worker rights. The Democratic political establishment is crystal clear about which side of the class struggle they take. "We're capitalist. And that's just the way it is," party leader Nancy Pelosi told a CNN town hall in 2017.[244]

---

244 [You Tube]. (2017, February 1). *Pelosi: Democrats are capitalists* [Video]. CNN Nancy Pelosi Town Hall. https://www.youtube.com/watch?v=MR65ZhO6LGA

A century and a half ago, Marx and Engels observed that the Paris Commune failed to survive because "the working class cannot simply lay hold of the ready-made state machinery, and wield it for its own purposes." Likewise, today's reformist socialists are badly mistaken in thinking that somehow they can wrest control of the Democratic Party and wield it as a weapon for transformational change; they should take Pelosi's statement at face value.

Reformism is not just non-productive; it is actively counterproductive to the socialist project. Trying to persuade people that the Democratic Party is something it can never be actually undermines the movement and—as we unfortunately saw in the 2024 election—creates political openings for extreme right-wing forces in society. Disillusioned by repeated Democratic Party failures, working people in the last generation have withdrawn from political engagement or fallen susceptible to right-wing carnival barkers and fascist opportunists. At least those politicians possess the candor to tell workers that they are being screwed over by state power.

We must also take stock of the weak and fractured state of working-class organizations. The breakup within Socialist Alternative following Sawant's departure from City Council is but one example of the internal challenges to scaling up socialist movements. The challenges are even greater in today's union movement. Notwithstanding high-profile organizing campaigns in recent years in low-wage industries, spearheaded largely by young workers, the US union movement overall continues its downward spiral. The percentage of US workers belonging to unions has fallen from a post-World War II high of more than one-third of all workers—including fully 69 percent of production workers—to an anemic 9.9 percent in 2024.[245] Beginning in 2018 and in the years following, strikes led by educators, hotel workers, delivery drivers, entertainment industry workers, and others inspired millions. Yet overall, major strikes and other work stoppages in the 2010s were down 95 percent compared to the post-World War II period.[246] Many unions are tied down fighting defensive battles against individual employers, too occupied to mount broader social justice campaigns. Most work in isolation, abstaining from the cross-union solidarity that could be decisive. The 2021 carpenters strike in Seattle, unfortunately, is not an isolated example of divided labor.

Likewise, community-based organizations like renter rights groups and LGBTQ, racial justice, and immigrant rights organizations are overwhelmed fighting back against the latest corporate or political attack or are pinned down fundraising to keep their doors open. On their back heels and bereft of significant resources to fight back, organizations find it nearly impossible to launch offensive campaigns. Many formulate inadequate responses because they lack a strong analysis of class and power. Obviously, a big part of this is by the design of economic and political elites, who work overtime to weaken working class power; the very success of neoliberal austerity depends upon

---

245 Brecher, J. (1972). Strike! (pp. 222-223). South End Press, and (2023, January 19). Union Members Summary. US Bureau of Labor Statistics. Retrieved May 21, 2025, from https://www.bls.gov/news.release/union2.nr0.htm

246 (2023, February 22). *Annual work stoppages involving 1,000 or more workers, 1947 - Present*. US Bureau of Labor Statistics. Retrieved June 28, 2023, from https://www.bls.gov/web/wkstp/annual-listing.htm

constraining, isolating, and crushing the organizations that could pose a threat to the capitalist order.

But that only explains part of the problem. The other problem is a widespread lack of vision, political analysis, and fortitude in movement leadership. This is especially true in labor, the most potent element of an organized, fighting left. Unfortunately, most top union officers today have abandoned the core purpose of unions—to fight unreservedly for the interests of workers; to be, as Book Workers Union member Jacob Schear declared at the Carpenters union strike, "a radical and disruptive force." They've exchanged that mission for a subservient and limited role in the capitalist economic and political order, focusing on the next round of contract negotiations or the next election. Most unions are structured along the lines of "business unionism," top-down bureaucracies in which well-paid staff provide representation services to the members. Local and national union principal officers settle into careerist positions, paying themselves multiples of what their own members earn while the actual members struggle to get by.

It's no surprise that many union members come to see the union not as their own democratically run organization, but as a third party mediating between them and their bosses. Members feel disempowered; they withdraw from activity.

In recent years, the AFL-CIO and other national union officers have given dramatic speeches declaring their absolute commitment to battle soaring corporate profits, worker concessions, and the loss of union members—half a million in the decade of the 2010s. Those troubles should have been clarion calls to throw every available resource into organizing and fighting back, but the lofty words have been largely empty gestures. In the last decade, union officers squirreled away working-class resources instead of investing in building a vibrant movement. Between 2010 and 2023, the net assets of unions rose 225 percent, to $35.3 billion, according to labor researcher Chris Bohner. Most of the increase was due to growth in unions' investment income and real estate holdings. Dues revenue also increased, in part to pay for exorbitant salaries—hundreds of thousands of dollars a year apiece—for national union presidents, a labor aristocracy utterly detached from the daily experiences of their own members. These assets could be thrown into new organizing fights; but as of early 2025, that is not the case. "If labor is facing an existential crisis, it is not reflected in labor's balance sheet," Bohner wryly observed.[247]

The scene is no better in the political arena, where the vast majority of union officers are wedded to the two-party duopoly. In 2023, in the wake of Biden's crushing the railroad workers' strike and ending COVID-era social protections while simultaneously bailing out Silicon Valley venture capitalists to the tune of $175 billion, AFL-CIO leaders announced that the labor federation was endorsing the Democrat's reelection.[248] Coming with no demo-

---

247 Bohner, C. (2022, June 5). *Now Is the Time for Unions to Go on the Offensive*. Jacobin Magazine. Retrieved June 27, 2023, from https://jacobin.com/2022/06/organized-labor-union-membership-finances-fortress-unionism-spending and Bohner, C. (2024, Sept. 2). *US Labor Unions Still Need to Get Serious About Organizing*. Jacobin Magazine. Retrieved April 8, 2025 from https://jacobin.com/2024/09/union-density-nlrb-law-harris

248 Allyn, B. (2023, March 14). *The White House is avoiding one word when it comes to Silicon Valley Bank: Bailout*. NPR. Retrieved June 28, 2023, from https://www.npr.org/2023/03/13/1163180140/silicon-valley-bank-is-it-a-bailout-barofsky and (2023, June 16). *AFL-CIO Votes to Endorse President*

cratic debate involving union members, and without even including a set of demands for Biden, the endorsement was a stunning but unsurprising display of business unionism's abject capitulation to the capitalist political order. The quick turn to Harris in the summer of 2024 only doubled down on this error.

In sharp contrast to this picture of a calcified labor bureaucracy, ordinary workers increasingly are agitating to fight back against capital and build struggle-based working-class organizations. Rank-and-file union members have called strikes in recent years over the objections of union officers. Some 10,000 John Deere workers struck after rejecting a contract negotiated behind closed doors between union officials and the tractor manufacturing company. The workers won substantial improvements over the initial offer.[249] Another 7,500 machinists at Spirit Aerosystems, a key Boeing contactor, rejected a contract recommended by their union leadership and struck. A week after shutting down production, the union workers won a better contract.[250] The statewide

Biden for Re-Election. AFL-CIO. Retrieved June 28, 2023, from https://afl-cio.org/press/releases/afl-cio-votes-endorse-president-biden-re-election

249 Furman, J. (2021, October 20). *'Let's Put a Wrench in Things Now': Deere Workers Strike as Company Rakes in Record Profits*. Labor Notes. Retrieved June 27, 2023, from https://labornotes.org/2021/10/lets-put-wrench-things-now-deere-workers-strike-company-rakes-record-profits

250 Leon, L. F. (2023, June 27). *Six Thousand Machinists Strike Aircraft Parts Giant in Kansas—Threatening Boeing Production*. Labor Notes. Retrieved June 27, 2023, from https://labornotes.org/2023/06/six-thousand-machinists-strike-aircraft-parts-giant-kansas-threatening-shut-down-boeing and Wronski, L. (2023, June 29). *Union members say 'yes': Machinists strike ending in Wichita*. KWCh-12 News. Retrieved June 29, 2023, from https://www.kwch.com/2023/06/29/union-members-say-yes-machinists-strike-ending-wichita/

West Virginia educators' strike in 2018, a movement led by rank-and-file union members over the objection of some of their own union leaders, wrested concessions from the state and sparked the national "Red for Ed" movement.

Rank-and-file union members in the UAW have fought for and won the right to directly elect their top union representatives, inspiring members in other unions to push for direct elections and democratic rights. The UAW's breakthrough Stand Up strike in auto in the fall of 2023 was a direct result of the union's democratization. Young workers, many of them socialists and often organizing independent of mainstream unions, have led creative organizing campaigns at Amazon and Starbucks, in higher education, and in retail industries. Immigrant workers have led militant strikes at hotels and other low-wage industries. These and other grassroots-led fights demonstrate a growing hunger by rank-and-file union members to disrupt business unionism and smash the union bureaucracy's allegiance to class collaboration. This is a hopeful starting point for building a new, fighting left in the US.

There is precedent for these developments germinating into a fully-grown movement. Marxist labor historian Bryan Palmer has noted that the industrial union upsurge in the 1930s "was led by dissidents, politically committed leftists." Major breakthroughs, he said, "will never happen unless there is in some ways an organized contingent of committed leftists who are both embedded in the trade union movement and willing to fight for new kinds of unionism, but also organized outside of it."[251]

---

251 Fong, B. Y. (2024, March 11). *Organize the Unorganized: The Rise of the CIO: Episode 9: Lessons*. Organize the Unorganized: The Rise of the CIO.

Where to now?

A few years back Sawant and I were meeting with a community member who exclaimed enthusiastically, "What we need is 1,000 Kshamas!" We both winced at his electoral focus. Sawant, ever gracious in these conversations with allies, thanked him and then replied that electing 1,000 Kshamas wouldn't solve the problems of the working class; to win radical change we need a powerful working-class movement, centered in the labor movement, that has strength, militancy, and political independence. The victories won during Sawant's term in office required grassroots movements and political discipline. Shortcuts like electing good people, even socialists, cannot substitute for the arduous movement-building work that is urgently needed.

Certainly, movements should take advantage of opportunities in the coming years to put up candidates who are backed by grassroots movements and who are committed to the three pillars of Marxist political insurgency. Even losing insurgent campaigns can build the movement if they use the electoral contest to make bold demands and draw new activists into the fight. But most political organizing energy must be devoted toward building working-class organizations, the foundation for societal transformation. We will have 1,000 Kshamas in political office when base working-class movements—unions, tenants' rights groups, immigrant organizations, and so on—are mature and strong enough to support those revolutionaries inside the halls of power.

Retrieved April 22, 2025, from https://podcasts.apple.com/us/podcast/episode-9-lessons/id1731878287?i=1000648844920

Unions are the indispensable foundation of this working-class movement. Collectively, workers have the power to bring the wheels of the capitalist economy to a halt by withholding their labor. Through strikes, unions have played decisive roles in the capitalist era, toppling dictators and winning democracy, squeezing economic and social concessions out of the political and business establishment, and leading national revolutions. Unions historically have been the wellspring for new working-class leaders.

But here is a conundrum: The primary work of nearly all unions today is fundamentally reformist. Workers organizing and bargaining for union contracts are simply trying to lessen the terms of their exploitation under capitalism. Outwardly, a union negotiations session does not look like a revolutionary project. The product of successful bargaining—a union contract—codifies class relations under capitalism. Yet union organizing and negotiations battles must be our starting point for the revolutionary socialist project. Union work contains the seeds of revolutionary political work because it starkly illuminates the conflicting interests between workers and bosses on wages, benefits, work rules, workplace control, and ultimately, the distribution of wealth and the organization of society.

In their book *Rules to Win By: Power and Participation in Union Negotiations*, Jane McAlevey and Abby Lawlor make the case for inviting all workers, even those who have opted out of joining the union, to attend union negotiations. "Open bargaining," as the authors call it, may be counterintuitive to union officials who are accustomed to a tightly controlled process. These officials may negotiate directly with management, without any members present, or bring only a select, small group of union members to the bargaining table. But open bargaining is critically important to building democracy within unions and activating members. It can be a step toward building a revolutionary organization.

By directly entering the bargaining room, workers move from a passive to an active role in the conflict over the allocation of resources and power. They see and hear the boss reject calls for adequate staffing, decent wages, or reasonable safety protections. Their enemy is unmasked as the idea of competing class interests moves from abstract to solid. As workers directly hear the boss swat away reasonable proposals to improve working conditions, they feel the crystallization of that intangible Marxist term, "alienation," the workers' feeling of estrangement as they realize that their employer sees their labor only as a commodity, not for its social worth. And they also recognize that to win their demands, they will need not some outside hero but their own unity in action.

In this milieu, workers can move from examining *what the conflict is about*—the material demands of the workers—to *why the conflict even exists*. In workplace struggles socialists must raise this latter question, and furthermore, build working-class consciousness by asking the next two questions: *Who is on our side, and who is against us?* And: *What, therefore, must workers do to prevail in this conflict?* There are vital steps in moving workers from passivity, through reformism, and then to a revolutionary orientation.

Bolder bargaining demands, especially ones that go beyond traditional workplace issues, are important as well to moving workers beyond reformist thinking. Bold demands point to the greater societal problems of capitalism and the inability of the political establishment to solve these problems. They demonstrate that the union is fighting for the interests of all workers. Educators fighting for smaller class sizes, public workers and construction workers demanding billionaire taxes to build social housing, and hospital workers fighting for better staffing, medical debt cancellation, and guaranteed healthcare for all are just some examples of how union members can elevate demands and inspire other members of the working class to come off the sidelines and join the fight.

The sharper the conflict, the greater the opportunity to develop political consciousness and engage new radical activists. Strikes in particular are outstanding training grounds for the next generation of revolutionary fighters. In this work, it's essential to recognize that contemporary unions are not intrinsically revolutionary organizations, nor are they likely to be in the foreseeable future. Rather, today's unions and their battles against employers create the environment in which revolutionary political activity can be instigated. As socialist author and trade unionist Sam Gindin has argued:

> "Building a fighting working class isn't a matter of taking over unions and making them into socialist organizations, since union membership is not based on common politics but the happenstance of sharing a workplace and concern with self-defense and material gains. It is instead a matter of strengthening unions and moving them toward being more open to class struggle and radical critiques of the capitalist system. This kind of transformation can in turn also strengthen movements for broader social change: e.g., turning unions into schools that introduce radical political ideas, seriously engaging union members in campaigns for universalist demands like health care and free education, and

through all this developing more promising recruitment grounds for left-wing parties."[252]

During the ten years of Sawant's tenure inside Seattle City Hall, the Marxist-led movement applied these same principles of union struggle in the political arena. Legislating, like union bargaining, is by nature a reform process. But by advancing bold demands and connecting them to a socialist vision, Sawant and the movement forced class conflict into the open, exposed opponents, fostered alliances, and built revolutionary class consciousness in a new generation of activists.

The challenge for socialist activists today is to extend that approach in new spaces: A dual strategy of waging immediate reform fights—in collective bargaining, in the legislative arena, and in the broader community—as a mean of exposing the class nature of the conflict, engaging new layers of activists, and preparing workers to demand broader social transformation.

Many critics will argue that America is not ready for socialism. Those on the left who say it's not yet time are stuck in a self-defeating cycle. They note decades of capitalist hegemony and systematic, even violent, repression of working-class institutions and leaders. Yet notwithstanding this suppression, the last decade has seen rising support for socialist ideas as conditions for working people spiral down—poverty wages, food scarcity, skyrocketing rents, healthcare crises, collapsing public education, crushing

252 Gindin, S. (2023, August 22). *In Failing to Strike at UPS, the Teamsters Missed a Big Opportunity*. Jacobin Magazine. Retrieved September 5, 2023, from https://jacobin.com/2023/08/ups-teamsters-part-time-workers-agreement-strike-ratification-strategy

debts, rampant racism, misogyny and homophobia, and a burgeoning climate catastrophe. In recent years people, especially young workers and students, have stood up to demand radical change. They recognize capitalism's failures. A 2021 poll showed that a majority of young adults in the US viewed socialism positively and capitalism negatively.[253]

That fact itself is remarkable. In the face of nonstop anti-socialist propaganda in the headquarters of world capitalism, how is *any* support for socialism possible? It is because of workers' lived experiences—the manager's whip-crack speedup, the eviction notice posted on your apartment door, the unpayable debt notices piling up in the mail, the racist traffic stops, your aching back at the end of a long day of multiple soul-sucking jobs, the unbearable smoke and heat and powerful storms of a raging planet. You could wipe out from history all the writings of Marx and Engels and still workers today, experiencing the sting of class oppression, would gravitate toward the socialist idea. The vitriol with which the far-right rails against socialism, and Marxism in particular, shows just how much the most ardent defenders of capital recognize the durability and potency of the vision of a society based on common good, not private profit.

But ideals don't manifest into reality just because they are good. It takes extraordinarily hard work, especially in the face of such powerful opposition. Contemporary union organizing, led by young workers, disproportionately people of color, many socialist, are a hopeful sign of the rebirth of a fighting labor movement; they require our dedicated encouragement and solidarity. These

253 Wronski, L. (2021, June 15). *Axios|Momentive Poll: Capitalism and Socialism*. SurveyMonkey.com. Retrieved June 29, 2023, from https://www.surveymonkey.com/curiosity/axios-capitalism-update/

campaigns are not yet enough to be called a historical movement. But they could become one, with sustained, grassroots organizing and by connecting to the related class struggles for housing, climate, and racial and gender justice.

For 10 years in Seattle, a movement of dedicated activists—construction workers and trans community members, immigrant mothers and graduate students, recovering addicts and faith ministers, tech workers and daughters of sharecroppers, nurses and baristas, and many more—came together and turned the political scene on its head. Many of them would not even describe themselves as socialist, but they took leadership from a committed group of Marxists who channeled the activists' anger and frustration into a fighting program for transformation.

Kshama Sawant and the movement proved that it's possible to win big by naming the underlying conflict between the bourgeoisie and the proletariat as they engaged in fights for immediate material needs—living wages, housing, a Green New Deal, renters' rights, racial justice, civil rights. The Seattle experience provides a template for activists trying to make sense of the world, a way to fight back, a ray of hope in the despairing miasma of 21st century capitalism. The new political revolutionary movement, if there is to be one, must build and expand on that decade of experience. It must raise the socialist banner not in an abstract or utopian way, but with conviction, purpose, and discipline. It must guard against expediency, shortcuts, and reformist temptations. And it must bridge immediate material battles to a clarion call to transform society and save our planet.

Afterword: The Fight for Socialism in the Age of Trump

More than a few mainstream pundits were shocked by how the 2024 elections unfolded. How is it that a misogynist, racist, billionaire felon could wing his way into the White House—again?

They shouldn't have been surprised. Trump 2024 rode to power atop the deep alienation felt by millions of ordinary Americans, drowning in a half-century of neoliberalism: the destruction of social supports, the privatization of public space, the exaltation of corporate profits over the planet, the abandonment—and aggressive policing—of working-class communities, and the violent repression of social movements.

I spent some time in the runup to the election in northern Kentucky, helping Amazon workers who were organizing at the company's main air cargo hub. These were the sons and daughters of farmers, local shop owners, mechanics, firefighters, and teachers. The

Amazon workers didn't aspire to riches. They hoped for decent lives. Instead, multinational logistics firms like Amazon colonized their rolling bluegrass farmlands and fed them poverty wages, job precarity, and brutal, unforgiving labor conditions. Multiple Amazon warehouses in the region spat out injured workers and wrecked spirits while ginning up mind-numbing profits for Jeff Bezos and his ilk.

Biden's four years had only given these low-wage Amazon workers more of the same: crumbling schools and health clinics, onerous student debt if they were lucky enough to get into college, mounting mental health and drug crises, the perpetual chase for enough money to pay next month's rent. Biden supporters' gushing claims about his pro-worker policies and accomplishments—Build Back Better, his pro-union appointments to the National Labor Relations Board, his fleeting appearance on an auto worker picket line—were so much gobbledegook to these workers, a foreign language with no practical meaning.

I spent the weekend before the 2024 election with Tom, an air cargo worker and union activist, driving around northern Kentucky and southern Ohio, visiting his coworkers to discuss the Amazon union drive. Cruising through working-class communities, we'd compare the number of Harris versus Trump signs. It was about an even split in some neighborhoods, but in most, Trump signs dominated. Tom was keenly aware that Trump was a bloviating egomaniac, fixated on his own wealth and stature. Tom thought college should be free, and he had a problem with for-profit healthcare. But over the previous four years his material conditions, never great, had worsened. Monthly COVID checks and eviction prevention protections had ended under Biden, his rent was up 25 percent, groceries cost more, and inflation had eaten away the meager raise he and his coworkers had wrested from Amazon through their union work. This was no decent way to live. Tom and most of his co-workers—if they even bothered voting at all—weren't voting blue. Democrats only promised more of the same; Trump was an economic gamble, but at least it would be *different.* Given the choice between the two, the riskier choice at least offered the possibility of betterment.

The Democratic Party deserted these workers not in 2024 or in 2016, but rather decades before, in the 1970s, when it abandoned its lukewarm commitment to New Deal economics and a haphazard allegiance to civil rights. It wasn't just Democrats, of course. The desertion was decidedly bipartisan, beginning in the late 1970s when Jimmy Carter and congressional Democrats eviscerated pension protections and deregulated the trucking and airline industries, which led to widespread union-busting. In 1981, Ronald Reagan and the GOP picked up where the Democrats left off, cutting taxes on the rich and unleashing even more union-busting after breaking the air traffic controllers' strike. Democrat Bill Clinton proudly led the campaign to end welfare programs and signed the job-killing NAFTA free trade pact into law; Republican George W. Bush steered the country into unending wars; Democrat Barack Obama spent his political capital rescuing Wall Street, as the streets of towns like those I visited in northern Kentucky got layoffs, foreclosures, and eviction notices. Meanwhile, the gilded elite luxuriated on enormous yachts and in splendid mansions, daydreamed about colonizing Mars, and flaunted their unimaginable riches on social media. Trump's ugly, kleptocratic reign is neither an aberration nor an anomaly—it's the culmination of the last 50 years of capitalist economics, an acceleration of its logical trajectory, a release of all restraints on the elite to steal from us and forsake our future.

As I write in mid-2025, the world is gyrating in trade wars. Trump's police are kidnapping and imprisoning immigrants and forcing others to leave the country; his shock troops, employed by the so-called Department of Government Efficiency (DOGE) and the Office of Management and Budget, are decimating federal workers' unions and eviscerating basic services with glee; Trump sycophants are following suit at the state level; and his minions attack transgender people and other marginalized communities. Trump speaks unabashedly about taking over Canada, Greenland, and the Panama Canal while providing bombs and political cover for Israel's genocide of the Palestinian people.

It's impossible to forecast how things will have developed by the time you read these words. Perhaps—one hopes—mass popular movements will have risen up to blunt Trump's worst excesses. But about this I am absolutely certain: At the moment you read this, there will be those in our ranks, people on the political left—perhaps people you deeply trust—who will argue that we mustn't talk about socialism now, and that instead, we must first focus all of our attention on defeating Trump or whatever iteration follows him. They will say attacking Democrats now, doing anything other than "Voting Blue," only helps Trump, and that we must fight this greater evil by supporting a lesser one. You will hear people make excuses for the Democrats' failures to mount any genuine resistance. They will argue against more radical agendas in favor of first getting "back to normal"—as if neoliberalism were ever a humane and sustainable way to manage the affairs of this planet.

Of course we must fight Trump. But it would be a fatal mistake to set aside the larger questions surrounding our present political and economic order. It is precisely that order—capitalism, and the political duopoly that steers it—which has led to this perilous stage in the first place.

Any temporary reversal of fortunes for Democrats—perhaps spurred by a new cohort of progressive candidates who aspire to "change the party from the inside"—will only buy a short respite before the grinding descent into capitalist savagery resumes. Calls to work within the Democratic Party to draw working-class voters back into the fold will fail exactly as they have before. Having been let down time and again by the Democrats, these voters are not coming back.

It's not, as mainstream pundits would have us believe, because workers are narrow-minded or duped by Fox News or preternaturally conservative, or because the Democrats lack the right messaging or need more door-knockers or need to become more adept at using the latest social media app. It's because workers are intelligent; because their lived experiences have hammered into their bones that the political duopoly, with Democrats and Republicans each playing distinct but mutually reinforcing roles, will never meet their needs. While Republicans are unabashed about their economic and social cruelty, Democrats claim to want a more humane capitalism but then capitulate or claim impotence to prevent harm to workers and the planet. Both of these parties are funded by and serve big business, from Wall Street executives to the George Petries of this world. Both are absolutely committed, in their symbiotic relationship of contesting-yet-colluding, to uphold capitalism. This duopoly screws workers, kills the human spirit and, unchecked, will snuff out life on this planet.

Today's treacherous juncture is not only an indictment of Democrats; it also implicates the socialist movement, which over the years has not done nearly enough to put forward an alternative to the Democrat versus Republican binary. I don't mean just in terms of ballot options, but in everyday life, in conversations on the street and in community spaces, at work and in union meetings, in schools and in places of worship. We must do more—much more—to impress on our neighbors, friends, and coworkers that there *is* an alternative. A small band of Marxists in Seattle showed us as much.

In the movements to Tax Amazon, for renters' rights, and for a $15 minimum wage, most of the people involved wouldn't even consider themselves socialists, much less Marxists. But they embraced Sawant's approach because they saw it was a way through the horrific fatalism that capitalism offers us. If we could, in a city home to many of the world's most powerful corporations, wrest victories under a socialist banner from the political establishment, then we certainly can do so elsewhere.

The Seattle experiment offers a template for the political revolution that is so urgently needed. It lifts the theory of Marxism off dusty bookshelves and brings it to vivid life.

I never intended, in writing this book, to offer a fixed roadmap for how to "scale up" the post-Seattle experience. That is a project we must undertake together, gleaning the lessons of Marxist insurgent struggle and applying them to our battles today. Seattle is not a formula or a recipe. It offers a set of principles and methods, ideologically grounded and diligently applied, that points to a hopeful outcome.

More than a century ago, during World War I, Rosa Luxemburg wrote that "bourgeois society stands at the crossroads, either transition to Socialism or regression into Barbarism." How painfully true this remains, especially today.

But we are not helpless observers in this drama, staring at the turbulent world behind some museum glass. We are direct actors. Which path we take at Luxemburg's parlous crossroads is up to us. We have ideas and energy, we have each other, and we have the knowledge and experience—borne out in places like Seattle, but not just Seattle—that we can take on and beat the most powerful adversaries, and that a better world, a socialist world, can be won.

Acknowledgements

There are three stages to any campaign or movement: We prepare, take action, then broadcast to others what we did. If you do the first two stages but forego that third one, any lessons gleaned from the struggle get lost to history. I wrote this book not as an author per se but as an organizer, aiming to spell out lessons and, in doing so, expand and strengthen our movement to win a new world. To do that third stage. While my name is on the cover, the book you are reading is the product of many, many people with whom I had the privilege of working on the first two stages. They did amazing, historic work.

First and foremost, I owe appreciation to the members of Socialist Alternative, who in 2013 had the chutzpah to run Kshama Sawant against the most powerful member of Seattle's political establishment ("Don't worry, it's not like you're going to win," one senior comrade had assured the reluctant candidate). Over the years, I have learned so much from so many of you, in Socialist Alternative and in Workers Strike Back. I also drew inspiration from area religious leaders, who brought moral clarity to the fights for workers and tenants and against racist gentrification and corporate greed: the Black Pastors of the Central District, Rev. Angela Ying of Bethany United Church of Christ, and my own spiritual leader, Rabbi David Basior of Kadima Reconstructionist Community. Credit also must go to those who played important roles in this remarkable decade of struggle: The SeaTac Airport workers—immigrants from Somalia, Ethiopia, Eritrea, Iran, Latin America, South Asia, and elsewhere—who made history in the fight for $15; the carpenters who formed the Peter J. McGuire Group, and all the other rank and file workers whose bravery and creativity inspired so many; the tenants who organized, like those at Seattle Housing Authority, in Carl Haglund-owned buildings, at the Chateau, Brighton, and Kenton Apartments, and at Halcyon Mobile Home Park; the Nickelsville and Northlake Tiny House Village residents, who modeled local democracy in their communities and direct action on the streets; and of course, everyone who marched, phone-banked, door-knocked, leafleted, petitioned, occupied, or otherwise organized with us to make Seattle a city for the multiracial working class, to help us hold office through four election campaigns, and to build international solidarity, especially solidarity with the Palestinian people.

I particularly appreciate the activists who sat with me for interviews. Whether your name is in the text or not, your ideas and perspectives had influence: Natalie Bailey, Sharon Crowley, Renee Gordon, Kathy Heffernan, Rev. Robert L. Jeffrey, Sr., Emerson Johnson, Arianna Laureano, Paula Lukaszek, Cat Ngo, Kailyn Nicholson, Barbara Phinney, Calvin Priest, Alycia Roberts, Kshama Sawant, Logan Swan, Nina Wurz, Kathy Yasi, Adam Ziemkowski.

As for the third stage, telling the story and gleaning lessons, it's true that the words are mine, but they wouldn't have become the book before you without the support of some amazing people: my colleagues at Hing Hay Coworks, who abided my asocial deadline single-mindedness; my patient and persistent agent, Diana Finch (I still don't understand how the book agent profession pencils out economically); Sam Gindin, Robin D.G. Kelley, and Rachel Forgash, each of whom gave me excellent feedback on manuscript drafts; Lapiz Digital Services for their typesetting expertise; and the crew of OR Books: Sam Russek, a delightful and laser-sharp editor; Colin Robinson, John Oakes, Olivia Heffernan, Zahra Khan, Ana Ratner, Aymen Qureshi, Antara Ghosh, Georgie Carr, and Fatema Merchant, for taking a chance on me; and creative cover artist Allie Rudin.

We've now come to the part where the author is supposed to offer a soul-bearing-but-not-too-treacly paean to their immediate family. I am deeply indebted to my mom, Rachel, and my dad, Myron (of blessed memory), who helped me set my moral compass in this world. I could not have undertaken this project without the love of my wife and life partner, Carolyn. She offered me unconditional support and incisive criticism in proper measure every step of the way. Carolyn was not the only household co-conspirator: She and I have engaged in Marx's process of "social reproduction." Natalya and Tamar, also both caring muses and essential critics throughout this book project, are about to be let loose on this world to fix everything that my generation doesn't get around to. They are both whip-smart and tough. You have been forewarned, capitalists. They, too, along with their peers, are coming for you and your rotten system.

Ah, the final paragraph. Here, the writer's glow of happiness is suddenly darkened by the penumbra of doubt. Did I forget to give someone credit? Short-change them? Misspell their name? The mind is wracked with anxiety: I don't remember what I don't remember. So I will say in advance: I'm very sorry. Any omissions and inaccuracies in this section, and indeed throughout this book, are my responsibility alone. Come talk to me, and if you're not too sharp, I'll do my best to make it up to you.

About the Author

Jonathan Rosenblum has caused trouble for the rich and powerful for over forty years. He's helped workers throughout North America organize, bargain, and strike in a wide range of industries—warehousing and logistics, higher education, healthcare, and public service.

A member of the National Writers Union and veteran newspaper reporter, he has published dozens of articles about organizing and is the author of *Beyond $15: Immigrant Workers, Faith Activists, and the Revival of the Labor Movement,* on his experience leading the first Fight for $15 campaign in SeaTac, Washington. During Kshama Sawant's decade on the Seattle City Council, he worked on her council staff and as an election campaigner. In 2018, he served as strategic advisor to COPE-Vancouver during their historic Rent Freeze campaign in

British Columbia, which led to the election of anti-poverty activist Jean Swanson to Vancouver City Council. In 2022, he served as an organizer and strategist for University of California graduate student and postdoctoral workers in the largest academic strike in US history. He's been an invited speaker in the US, Canada, and Europe. Beginning in early 2025, as Activist in Residence at Arizona State University's Center for Work and Democracy, he has expanded his prior work helping Amazon workers organize in the US and internationally.

He lives with his family in Seattle, Washington, and has worked at various times as an Amazon delivery driver and a stagehand.

www.ingramcontent.com/pod-product-compliance
Lightning Source LLC
Jackson TN
JSHW080711150226
97672JS00004B/6

* 9 7 8 1 6 8 2 1 9 6 3 6 6 *